Red Jack Saloon
near condo

ZAGATSURVEY®

2005/06

SAN FRANCISCO NIGHTLIFE

Local Editor: Kurt Wolff

Editor: Randi Gollin

Published and distributed by
ZAGAT SURVEY, LLC
4 Columbus Circle
New York, New York 10019
Tel: 212 977 6000
E-mail: sfnightlife@zagat.com
Web site: www.zagat.com

Acknowledgments

We thank John Adams IV, Kathy Batt, Eleanor Bertino, Susie Biehler, Todd Cote, Phil Cusick, Tara Duggan, Tom Erikson, Elgy Gillespie, Dema Grim, Nicholas Helfrich, Jeanne Kearsley, Amy Marr, Kevin Odle, Pat Ryan, Maria Sample, Steven Shukow, Nick Tangborn, Amy Ventura, Tom Walton, Craig and Vivienne Von Wiedorhold, Mike "Guitar" Wolf and Carolyn Wolff. We are also grateful to our assistant editors, Emily Parsons and Victoria Elmacioglu, as well as the following members of our staff: Reni Chin, Larry Cohn, Schuyler Frazier, Jeff Freier, Shelley Gallagher, Natalie Lebert, Mike Liao, Dave Makulec, Robert Poole, Thomas Sheehan, Joshua Siegel and Sharon Yates.

Contents

About This Survey

This *San Francisco Nightlife Survey*, covering 650 bars, clubs and lounges, is an update reflecting significant developments since our last *Survey* was published. To bring this guide up to the minute, we have added 59 newcomers and made changes throughout to indicate new addresses and phone numbers, as well as closings.

This marks the 26th year that Zagat Survey has reported on the shared experiences of people like you. What started in 1979 as a hobby involving 200 of our friends rating local NYC restaurants has come a long way. Today we have over 250,000 active surveyors and now cover entertaining, golf, hotels, resorts, spas, movies, music, nightlife, shopping, sites and attractions as well as theater. All of these guides are based on consumer surveys. Our *Surveys* are also available on PDAs, cell phones and by subscription at zagat.com, where you can vote and shop as well. Not incidentally, our newly redesigned Web site now features nightlife content for the first time.

By regularly surveying large numbers of avid customers, we hope to have achieved a uniquely current and reliable guide. More than 2,600 people participated in this *Survey*; since they go out an average of 2.1 times per week, our results are based on roughly 290,000 evenings out per year. Our editors have synopsized surveyors' opinions, with their comments shown in quotation marks. We sincerely thank each of these people; this book is really "theirs."

We are especially grateful to our local editor, Kurt Wolff, an author and journalist who, when he's not checking out the scene, writes about country music and, as an antidote to all those cool bars, national parks.

To help guide you to the places that best fit your individual needs, we have prepared a number of lists for specific occasions. See Most Popular (page 9), Top Ratings (pages 10–16) and Best Buys (page 17). In addition, we have provided 71 handy indexes.

To vote in any of our upcoming *Surveys*, just register at zagat.com. Each participant will receive a free copy of the resulting guide (or a comparable reward). Your comments and even criticisms of this guide are also solicited. There is always room for improvement with your help. Just contact us at sfnightlife@zagat.com.

New York, NY
June 21, 2005

Nina and Tim Zagat

What's New

It may be premature to shout that boom times are here again, but if the profusion of new hot spots is any barometer, the Bay Area's economy is bounding back big time. In fact, our surveyors, besides eating out regularly, go to night-spots 2.1 times a week, living the high life at plush clubs or just kicking back at neighborhood dives.

Neighborhood Watch: The revitalized Embarcadero remains a magnet, with the Americano Restaurant & Bar in the new Hotel Vitale the latest waterfront lure. Meanwhile, out-of-the-way haunts continue to draw the club crowd: Mighty brings world-class DJs to half-industrial, half-residential Potrero Hill, while Riptide gives Outer Sunset inhabitants a cozy, lodgelike home. With a freeway off-ramp close to completion, a once-lonesome stretch of Octavia Boulevard near Hayes Valley is primed for major transformation, and Third Street is becoming a more desirable vicinity thanks to the upcoming light-rail system extension, which will swiftly run passengers south from SBC Park. Across the bridge in Oakland, lounge lizards and punk rockers head to At Seventeenth, the Golden Bull and Luka's Taproom. And come the weekend, a carefree crowd plunges onto the dance floors at the Deep in San Jose.

Shaken and Stirred: Our night-owl surveyors may pony up an average of $7.27 for a drink, but they oftentimes get something exceptional in return. Circolo, Lime and Oola tempt cocktail aficionados with tropical concoctions like lychee gimlets, coconut mojitos and watermelon Cosmos. Bar 821 and RX Gallery draw foam fans with Belgian brews, while Nectar Wine Lounge and VinoVenue take a page from *Sideways,* offering memorable flights aplenty. Concurrently, bottle service has taken off at clubs like Frisson and Prive, with luxe-lovers reaching into deep pockets for perks like guaranteed admission and reserved seating.

Fresh Faces: Spanking new spots continue to surface, replacing gone-but-not-forgotten favorites citywide. The laid-back lesbian hang Chaise Lounge sprung up in the former Charlie's Club digs; Bay-side haunt La Suite put its elegant imprint on the Slanted Door's former space; Trader Vic's sprinkled tiki dust on the old Stars' site; and Winterland, named for the long-defunct rock arena, took root in a condo on the venue's former location.

Up and Coming: Debuts on the horizon include Supper Club in SoMa and Tres Agaves near SBC Park, a Mexican tequila joint partly owned by rocker Sammy Hagar. In Sausalito, the wine bar Cork is about to pop, and the historic 1928 Fox Theatre in Oakland is set to reopen as a performing arts center in 2007. In sum, the future looks bright – cheers.

San Francisco, CA
June 21, 2005

Kurt Wolff

subscribe to zagat.com

Ratings & Symbols

Name, Address, Phone Number & Web Site

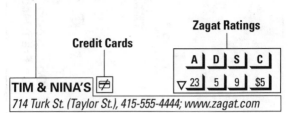

Zagat Ratings

Credit Cards

A	D	S	C
▽ 23	5	9	$5

TIM & NINA'S ⌷

714 Turk St. (Taylor St.), 415-555-4444; www.zagat.com

"Bukowski would've loved" this "screw-top chic" Tenderloin wine bar that tenders "flights of rotgut" "aged in the basement"; while the viti-cultured are "shocked" at the "surly staff" and shun the "uncomfy furniture made from old barrels", barflies boast "after two glasses of plonk" "your tush won't feel a thing."

Review, with surveyors' comments in quotes

Nightspots with the highest overall ratings and greatest popularity and importance are printed in CAPITAL LETTERS.

Credit Cards: ⌷ no credit cards accepted

Ratings are on a scale of 0 to 30. **Cost (C)** reflects our surveyors' estimate of the price of a typical single drink.

A Appeal	D Decor	S Service	C Cost
23	5	9	$5

0–9 poor to fair	**20–25** very good to excellent	
10–15 fair to good	**26–30** extraordinary to perfection	
16–19 good to very good	▽ low response/less reliable	

For places listed without ratings, such as a newcomer or survey write-in, the price range is indicated as follows:

I	below $5	**E**	$9 to $11
M	$5 to $8	**VE**	more than $11

Most Popular

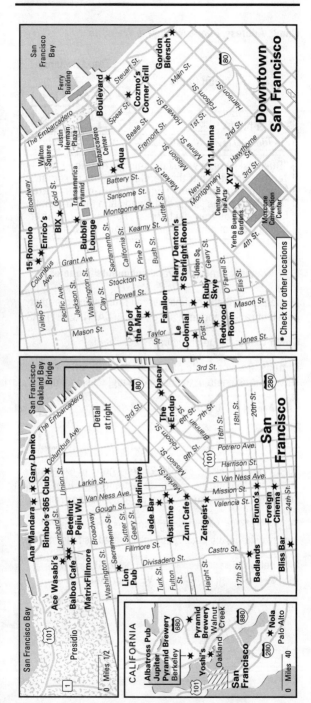

San Francisco Bay

Ferry Building

Gordon Biersch ★★

Main St.

80

Steuart St.

Boulevard ★

Cozmo's Corner Grill ★★

Spear St.

Beale St.

Fremont St.

1st St.

Howard St.

Folsom St.

Harrison St.

The Embarcadero

Justin Herman Plaza

Embarcadero Center

Mission St.

Minna St.

111 Minna ★

2nd St.

Hawthorne St.

Downtown San Francisco

Walton Square

Aqua ★

Battery St.

New Montgomery

XYZ ★

3rd St.

Broadway

Gold St.

Sansome St.

Transamerica Pyramid

Montgomery St.

Market St.

Center for the Arts

Moscone Convention Center

Yerba Buena Gardens

4th St.

15 Romolo ★★

Enrico's ★

BiX ★

Bubble Lounge ★

Kearny St.

Sacramento St.

California St.

Sutter St.

Harry Denton's Starlight Room ★

Columbus Ave.

Grant Ave.

Pine St.

Bush St.

Geary St.

Union Sq.

Ruby Skye ★

* Check for other locations

Vallejo St.

Pacific Ave.

Jackson St.

Washington St.

Clay St.

Stockton St.

Powell St.

Farallon ★

O'Farrell St.

Ellis St.

Mason St.

Mason St.

Top of the Mark ★

Taylor St.

Le Colonial ★

Post St.

Redwood Room ★

Jones St.

San Francisco-Oakland Bay Bridge

3rd St.

80

280

The Embarcadero

Detail at right

bacar ★

7th St.

18th St.

20th St.

Columbus Ave.

3rd St.

The Endup ★

6th St.

5th St.

Bryant St.

16th St.

Potrero Ave.

Harrison St.

101

San Francisco

Ana Mandara ★ ★ Gary Danko

Bimbo's 365 Club ★

Larkin St.

Jardinière ★

Van Ness Ave.

S. Van Ness Ave.

Mission St.

Bruno's ★

24th St.

Betelnut Pejiu Wu ★

Gough St.

Jade Bar ★

Market St.

Valencia St.

Foreign Cinema ★

Lombard St.

Broadway

Sacramento St.

Fillmore St.

Absinthe ★

Zuni Cafe ★

Zeitgeist ★

Ace Wasabi's ★

Balboa Cafe ★

MatrixFillmore ★

Geary St.

Divisadero St.

Castro St.

17th St.

Badlands ★

Bliss Bar ★

San Francisco Bay

Presidio

101

1

Lion Pub ★

Turk St.

Fulton St.

Haight St.

0   Miles 1/2

CALIFORNIA

Albatross Pub ★

Jupiter ★

Pyramid Brewery

Berkeley

680

Pyramid Brewery

Walnut Creek

880

Nola ★

Palo Alto

101

Yoshi's ★

Oakland

San Francisco

280

0   Miles 40

Most Popular

Places outside of San Francisco are marked as follows:
E=East of SF; N=North; and S=South.

1. Redwood Room	21. Ace Wasabi's
2. Boulevard	22. Absinthe
3. MatrixFillmore	23. Bruno's
4. Betelnut Pejiu Wu	24. Ana Mandara
5. BIX	25. Nola/S
6. Bimbo's 365 Club	26. Jardinière
7. Aqua	27. Ruby Skye*
8. Bubble Lounge*	28. Lion Pub
9. Top of the Mark*	29. Zuni Cafe*
10. XYZ*	30. Bliss Bar
11. bacar	31. Jupiter/E*
12. Yoshi's/E	32. Foreign Cinema
13. Gordon Biersch/S/SF	33. Farallon
14. Zeitgeist	34. Harry Denton Starlight*
15. Le Colonial	35. Endup
16. Balboa Cafe	36. 15 Romolo*
17. Cozmo's Corner	37. Albatross Pub/E
18. 111 Minna	38. Enrico's Sidewalk*
19. Badlands	39. Pyramid Brewery/E*
20. Jade Bar*	40. Gary Danko

It's obvious that many of the places on the above list are among the most expensive, but Bay Area night-owls also love a bargain. Were popularity calibrated to price, we suspect that a number of other places would join the above ranks. Thus, we have listed 40 Best Buys on page 17.

Cigars:
P. 44

---

* Indicates a tie with place above

Top Ratings

Excluding places with low voting.

Top 40 Overall Appeal

29 Paramount Theater/E
28 Auberge du Soleil/N
Highlands Inn/S*
27 Atlas Cafe
Gary Danko
Plush Room
26 Hôtel Biron
Parkway Speakeasy/E*
Freight & Salvage/E
Mandarin Lounge
Martini House/N
Top of the Mark
Lobby/Ritz-Carlton
Farallon
Yoshi's/E
Boulevard
Jardinière
Sushi Ran/N
25 Great Amer. Music
Slow Club

Lark Creek Inn/N
Seasons Bar
Aqua
BIX
Pied Piper Bar
Jade Bar
suite one8one
Tony Nik's*
Pelican Inn/N
Specs Bar
Bouchon/N
Cole's Chop House/N
Jazz at Pearl's*
Albatross Pub/E
24 Bimbo's 365 Club
Calistoga Inn/N
Absinthe
Tra Vigne/N
Kokkari Estiatorio
Buckeye Roadhouse/N

By Special Appeal

After Work
25 Aqua
Pied Piper Bar
Specs Bar
24 Moose's
Ozumo

Bars
26 Hôtel Biron
25 Jade Bar
Tony Nik's
Specs Bar
Albatross Pub/E

Beautiful People
26 Farallon
Boulevard
Jardinière
25 Aqua
BIX

Blues Clubs
24 Sweetwater Saloon/N
22 Lou's Pier 47
21 Boom Boom Rm.
Slim's
19 Biscuits & Blues

Coffeehouses
27 Atlas Cafe
23 Cafe Flore
Grove
22 Caffe Trieste/E/N/SF
Steps of Rome

Dance Clubs
25 suite one8one
24 Mezzanine
23 Bissap Baobab
El Rio
22 Endup

Dives
24 Odeon
Alley/E
21 Club Mallard/E
20 500 Club
Doc's Clock

Fine Food Too
28 Auberge du Soleil/N
Highlands Inn/S*
27 Gary Danko
26 Martini House/N
Farallon

Top Appeal

Frat House
- **24** Redwood Room
- **23** Jupiter/E
- **22** Sam's Anchor Cafe/N
  850 Cigar Bar
- **20** Fuse

Gay
- **24** Mecca
- **23** Cafe Flore
  Whiskey Lounge
  Martuni's
- **22** Eagle Tavern

Good Beer Selection
- **25** Albatross Pub/E
- **23** Jupiter/E
- **22** Dalva
  Suppenküche
- **21** Toronado

Grown-Ups
- **29** Paramount Theater/E
- **28** Auberge du Soleil/N
  Highlands Inn/S*
- **27** Gary Danko
- **26** Freight & Salvage/E

Hotel Bars
- **28** Auberge du Soleil/N
  Auberge du Soleil
  Highlands Inn/S*
  Highlands Inn
- **26** Mandarin Lounge
  Mandarin Oriental
  Top of the Mark
  Mark Hopkins
- **25** Pied Piper Bar
  Palace Hotel

Irish
- **22** Little Shamrock
  O'Reilly's Irish Pub
- **20** Plough & Stars
  Beckett's Irish/E
- **19** Johnny Foley's

Jazz Clubs
- **26** Yoshi's/E
- **25** BIX
  Jazz at Pearl's
- **23** Bruno's
  Enrico's Sidewalk

Jukeboxes
- **24** Zeitgeist
- **23** Zam Zam
  Tosca Cafe
  El Rio
  Vesuvio

Latin
- **22** Puerto Alegre
- **21** Tommy's Mexican
  Maya
- **20** Alma
- **18** La Rondalla

Lesbian
- **23** Cafe Flore
  Wild Side West
- **17** Café
- **–** Cherry Bar
- **–** Lexington Club

Live Music Clubs
- **29** Paramount Theater/E
- **27** Plush Room
- **26** Freight & Salvage/E
  Yoshi's/E
- **25** Great Amer. Music

Lounges
- **26** Mandarin Lounge
  Lobby/Ritz-Carlton
- **25** Seasons Bar
- **24** Ana Mandara
  Le Colonial

Meat Markets
- **24** Redwood Room
- **23** Red Devil
- **22** Betelnut Pejiu Wu
  Harry Denton Starlight
  Steps of Rome

Mixed Drinks/Cocktails
- **27** Gary Danko
- **26** Mandarin Lounge
  Boulevard
  Jardinière
- **25** Seasons Bar

Newcomers/Unrated
- Frisson
- La Suite
- Madrone Lounge
- Mighty
- RX Gallery

Top Appeal

Quiet Conversation
28 Highlands Inn/S
27 Atlas Cafe
26 Hôtel Biron
    Mandarin Lounge
    Lobby/Ritz-Carlton

Roadhouses
24 Sweetwater Saloon/N
21 Toronado
20 Casanova
19 Thee Parkside
17 Ivy Room/E

Sports Bars
21 Conn. Yankee
    Gino & Carlo
20 Greens Sports Bar
19 Horseshoe
    Kezar Pub

Theme Bars
26 Farallon
24 C. Bobby's Owl Tree
21 Bigfoot Lodge
    Tonga Room
    Shanghai 1930

Wine Bars
26 Hôtel Biron
    Sushi Ran/N
24 Tra Vigne/N
23 Eos
22 Azie

Wine by the Glass
27 Gary Danko
26 Hôtel Biron
    Martini House/N
24 Tra Vigne/N
    bacar

Most Visited

By Gender

Female
1. Betelnut Pejiu Wu
2. Bubble Lounge
3. Gordon Biersch/S/SF
4. MatrixFillmore
5. Redwood Room

Male
1. Gordon Biersch/S/SF
2. Aqua
3. Boulevard
4. Betelnut Pejiu Wu
5. Redwood Room

By Age

Twentysomethings
1. MatrixFillmore
2. Betelnut Pejiu Wu
3. Blondie's Bar
4. Bubble Lounge
5. Bar None
6. Gordon Biersch/S/SF*

Thirtysomethings
1. Gordon Biersch/S/SF
2. Betelnut Pejiu Wu
3. Bubble Lounge
4. 111 Minna
5. Redwood Room

Fortysomethings
1. Gordon Biersch/S/SF
2. Boulevard
3. Betelnut Pejiu Wu
4. Aqua
5. Zuni Cafe*

Fiftysomethings
1. Aqua
2. BIX
3. Boulevard
4. Buena Vista
5. Fog City Diner*

By Neighborhood

Downtown/Embarcadero
- **27** Plush Room
- **26** Mandarin Lounge
  Farallon
  Boulevard
- **25** Seasons Bar

Fisherman's Wharf
- **27** Gary Danko
- **24** Buena Vista
  Ana Mandara
- **22** Lou's Pier 47
- **21** McCormick/Kuleto's

Haight-Ashbury/Cole Valley
- **23** Zam Zam
  Eos
- **22** Hobson's Choice
- **21** Milk Bar
- **20** Kan Zaman

Hayes Valley/Civic Center
- **26** Hôtel Biron
  Jardinière
- **25** Jade Bar
- **24** Absinthe
  Zuni Cafe

Lower Haight
- **23** Movida Lounge
- **22** Noc Noc
  Nickie's BBQ
- **21** Toronado
- **19** Mad Dog in Fog

Marina/Cow Hollow
- **24** Brazen Head
- **23** Black Horse Pub
  Grove
- **22** Betelnut Pejiu Wu
- **20** Liverpool Lil's

Mission
- **27** Atlas Cafe
- **25** Slow Club
- **24** Odeon
  Ramblas
  Zeitgeist

Nob Hill
- **26** Top of the Mark
  Lobby/Ritz-Carlton
- **23** Big 4
- **21** Tonga Room
- **17** Front Room

Noe Valley/Castro
- **23** Cafe Flore
  Whiskey Lounge
  2223 Restaurant
- **20** Bliss Bar
- **19** Badlands

North Beach
- **25** Tony Nik's
  Specs Bar
  Jazz at Pearl's
- **24** Bimbo's 365 Club
  Moose's

Pacific Heights/Upper Fillmore
- **23** Lion Pub
- **22** Florio
- **20** g bar
- **19** Harry's
  Fish Bowl

Richmond/Inner Richmond
- **21** Tommy's Mexican
- **20** RoHan Lounge
  Trad'r Sam's
  Cliff House
  Plough & Stars*

SoMa
- **24** Public
  Mezzanine
  XYZ
  bacar
- **23** Wish

Tenderloin
- **25** Great Amer. Music
  suite one8one
- **24** Mitchell Bros.
- **22** Bambuddha Lounge
- **21** Olive Bar

Van Ness Corridor
- **23** Red Devil
- **22** Harris'
  Lush Lounge
- **21** Hemlock Tavern
  R Bar

Western Addition
- **24** Fillmore
- **21** Boom Boom Rm.
  Fly
- **20** Cafe Abir
  Rasselas Jazz Club

Top Appeal

East of SF – Berkeley

26 Freight & Salvage
25 Albatross Pub
23 César
   Jupiter
   Skates on Bay

East of SF – Oakland

29 Paramount Theater
26 Parkway Speakeasy
   Yoshi's
24 Alley
   Fat Lady

North of SF

28 Auberge du Soleil
26 Martini House
   Sushi Ran
25 Lark Creek Inn
   Pelican Inn

South of SF

28 Highlands Inn
24 Evvia
23 Zibibbo
   Tarpy's Roadhouse
22 Spago Palo Alto

Top 40 Decor

29 Paramount Theater/E	Le Colonial
28 Farallon	Campton Place
Hôtel Biron*	Pelican Inn/N
Jardinière	Red Room
Highlands Inn/S	MatrixFillmore
27 Redwood Room	Absinthe
Martini House/N	Cole's Chop House/N
Auberge du Soleil/N	C. Bobby's Owl Tree
26 BIX	**24** bacar
Jade Bar	Big 4
Pied Piper Bar	Bambuddha Lounge
Ozumo	Great Amer. Music
Ana Mandara	Fat Lady/E
Lobby/Ritz-Carlton	Monkey Club
Gary Danko	Spago Palo Alto/S
Boulevard	Blowfish Sushi/S/SF
Aqua	Zam Zam
25 Seasons Bar	Fifth Floor
Kokkari Estiatorio	Mecca
XYZ	Noc Noc

Old Bay Area

Balboa Cafe	John's Grill
Buena Vista	Little Shamrock
Cliff House	Saloon
Elixir	San Fran. Brewing
Gold Dust Lounge	Specs Bar
Great Amer. Music	Tadich Grill
Heinold's Saloon/E	23 Club/S
House of Shields	Vesuvio

Outdoors

Atlas Cafe	Pier 23 Cafe
Cafe Flore	Pilsner Inn
Eagle Tavern	Ramp
El Rio	Rancho Nicasio/N
Enrico's Sidewalk	Sam's Anchor Cafe/N
Forge in Forest/S	Wild Side West
Guaymas/N	Zeitgeist

Romance

Ana Mandara	Bruno's
Auberge du Soleil/N	Hôtel Biron
Avalon Bar	Pied Piper Bar
Big 4	Seasons Bar

Views

Auberge du Soleil/N	Equinox
Beach Chalet	Grandviews Lounge
Carnelian Room	Harry Denton Starlight
Cityscape	Highlands Inn/S
Cliff House	Top of the Mark

Top 40 Service

27 Gary Danko
Lobby/Ritz-Carlton
26 Seasons Bar
Auberge du Soleil/N
R Bar
Mandarin Lounge
25 Campton Place
Fifth Floor
Boulevard
Aqua
24 Hawthorne Lane
Martini House/N
Brazen Head
Highlands Inn/S
Slow Club*
Tarpy's Roadhouse/S*
Big 4
Lark Creek Inn/N
Jardinière
Kokkari Estiatorio

Plush Room
Farallon
Fat Lady/E
23 Lush Lounge
Ramblas
Roy's/S/SF*
Moose's
Evvia/S
Calistoga Inn/N
Black Horse Pub
Hôtel Biron
Spago Palo Alto/S
Buckeye Roadhouse/N
Cole's Chop House/N*
Tra Vigne/N
Rubicon
Oliveto Cafe/E
22 2223 Restaurant
Sushi Ran/N
Buzz 9

subscribe to zagat.com

Best Buys

1. Odeon
2. Specs Bar
3. Zeitgeist
4. Club Mallard/E
5. Black Horse Pub
6. Little Shamrock
7. Wild Side West
8. Blue Danube Coffee
9. Eagle Tavern
10. Gino & Carlo
11. Atlas Cafe
12. Albatross Pub/E
13. Vesuvio
14. Parkway Speakeasy/E
15. Noc Noc
16. C. Bobby's Owl Tree
17. 500 Club
18. Cafe Abir
19. Paramount Theater/E
20. Lone Palm
21. Tony Nik's
22. Latin Amer. Club
23. Cafe Flore
24. Grumpy's Pub
25. Molotov
26. Hush Hush Lounge
27. Hemlock Tavern
28. R Bar
29. Mr. Bing's
30. Puerto Alegre
31. El Rio
32. Caffè Greco
33. Movida Lounge
34. Bigfoot Lodge
35. Liberties
36. Great Amer. Music
37. Gold Cane
38. Kennedy's Irish
39. Dalva
40. Attic Club

Nightlife Directory

City of San Francisco

	A	D	S	C

Abbey Tavern 🚭
4100 Geary Blvd. (5th Ave.), 415-221-7767;
www.abbeytavern-sf.com

| 12 | 9 | 14 | $6 |

"Expect to dance, spill your drink", play pool and "have lots of unintelligible conversations with strangers" say regulars who can't resist the "contagious Irish ambiance" of this "established neighborhood bar" in the Outer Richmond; late in the evening it's "mobbed" by a "rowdy crowd" boogeying to "sub-average" bands, but acolytes aver "sometimes cheesy music is what you need."

ABSINTHE
398 Hayes St. (Gough St.), 415-551-1590; www.absinthe.com

| 24 | 25 | 21 | $9 |

"Engulf your date in the aura of Old Europe as you discuss the night's entertainment" (the opera and symphony are nearby) at this "swanky bar" and brasserie in "hip Hayes Valley"; "excellent retro cocktails" like the "fabulous Ginger Rogers" keep the "grown-up" and "well-heeled crowd" smiling as they sink into the "luxurious interior" marked by "red walls and dim lighting" that's straight "out of *Moulin Rouge*"; P.S. celeb spotters can watch for the occasional "movie or rock star sitting in the window."

ACE WASABI'S
3339 Steiner St. (bet. Chestnut & Lombard Sts.), 415-567-4903

| 20 | 16 | 18 | $8 |

"Fun"-seekers in search of "sushi and a scene" ensure that this "rocking" Marina bar/restaurant is "full every night" with "good-looking singles" swilling "great sake cocktails" in the "tiny" bar area; while some wail it's "so loud you can't taste the beer", "let alone hear what your date is saying", more are enamored of the "friendly staff" and "party" atmosphere.

Acme Chophouse
SBC Park, 24 Willie Mays Plaza (3rd St.), 415-644-0240;
www.acmechophouse.com

| 20 | 19 | 19 | $10 |

There's nothing "rookie" about Traci Des Jardin's South Beach steakhouse that's a "civilized setting" for "pre-game cocktails", not to mention "convenient", as it's tucked right into the walls of SBC Park; pleased patrons pitch it's the "best upscale sports bar in SF" for its "big drinks" from a "traditional" cocktail menu, "fantastic wine list" and "diamond-in-the-rough" food including "terrific burgers", even if the room itself is "relatively nondescript."

Alma
1101 Valencia St. (22nd St.), 415-401-8959;
www.almacomida.com

| 20 | 19 | 20 | $8 |

"Have mojitos and plantain chips" or sup on an "awesome seviche sampler" at the wood-and-"wrought-iron bar" (it's "small" but "somehow works") inside this "beautiful" Nuevo Latino in the Mission; the "excellent wine list" is "full of interesting Portuguese and Spanish offerings" (let the "impressively knowledgeable staff" help you choose), and the "cocktails fit the mood", though most admit it's more of a "romantic" restaurant than a drinks destination.

A	D	S	C

Alpha Bar & Lounge
- | - | - | M
(fka Pat O'Shea's Mad Hatter)

3848 Geary St. (3rd Ave.), 415-831-8838; www.alphabarsf.com
Alpha and beta types alike are drawn to this hip Inner Richmond newcomer, in the former home of Pat O'Shea's; a young, mixed crowd mingles over cocktails, and a DJ spins in a spacious room that's more red than green these days, with black, white and gray leather couches adding a modern touch to the moody atmosphere that's as ideal for midweek conversations as it is for weekend mash-ups.

Amber ⌁
21 | 21 | 20 | $7
718 14th St. (bet. Belcher & Church Sts.), 415-626-7827
"Inhale and enjoy" at this "mellow, comfy cocktail lounge" "in low-key Upper Market" because it's "one of the city's few bars" that permits nic fiends to indulge; it can be "a tad pretentious" at times, but the "dim lighting", "funky couches", "delicious, inventive drinks" and "fun staff" add puff to the fluff and "more than make up for" any smoke that may get in your eyes.

Americano Restaurant & Bar
- | - | - | E
Hotel Vitale, 8 Mission St. (The Embarcadero), 415-278-3777; www.hotelvitale.com
Join the trendy crowd and beat a path to this swanky Embarcadero hideout, a neo-minimalist circular lounge tucked inside the new, deluxe Hotel Vitale's Americano restaurant; slide into a cushy, ultrasuede seat, indulge in a cocktail or glass of wine with antipasti, drink in the dazzling Bay Bridge view and outdoor aromatherapy garden, and in no time you'll be murmuring 'serenity now', just like Jerry Stiller in the famous *Seinfeld* episode.

Amnesia ⌁
18 | 16 | 18 | $6
853 Valencia St. (bet. 19th & 20th Sts.), 415-970-0012; www.amnesiathebar.com
There may be no spirits served at this "small, dark and secretive" spot in the Mission, but the "extensive beer list" (some claim it's the "best Belgian selection in town") and the "I-just-came-to-get-my-groove-on" attitude (it does a bang-up job "supporting local DJs" and live bands on weekends) definitely "set this place apart"; spend too much time staring at the "crazy red walls", though, and you may wake up wondering "what the hell happened last night?"

ANA MANDARA
24 | 26 | 20 | $9
Ghirardelli Sq., 891 Beach St. (Polk St.), 415-771-6800; www.anamandara.com
It's "smack in the middle of the madding crowds" of Ghirardelli Square, but the "gorgeous", "romantic" and "spacious" upstairs bar inside this "stunning", "movie-set" "haven" "makes you feel you've traveled to Vietnam" with its "lovely furniture" and "open-air" space; though it's admittedly "pricey", ana-mated admirers assert its "amazing Cosmos" plus "superb jazz" and "excellent service" equal one seriously "sexy date bar."

An Bodhran
18 | 13 | 20 | $5
668 Haight St. (Steiner St.), 415-431-4724; www.anbodhran.com
Brogue-meisters longing to "hear Irish accents" head to this "understated" tavern, a "good all-around pub in the bohemian Lower Haight"; the "exceptionally capable" staff "pours better

Guinness than most places in the city", and while the traditional Gallic "music tends to be cheesy", dancing is still plenty "fun if you have enough booze in you."

Andalu
22 | 21 | 19 | $8

3198 16th St. (Guerrero St.), 415-621-2211; www.andalusf.com
"Great for groups", this "beautiful", "stylish" Mission "fave" attracts "hipsters" with its "original" menu of "tasty" "international tapas", "amazing wines by the glass", "fantastic red and white sangrias" and "good, strong cocktails made with soju" served by "attentive bartenders"; the "friendly atmosphere" can escalate into "noisy", however, so you may "have to yell" in order "to talk in-depth", but that doesn't trouble its "trendy" patrons.

Annie's Cocktail Lounge
▽ 16 | 13 | 19 | $6

15 Boardman Pl. (Bryant St.), 415-703-0865; www.urbanlogic.com/annies/annies.htm
"Hidden" in a SoMa alley across from the Hall of Justice, this "punk-rock" haven helmed by veteran scenester Annie Whiteside keeps its "hip crowd" happy with pool, karaoke, DJs, a bopping jukebox, occasional music celeb sightings and a passel of potent potables; sure, it has a certain "bike messenger appeal" but that's exactly what delights groupies of "great dives."

Anú
22 | 20 | 21 | $6

43 Sixth St. (bet. Market & Mission Sts.), 415-543-3505; www.anu-bar.com
It's "worth trekking through a scuzzy neighborhood" for a spot inside the "safe retreat" of this "swank" SoMa lounge that's a "cool locals' scene" serving "real drinks to real people"; "good DJs" spinning "great music" means the "tiny dance floor in the back" does "get packed to the brim", but the "dark" bar area up front is "perfect for an illicit affair."

AQUA
25 | 26 | 25 | $11

252 California St. (bet. Battery & Front Sts.), 415-956-9662; www.aqua-sf.com
"You want to live it up? this is the place" proclaim aqua-nuts of this "sublimely decorated", "sophisticated" seafooder "frequented by the Downtown power elite" ("pull out the fake Rolex if you're unemployed"); true, drinks are "quite pricey", but the trade-off is "first-class service", an "amazing wine list", "fabulous flowers" and "exquisite food even at the bar", and if it's "a little too full of itself", well, "you can't quite blame it."

Argus Lounge ⇗
▽ 20 | 14 | 21 | $5

3187 Mission St. (Valencia St.), 415-824-1447; www.arguslounge.com
An "Outer Mission mélange of artists, minimum-wage workers, computer geeks and freaks" populate this "well-hidden gem" (its "exterior sign has no text", just a big neon peacock feather) that converts claim is "one of the last great neighborhood bars"; it's "smallish" but "laid-back", "homey" and "worth it for the jukebox alone", and now live music too, and after a few visits, "everyone really does seem to learn your name."

AsiaSF
22 | 19 | 20 | $9

201 Ninth St. (Howard St.), 415-255-2742; www.asiasf.com
"How can you go wrong with drag queens who lip synch", "blow kisses from the stage" and then "get you drinks"? marvel mavens of this "endlessly entertaining" "gender-bending" club/restaurant

in SoMa; a few shrug it's a "onetime-only type of place", though most offer bravas to the "brilliant concept", "beautiful 'waitresses'" and "excellent" cocktails, adding it's the "perfect place to take out-of-towners."

ATLAS CAFE

27 | 19 | 22 | $6

3049 20th St. (Alabama St.), 415-824-0298; www.atlascafe.net
Expect "fantastic people-watching" on the "awesome patio" of this "relaxing bohemian cafe" in the Outer Mission; "nurse a beer or coffee for hours", sip a "good drink", like ginger-infused lemonade (no liquor), or indulge in "the most creative sandwiches in the city" while "perusing the fabulous reading selections", logging on the free wireless or changing directions with "great" bluegrass.

Attic Club

20 | 14 | 18 | $5

3336 24th St. (Mission St.), 415-643-3376
This "low-key hole-in-the-wall" may be as "dark" and "tiny" as the average crawlspace – not to mention "crowded" and "loud" – but it's also "one of the best spots in the Mission", attracting a "friendly, mixed" group of "regulars" with its "intimate" vibe, art openings and "awesome DJs" (including one spinning 78s); "it isn't the flashiest but that's exactly the appeal", and if you have too many of the "great", "inexpensive drinks", "you can literally crawl" across the street to BART.

Aunt Charlie's

– | – | – | I

133 Turk St. (bet. Jones & Taylor Sts.), 415-441-2922;
www.auntcharlieslounge.com
It may be situated in the "dicey" Tenderloin, but this "friendly, unpretentious" and "always-amusing" venue features DJs twice a week and "old-school" performers on other nights who are all about "guts, glitz and glamour"; however, while buffs boast it's "simply the best drag-show lounge in the entire universe", a few prodigal nephews retort "watching over-50 gay bikers sing Barbra Streisand [tunes] is now off my to-do list."

Avalon Bar

– | – | – | E

Hotel Majestic, 1500 Sutter St. (Gough St.), 415-441-1100;
www.thehotelmajestic.com
Tucked inside the century-old Majestic in Pacific Heights, this small and "luscious hiding spot" is "perfect for an intimate rendezvous", illicit or otherwise; with its classic cocktails, extensive butterfly collection and vintage Edwardian appointments, the experience is "like a beautiful form of time travel."

Azie

22 | 23 | 19 | $9

826 Folsom St. (bet. 4th & 5th Sts.), 415-538-0918
"If you have a cute cocktail dress" hanging idle in the closet, this "glamorous" SoMa bar/eatery supplies an "excellent" excuse to swan through the "swanky crowd" sipping "inventive" cocktails in a "warm", "sexy atmosphere"; some say it's "overhyped and overpriced", but supporters of this sister to next-door Restaurant Lulu insist the "wonderful" French-Asian fare and "stunning" decor make it "great for special occasions."

BACAR

24 | 24 | 21 | $10

448 Brannan St. (bet. 3rd & 4th Sts.), 415-904-4100; www.bacarsf.com
"Your Gucci shoes will feel at home" in this "beautiful", "modern" SoMa restaurant and wine bar; with live jazz every night (except

Sunday) in the upstairs lounge, it's an "excellent place for grown-ups (especially if someone else is paying)", and the "extremely knowledgeable staff will help you pick the perfect" vintage from a "premier" list of 100 by the glass (or a roster of 1,400 bottles that wags tag the "encyclopedia vitanica"); no wonder the wowed declare this "Dionysian fantasy" is "aging well"; N.B. the salon downstairs is open only for private parties.

Bacchus Kirk – | – | – | M
925 Bush St. (bet. Jones & Taylor Sts.), 415-474-4056
Watch the game from the bar, shoot some pool in the back or just cold kick it by the fireplace that's the centerpiece of this local hangout Downtown; the wood-beamed ceiling, accented by red lamps and a '70s-style stone wall, creates a cozy ski lodge feel – though 'mountain chapel' may be a more appropriate metaphor as one of the definitions of 'kirk' is 'Scottish church.'

Bacchus Wine & Sake Bar 21 | 21 | 21 | $11
1954 Hyde St. (Union St.), 415-928-2633
"This low-key wine bar" ("the coolest in town", or at least on Russian Hill) is about "as big as your bathroom", but "if you can get a seat" it works well "for a drink and conversation"; "most people are here for a quick sake cocktail while waiting for a table" at nearby sib Sushi Groove, although "locals" affirm a "friendly staff" and "great selection" will "make you feel all warm and fuzzy inside."

BADLANDS ⊅ 19 | 18 | 17 | $6
4121 18th St. (Castro St.), 415-626-9320; www.badlands-sf.com
A time-honored formula of "beer, cruising and dancing" ensures the "popularity" of this "LA-style video bar" in the Castro that attracts a "diverse" crowd from "barely legal East Bay boys" to "leather daddies", all downing "cheap", "strong" drinks in the "spaceship"-style interior; "mainstream gay disco music" (read: "Europop") irritates elitists, not to mention the "long lines" outside, but "for those looking to hook up" in the neighborhood, "this is the place."

BALBOA CAFE 19 | 16 | 18 | $8
3199 Fillmore St. (Greenwich St.), 415-921-3944; www.plumpjack.com
"The upwardly mobile Cow Hollow crowd" still flocks to this 91-year-old "SF original" (now owned by the PlumpJack restaurant group, founded by Mayor Gavin Newsom) that's "a constant favorite" for its "attentive service, traditional atmosphere" and "excellent burgers"; critics cringe that especially on weekends "it's a zoo" full of too many "aging yuppies looking for love", but stalwarts insist that, no matter how many "Porsche-driving middle-aged men" are "on the prowl", "the appeal never fades."

Bamboo Hut 18 | 19 | 17 | $7
479 Broadway (bet. Kearny & Montgomery Sts.), 415-989-8555; www.maximumproductions.com
"Pretend you are on a faraway island and go crazy" at this "cheeky" North Beach "hangout" serving "delicious" "big drinks in coconuts" and appropriately "kitschy tiki-style decor"; "booming '80s tunes hit you" as you "work your way past drunk fraternity boys and sorority girls" on the "ridiculously cramped" dance floor, but the "hilarious" Thursday theme night 'Rockin' Like Dokken' and the crew of "laid-back" bartenders "make up for" any shortcomings.

Bambuddha Lounge   22 | 24 | 17 | $9

Phoenix Hotel, 601 Eddy St. (Larkin St.), 415-885-5088; www.bambuddhalounge.com
"Imagine yourself as a model in *Wallpaper* magazine" as you "sip refreshing" guavapolitans poolside or "relax on comfy chairs", pillows or even beds in the "multiple rooms" of this "cool", "serene" slice of "South Beach" in the Tenderloin's Phoenix; the "beautiful" "Zen decor", "hot DJs" and "healthy" Southeast-Asian nibbles attract a "sophisticated", "young", *"Melrose Place"*-esque crowd that can choose to "chill" or "party"; N.B. the outdoor area closes early for the sake of hotel guests.

Bar 821 ⌀   – | – | – | M

821 Divisadero St. (Fulton St.), unlisted phone; www.bar821.com
Ssshh, don't tell a soul, because this handsome hangout in the Western Addition offering a laid-back, friendly respite from the busy street outside is a neighborhood secret (the blue lights outside are its only 'sign'); with its ink-colored walls, gentle orange lighting and tasty tap selection, including Belgian brews like Leffe and Chimay, this well-designed space (offering beer and wine only) is just right for night-owls who prefer to roost on the down-low; N.B. the bar closes at 11 PM.

Bar None   11 | 8 | 13 | $6

1980 Union St. (Buchanan St.), 415-409-4469; www.barnonesf.com
Shots are the preferred tipples at this "loud" "hole-in-the-wall" Marina "basement bar" that feels "like college all over again" (to wit: "Bon Jovi at distortion-level volumes", "greasy fried food", "horny" superannuated "frat boys" and the "drunk chicks" who love them); on the plus side, "you can stand in the courtyard and smoke", but nonetheless, "if you're over 24, forget about it."

Bar on Castro ⌀   19 | 13 | 18 | $6

456B Castro St. (bet. 18th & Market Sts.), 415-626-7220
After a 2003 remodel, "the bar is darker, the crowd is bolder" and the "gropes go further" at this "cozy" bar in the Castro, whose new decor is described as very "red", "sexy" and sort of *"Barbarella* meets *Down With Love"* swank"; the "music's too loud to have much of a conversation", but it's still a "fun place to go" for the "cute boys", "relaxed vibe" and "reasonably priced drinks", including "killer frozen Cosmopolitans."

Bayside Sports Bar & Grill   16 | 11 | 15 | $6

1787 Union St. (Octavia Blvd.), 415-673-1565
"Get ready to rumble at this Cow Hollow spot", an "excellent place to watch sporting events" because of the "good, greasy bar food and cheap pitchers of beer", not to mention "tons of TVs" hooked to a dish so "you can literally see any game you want"; "wear your team's colors if you want to blend in", and "be prepared for large crowds elbowing for space."

Bazaar Café ⌀   – | – | – | I

5927 California St. (bet. 21st & 22nd Aves.), 415-831-5620; www.bazaarcafe.com
"The garden in back is a haven of serenity" at this "quirky but fun" "coffeehouse with zip" (i.e. beer and wine) that's "one of the few places in the Richmond to enjoy a drink outside"; it also cultivates "a sense of community", with a "friendly staff" that makes a point

to "learn your name", "yummy nibbles" as well as a nightly roster of "surprisingly good" local music that "adds to the warm feeling" inherent in this "cozy place."

Beach Chalet Brewery   19 | 18 | 13 | $7

1000 Great Hwy. (bet. Fulton St. & Lincoln Way), 415-386-8439; www.beachchalet.com

If there's a "full moon" outside yet you "want to stay warm while watching the waves", then this brewpub and "tourist mecca" in the Outer Richmond, directly across from Ocean Beach, is definitely "the place to go" for "great" ales and "gorgeous views"; those who beach about the "less-than-inspiring" food and "unfriendly" service may shore up renewed support thanks to the opening of the new glass-walled Park Chalet restaurant below; N.B. don't miss the scenic WPA murals downstairs.

Beale Street Bar & Grill   16 | 10 | 19 | $5

133 Beale St. (Mission St.), 415-543-1961; www.bealestreetsf.com

Boasting the "best mix of people", this "no-attitude bar" above an Embarcadero diner is a "great place to just be yourself" when "hanging out after work"; it's a "regular haunt for construction crews", "well-heeled businesspeople" and "leather-clad biker chicks", even though a few aesthetes lament it "looks like a mobile home being humped by a tent"; N.B. open for private events only on weekends.

Beat Lounge   – | – | – | M

501 Broadway (Kearny St.), 415-982-5299

Located downstairs from North Beach restaurant Jitney's, this little lounge is a "great place to chill and see some live music" that's heavy on jazz but also includes funk and groovy DJ action; the vibe is "charming and quiet during the week" but more "hell"-ish on weekends, though the "unbelievable service" keeps many hungry (and thirsty) hearts beating; N.B. open Thursday–Sunday.

Beauty Bar   19 | 18 | 14 | $7

2299 Mission St. (19th St.), 415-285-0323; www.beautybar.com

"All of the charm but none of the peroxide" of a '50s-era beauty parlor seduces a hair-brained horde of "hipster" "multitaskers" at this "high-concept" "drink-and-a-manicure" mecca in the Mission; with its "kitschy-cool" salon fixtures, "eclectic mix of DJs who keep it danceable" and "huge martinis", it's a magnet for "stylish chicks and dudes" as well as the inevitable "bachelorette parties"; those who snipe that it "needs a makeover for itself" may reassess now that's it's undergone a minor nip, tuck and paint job.

Bell Tower   17 | 15 | 21 | $6

1900 Polk St. (Jackson St.), 415-567-9596

A "sweet", "unpretentious" staff serving "reasonably priced", "nononsense drinks" keeps patrons primed at this "comfortable" "locals' paradise" on Polk Street; it's a "mellow place to meet up with friends" with a "nice patio" and an "excellent menu of high-quality food", and even though a few buzz-seekers say "zzzzz", bar belles boast "every neighborhood should have one."

Benders ⌓   – | – | – | I

806 S. Van Ness Ave. (19th St.), 415-824-1800; www.bendersbar.com

Futurama robot star Bender (in bust form) glares at the booze hounds animating the bar of this spacious Mission tavern that has otherwise barely changed since its Sacrifice days; booths beckon from the dark corners, and it's still a neighborhood favorite ("I go there way too often") for those who dig pool, cheap Pabst in a can, rock 'n' roll from a "killer jukebox" and now live music too.

BETELNUT PEJIU WU　　22 | 23 | 18 | $9 |
2030 Union St. (Buchanan St.), 415-929-8855;
www.betelnutrestaurant.com
Its "potent", "exotic" cocktails, including "great group drinks" such as "wicked scorpion bowls", only enhance the "killer" tropical decor and "breezy environment" at this Cow Hollow Pan-Asian; the "beautiful" crowd makes for "people-watching galore", and the "snobby staff" and "overflowing" conditions are almost redeemed by the "excellent" food and libations; P.S. "get a table outside."

B44　　19 | 17 | 19 | $9 |
44 Belden Pl. (bet. Bush & Pine Sts.), 415-986-6287; www.b44sf.com
"Takes me back to Barcelona" sigh those with a sparkle in their Spanish eyes for this "energetic" Catalan bistro Downtown; "on a warm evening" the outdoor seating along "European-style alley" Belden Place is "enticing", offering "brilliant wines and small plates" to go with the "great people-watching", and even when it's "busy" you can count on "friendly" service.

Bigfoot Lodge　　21 | 23 | 20 | $6 |
1750 Polk St. (Washington St.), 415-440-2355; www.bigfootlodge.com
Let the "log-cabin walls take you away from the city" at this "tons-of-fun bar" in Russian Hill, which "fans of camp" claim "a gem to be stumbled upon" for the female staff members in "great scout uniforms" and the "life-size Bigfoot" standing "hairy and tall" near the fireplace in back; others praise the "dim lighting" that's "cozy for dates" and "cheesy '80s" tunes that pump up the "kitschy" vibe.

Big 4　　23 | 24 | 24 | $10 |
Huntington Hotel, 1075 California St. (Taylor St.), 415-771-1140;
www.huntingtonhotel.com
"Feel like a millionaire just having a drink" at this "old-money classic" that ranks as "the king of Nob Hill bars" for its "elegant space" in the Huntington Hotel, "discreet service", "excellent" pianist and "sophisticated crowd"; displaying memorabilia related to California's past (the so-called 'Big Four' founded the Central Pacific Railroad), it "oozes history" best captured by "sinking into a leather chair with a brandy."

BIMBO'S 365 CLUB ⇗　　24 | 23 | 18 | M |
1025 Columbus Ave. (Chestnut St.), 415-474-0365;
www.bimbos365club.com
"You expect the Rat Pack to walk" into this "gorgeous" North Beach club that's been run by the same family since 1931; guys and dolls adore the "creative bookings" of "all musical genres", from the Brazilian Girls to Macy Gray to local faves, the "terrific bathroom attendants", the "acres of red velvet" ("could it get any swankier?") and the legendary "babe swimming in the fish tank behind the bar"; sure, it's "expensive", but the "cool vibe keeps you going back."

Biscuits & Blues　　19 | 13 | 15 | $9 |
401 Mason St. (Geary St.), 415-292-2583
This "friendly", "intimate" and "unpretentious" Downtown club downstairs from the restaurant offers what may be the "best blues

in town" thanks to the "top-notch" bookings and "excellent acoustics" along with some "homey Southern food"; if a few blast the "basic decor and service" and "sardine can" feeling, even they may reassess following a recent renovation.

Bissap Baobab   23 18 19 $7

2323 Mission St. (19th St.), 415-826-9287; www.bissapbaobab.com
"Beautiful, down-to-earth people" from around town and all over the world savor this Senegalese bar and restaurant that offers a "change of pace" in the "typically cooler-than-thou Mission"; it may be "tiny" but it's "worth finding" for the "affordable", "terrific food", dancing ("you'll never be at a loss for a partner") and "original" cocktails zinged up with tamarind and hibiscus; the "tropical back-porch" decor and "gorgeous staff" heat up the "warm" ambiance; N.B. sib Little Baobab nearby offers drinks and dancing until 2 AM.

Bitter End   18 15 19 $5

441 Clement St. (bet. 5th & 6th Aves.), 415-221-9538
There's really "nothing fancy about" this "cozy" Inner Richmond "hangout", but the "people provide the atmosphere" and a "great staff" supplies "true" pints of "Dublin-caliber" Guinness and "fine single malts"; there's also "one of the best pub quizzes in the city" on Tuesday nights, when "dedicated pop culture enthusiasts" compete "for honor", small prizes, moolah and the chance to "hear their sexually pointed team names read over the microphone."

BIX   25 26 22 $10

56 Gold St. (bet. Montgomery & Sansome Sts.), 415-433-6300; www.bixrestaurant.com
All are "treated like royalty" at this "spectacular" Downtown restaurant, jazz lounge and "metrosexual magnet" "nestled down a narrow", "romantic" alley between the Financial District and North Beach; with its "high ceilings", "huge murals" and "beautiful deco" details, it's a "swank place to impress" dates or guests and indulge in "the ultimate martini" (mixed by "lovely bartenders"), and even if it's "a zoo after work", it's always "special" to "get Bixed."

Black Horse London Pub ⚑   23 21 23 $5

1514 Union St. (bet. Franklin St. & Van Ness Ave.), 415-928-2414
Choose from a mere handful of barstools and five "excellent beers" ("they serve nothing else" save a "fantastic" cheese plate) at this "comically small" English pub in Cow Hollow; size matters not, though, as it's "super charming" and "you're guaranteed a great time chatting" and horsing around with your neighbors who, like it or not, are "packed in next to you"; N.B. James King, the cousin of former owner Joseph Gilmartin, now holds the reins to the stable.

Black Magic Voodoo Lounge ⚑   17 13 16 $6

1400 Lombard St. (Van Ness Ave.), 415-931-8711
Don't be spooked by the voodoo dolls and posters decorating the walls of this "unpretentious" hangout in the Marina, as the staff is "nice" and the vibe's "as goofy as its name"; no magic of any color, however, can keep critics from crying it's "pretty much a dump", though if there's a "good crowd" in the house it "can be fun."

Blackthorn Tavern   – – – M

834 Irving St. (bet. 9th & 10th Aves.), 415-564-6627; www.sfblackthorn.com
No, you're not in Dublin – this "dive pub" sits instead in the Inner Sunset, though it shares "comfortable" traits with many a classic

Irish tavern; "the friendly bartenders serve drinks promptly", and the bands supply "great entertainment" on open-mike nights.

BLISS BAR   20 | 22 | 18 | $7 |
4026 24th St. (bet. Castro & Noe Sts.), 415-826-6200; www.blissbarsf.com
A "suave" and "seductive" lounge in the otherwise "staid", "dog-leash-and-stroller" nabe of Noe Valley, this "date" destination delights "pretty people" with "high-style" decor including "plush" seating, a fireplace and "hip music"; "tasty little snacks", "fancy" (albeit "pricey") cocktails and a "chilled vibe" are other reasons it's "properly named"; P.S. the "secret" Blue Room to the rear is a favorite for private parties.

Blondie's Bar & No Grill ⊄   15 | 11 | 16 | $7 |
540 Valencia St. (bet. 16th & 17th Sts.), 415-864-2419
It's "fun to sit and watch the world go by" from the open windows at this "no-frills" Mission watering hole serving "massive martinis" in "many flavors" ("don't let the price fool you" as "all are doubles" and "served in a pint glass with your own strainer"); beware the weekends, however, when "locals" back off and "sweaty Marina imports clog up" the "little dance floor", creating a vibe that's "like going back to Cancún."

Blowfish Sushi to Die For   23 | 24 | 20 | $9 |
2170 Bryant St. (bet. 19th & 20th Sts.), 415-285-3848;
www.blowfishsushi.com
"Is it sushi or is it MTV?" ask anime-niacs about this "ultrahip hangout" in the Mission serving up "blasting" "techno-electronica" and "pornographic Japanimation" to accompany the "delicious", "creative" raw fish ferried by a "hot" staff that could "double" as walking "body-art exhibits"; a "young", "trendy" crowd doesn't mind the "too-loud" scene, especially after sampling the "ample sake selection" or the "fabulous" drinks with flavors that range from "timid to bold"; N.B. its new San Jose offshoot is unrated.

Blue Danube Coffeehouse ⊄   19 | 17 | 18 | $4 |
306 Clement St. (4th Ave.), 415-221-9041
When the "young, hip and unpretentious" who lack the benefit of "daddy's wallet" need to "hit the town", this "cool" coffeehouse in the Inner Richmond with heated lamps warming the outdoor seating area and free WiFi access is "everything the Redwood Room is not (and that's a good thing)"; it's a "cozy" "local spot" for "catching up" with pals over a latte, beer or glass of wine as well as watching live music and Thursday comedy acts; N.B. closes 11 PM on weekends.

Blue Light   14 | 12 | 14 | $6 |
1979 Union St. (bet. Buchanan & Laguna Sts.), 415-922-5510
"Fairly small" and "busy", this now-loungey "watering hole for the young and frisky" draws a "diverse (for Cow Hollow) crowd" that "comes to party", especially on Taco Tuesdays for "unbeatable" Mexican food and beer discounts; some sneer that "it may be full of pretty people and famous as the Fajitagate" joint (so named after a group of cops got tangled in a late-night fight over a bag o' tortillas), "but it still sucks"; N.B. a recent refurb may impact the Decor score.

Blur   _ | _ | _ | E |
1121 Polk St. (Hemlock St.), 415-567-1918; www.blursf.com
Brought to you by the owners of Tongue & Groove, this blur-the-lines Polk Street nigiri joint jumps on the successful trend of

blending fresh sushi with live DJs and sophisticated cocktails – features that stick together like rice and tingle like wasabi on a tekka maki; slide into a soft red banquette for a few rolls or belly up to the fully stocked bar and lap up a vodka-sake concoction called the Blurry Dog; N.B. sushi served Tuesday–Saturday only.

Bocce Cafe
19 | 20 | 17 | $7

478 Green St. (Grant Ave.), 415-981-2044
A "hidden treasure" humming "in the heart of North Beach", this Italian trattoria offers a garden that's "perfect" for "big group dinners and cheap Chianti", as well as a bar area that's "great for late-night drinks"; while it's "awfully crowded", especially on weekends, "it always seems like you've just wandered into a private party where everyone is delighted to see you."

Bohemia Bar & Bistro ⌐
13 | 12 | 15 | $6

1624 California St. (bet. Polk St. & Van Ness Ave.), 415-474-6968;
www.bohemiasf.com
"Night after night", this "low-key", "rather large" two-floor place near Polk filled with couches and game tables draws a "lively crowd" quaffing German and Czech beers; foes fume it's a "frat bar" "scene" that "needs a makeover", advising if "getting up on benches to dance" isn't your bag, just "visit for happy hour and then head out"; N.B. a recent renovation may impact the Decor score.

Boom Boom Room ⌐
21 | 17 | 18 | $6

1601 Fillmore St. (Geary Blvd.), 415-673-8000;
www.boomboomblues.com
"There's always something happening" on stage at this "classic juke joint" and former speakeasy in the Western Addition where the ghost of onetime owner John Lee Hooker "is still sipping bourbon" at the bar; "excellent", "top-name" blues, jazz, funk and R&B bands ensure lots of "moneymaker shaking", and though the "small" space gets "jammed", it's still a "great place for a second date."

Bottom of the Hill
22 | 14 | 16 | $7

1233 17th St. (bet. Missouri & Texas Sts.), 415-621-4455;
www.bottomofthehill.com
"Punk, indie, whatever", this "mecca for music fans" at the base of Potrero Hill is a "kick-ass venue" to see "amazing local and national bands" "on their way up", thanks to its "intimate" vibe and the "energy generated by the clientele"; fans sometimes get "packed in like sardines", but with bonuses like "cheap beer", a "great" patio in the summertime and "awesome Sunday BBQ" with "free burgers and dogs" "included in the price of your ticket", it's no wonder that the bottom line remains "it rocks."

BOULEVARD
26 | 26 | 25 | $11

1 Mission St. (Steuart St.), 415-543-6084;
www.boulevardrestaurant.com
The "lovely people-watching" includes San Francisco's "power players, gold diggers", "well-dressed" "expense-accounters" and other "smiling" supporters of this "ultimate city destination" in the Embarcadero, where Pat Kuleto's "elegant", "beautiful" and "comfortable" belle epoque–style interior is complemented by "delicious" food, "wonderful" wines and a "skillful, engaging" staff; *bien sûr,* the bar area's "small" and you'll spend "beaucoup bucks", but it's "worth the hype" *parce que* "nightlife doesn't get much better than this."

Bow Bow Cocktail Lounge
16 | 16 | 18 | $8

1155 Grant Ave. (bet. Broadway & Pacific Ave.), 415-421-6730
"It's easy to imagine WWII soldiers on leave and drinking" in this Chinatown "institution", where "sweet", "welcoming" bartender-owner Candy Wong "knows exactly what you want without asking"; it may be a "dive", but it has "wonderful ambiance" abetted by "good jukeboxes" and karaoke every night, and you can always "throw down some dice" with the aforementioned proprietress.

Brainwash
20 | 15 | 18 | $6

1122 Folsom St. (bet. 7th & 8th Sts.), 415-255-4866; www.brainwash.com
"Multitaskers" can "do laundry and settle in for a glass of wine" or beer and even "good food" at this "utilitarian" yet "homey" cafe and washeteria in SoMa; at night, a "fun, young crowd" awaiting the spin cycle can hear "poets and assorted groovy folks doing their thang" (music, readings, comedy) at this "alternative hangout."

Brazen Head ⊅
24 | 20 | 24 | $7

3166 Buchanan St. (Greenwich St.), 415-921-7600;
www.brazenheadsf.com
"If you can find this tiny" unmarked Cow Hollow bar and eatery tucked "behind shrubs and white lights", the "warm atmosphere" and "friendly, laid-back staff" are sure to make you "feel like an insider" who's privy to the "ultimate local hideaway"; it's "darker than dark" and it "doesn't seat many", but those it does tend to be "sociable" types "who can hold" both "booze and a conversation", always a plus; P.S. it gets "bonus points for serving food until 1 AM."

BRUNO'S
23 | 21 | 19 | $7

2389 Mission St. (20th St.), 415-648-7701; www.brunoslive.com
Relive the heyday of the "Rat Pack" at this "dark, quiet" and genuine "old-school, Vegas-style lounge" (albeit "without the cheese") in the Mission; thanks to a recent renovation, the "dimly lit", "super-swank" surroundings have a more open feel, with fewer rows of the "irresistible" red-and-white vinyl booths, making it swell for imbibing "great vintage cocktails", nibbling on small plates of Southern food and listening to "some of the city's best jazz."

BUBBLE LOUNGE
21 | 23 | 17 | $11

714 Montgomery St. (bet. Jackson & Washington Sts.), 415-434-4204;
www.bubblelounge.com
"Champagne is the game" at this "classy joint" in the Financial District that offers a "veritable bible" of "spectacular" by-the-glass and -bottle bubbly (25 and 250, respectively) and appetizers, all served in a "luscious luxe setting" ("high ceilings", "plush sofas") that makes you "feel like a socialite"; yes, it's "horrendously expensive" and "servers are a bit snobby", but most agree it's a real "treat-your-girl-right kind of place" and you "can't miss at happy hour", plus there are DJs to boot.

Buddha Bar ⊅
19 | 14 | 17 | $7

901 Grant Ave. (Washington St.), 415-362-1792
This "small", "hopping" "hole-in-the-wall" is "worth the trip to Chinatown" simply for the "lunatics behind the bar", whose "entertaining" theatrics "add to the charm" of the refreshingly "shabby", "gangster-movie" digs; a "mix of locals and hipsters" hail the "great jukebox", "cheap" beverages and "happy vibes", but warn "you'd better be ready to join the drinking team."

Buena Vista Cafe 24 | 17 | 19 | $7
2765 Hyde St. (Beach St.), 415-474-5044; www.thebuenavista.com
Despite its location on the "major tourist thoroughfare" near
Fisherman's Wharf, even "locals" succumb to the "guilty pleasure"
of popping into this "classic SF watering hole" for a "fantastic" Irish
coffee, the drink it "introduced to America" over 50 years ago and
upon which it still "hangs its hat"; the decor "hasn't changed since
it opened" in 1898, making for a "comfortable ambiance", and some
of the "legendary" staff will regale you with "stories if you ask."

Bus Stop 15 | 11 | 17 | $6
1901 Union St. (Laguna St.), 415-567-6905; www.busstopbar.com
Die-hard "heterosexuals" deem this Cow Hollow "institution" the
"definitive sports bar", with new high-definition flat-screen TVs,
pool tables, "cheap booze" and a "constant flow of regulars and
tourists" creating a "friendly" vibe; when the game's over, it
becomes a full-on "pickup scene" that's "frat-boy heaven or hell",
depending on your point of view, and its "rowdiness" played a role
in the 2003 Fajitagate incident, as the cops involved allegedly got
their buzz on here.

Butter 17 | 16 | 17 | $7
*354 11th St. (bet. Folsom & Harrison Sts.), 415-863-5964;
www.smoothasbutter.com*
"A bit of Peoria" in SoMa, this "awesome" "temple to trailer trash"
is now under new ownership but still supplies a taste of the
NASCAR lifestyle with PBR on tap, Jello shots, specialty drinks and
"excellent" "microwaved junk food" like White Castle burgers, corn
dogs and tater tots; a "young crowd" shakes its Daisy Dukes to
"great" tunes in the "small" space, although a few post-ironists
yawn it's "so far from cool it hurts."

butterfly 20 | 21 | 16 | $9
Pier 33 (Bay St.), 415-864-8999; www.butterflysf.com
"Well-dressed", "sexy" social butterflies swarm this "hipster
paradise" on the Embarcadero where the "warehouse look" is
warmed up with "grand Bay views"; though cynics caterwaul about
"obtrusive DJs" and "slow service", the "drinks are tops", the
food's "great", the live jazz is "cool" and the "feng shui's soothing";
N.B. the Mission original closed and morphed into Levende.

Buzz 9 20 | 20 | 22 | $6
139 Eighth St. (Minna St.), 415-255-8783; www.buzz9.com
Its "lively mix of journos, artists, judges, Euros" and "theater"-goers
adds to the buzz at this bi-level cafe and club located "within
walking distance of the Orpheum" in SoMa; "awesome bartenders
just want to get you liquored up" in the "cool underground lounge"
(a former speakeasy), and despite (or because of) the "cramped"
quarters, it provides an "intimate spot for hiding away with a new
significant other" or "dancing with a few friends."

Café ⌨ 17 | 13 | 16 | $6
2367 Market St. (Castro St.), 415-861-3846; www.cafesf.com
"After a much-needed face-lift", this "Castro mainstay continues
to draw crowds" with "cute boys", "circuit queens" and lesbians
vying for space on the "bumpin'" dance floor, "cool balcony",
"nice" smoking patio or at the new pool tables; the bartenders are
"the hottest", the drinks are "potent" and even if a few fume about

the "flashback mixes" and profusion of "out-of-town twinkies" ("Hostess must own stock"), more insist it's "aging gracefully"; N.B. the redo may outdate the Decor score.

Cafe Abir　20 | 17 | 18 | $5
1306 Fulton St. (Divisadero St.), 415-567-6503; www.tsunami-sf.com
"Students, ex-hippies and business folks" all flock to this "chill space" and "indie cafe" in the Western Addition for "great coffee", "yummy wine" and "good food"; perhaps it's "a little run-down at the edges", but its "funky atmosphere" is exactly the appeal, and with the "attached magazine shop", it becomes "a destination where you could spend a whole day" or evening.

Cafe Bastille　20 | 16 | 19 | $7
22 Belden Pl. (bet. Bush & Pine Sts.), 415-986-5673; www.cafebastille.com
"Hoist yourself onto a stool at the zinc bar" and order a glass of pastis to enhance that "authentic French feeling" you get at this Downtown bistro; the "fun Euro atmosphere" is amplified by "great" outdoor seating, "good" drinks and "charming" waiters, even though a few foes storm about the "faux"-ness of it all.

Café Claude　19 | 17 | 18 | $8
7 Claude Ln. (Bush St.), 415-392-3505; www.cafeclaude.com
"Lively" and "mellow", this "charming" French bistro Downtown offers "authentic" ambiance in the form of outside tables, "adorable snooty waiters", "tasty food and drinks" and "occasional live jazz"; the "tiny" bar is "cozy", making it a "favorite place to hide" (or "impress your girlfriend").

Cafe Cocomo　21 | 19 | 18 | $6
650 Indiana St. (bet. Mariposa & 19th Sts.), 415-824-6910; www.cafecocomo.com
"Get your salsa on" at this "excellent", recently expanded, "very Copacabana" venue in Dogpatch that hosts "wonderful" bands and assorted DJs (call before heading out, as the lineup changes frequently); "Thursday and Saturday nights are meant for hard-core" movers and shakers ("scarily good"), but even folks with two left feet find the vibe "friendly" and can retreat to the "cozy patio" or new second-level deck or opt for "fun" dance lessons if they "go early"; N.B. the dress code prohibits sneakers, T-shirts and caps.

Café du Nord　24 | 21 | 20 | $6
2170 Market St. (bet. Church & Sanchez Sts.), 415-861-5016; www.cafedunord.com
Renovations and a "change of ownership" brought "new life" to this "wonderful little" "underground" Upper Market "speakeasy" whose "retro" stylings and "deep-red" hues inspire cineastes to don their "best film-noir duds"; "fab drinks", "superb" musicians ("swing, jazz, indie") and "excellent acoustics" help supply an answer to the "'what should we do tonight' question."

Cafe Flore　23 | 19 | 18 | $5
2298 Market St. (Noe St.), 415-621-8579; www.cafeflore.com
You can "hang with your friends" or check out the boys while sipping "good house wine" or cocktails and "pretending to read" at this "excellent" Castro "landmark" that cognoscenti claim is the "queerest spot on Market Street"; with a "great outdoor space", it's "one of the best places in the city to people-watch", which is why, "to paraphrase *Casablanca,* everybody comes to Flore."

Cafe International ∅   ▽ 21 | 13 | 23 | $4
508 Haight St. (Fillmore St.), 415-552-7390; www.cafeinternational.com
"Grab a couch and a brew", a "great smoothie" or dinner and "enjoy a slice of Lower Haight culture" at this "cool" coffeehouse whose "sweet" owners are "two of the most fascinating people you'll ever come across"; "colorful murals", "fantastic" jazz and open-mike nights and a "mellow" vibe make it a "relaxing place to hang out."

Cafe Lo Cubano   – | – | – | M
3401 California St. (Laurel St.), 415-831-4672; www.cafelocubano.com
Lively conversation, live music and genuine Cuban coffee concoctions keep beanophiles buzzing until midnight at this Laurel Heights cafe; purr to live Latin and jazz as you indulge in hot pressed sandwiches and strong café con leche or, if zing is your thing, a tangy Michelada de Jerry (beer with dashes of Worcestershire, Tabasco, pepper and lime) with a salt-lick rim.

Cafe Macondo ∅   ▽ 22 | 21 | 21 | $4
3159 16th St. (bet. Albion & Guerrero Sts.), 415-431-7516
"Natural fibers" and a "progressive attitude" are the dress code when coming for coffee at this "authentic revolutionary cafe" in the Mission that now also offers beer and wine too; comrades commend its "kooky leftist" vibe and "cozy", "comfortable feel" complete with "non-matching tables and chairs", all the better for "hanging out for hours on a rainy day."

Café Niebaum-Coppola   19 | 22 | 19 | $10
916 Kearny St. (Columbus Ave.), 415-291-1700;
www.cafeniebaum-coppola.com
"Watch the world go by" while sampling "lots of good" vinos at Francis Coppola's "fun wine bar" located in the Sentinel building, an "architectural landmark" in North Beach (with a sequel in Palo Alto) that doubles as his film company headquarters; the outdoor tables on heated sidewalks are "lovely" for Tuckered types and the ambiance is "wonderful", but the "pretentious" staff and "overrated" offerings can be Conversation stoppers.

Café Prague ∅   21 | 19 | 18 | $7
584 Pacific Ave. (Columbus Ave.), 415-433-3811
"It could be the set from *The Little Shop Around the Corner*" claim Ernst enthusiasts of this "inviting" North Beach "haunt" that exudes "old-world charm"; "Czechs know their beer and it's easy to see why" here, and it also offers "great coffee", wines and "hearty food"; even though it's not exactly a "destination", there's disco music on Saturday nights, and "European expats" proclaim it the "perfect place to chill out."

Café Royale   – | – | – | M
800 Post St. (Leavenworth St.), 415-441-4099;
www.caferoyale-sf.com
"In a neighborhood dominated by old-school dives", this "lovely" Tenderloin "gem" is a "real draw" for an "interesting, eclectic mix" of mavens who enjoy "sophisticated beer and wine" selections along with "great" soju and sake cocktails; "comfortable" couches, an "intimate balcony for dates", "endless music choices" from the occasional DJs and live bands, plus "cordial" service help create a "fantastic hangout."

Caffè Greco 🚭   22 | 17 | 19 | $5
423 Columbus Ave. (bet. Green & Vallejo Sts.), 415-397-6261
"The staff greets everybody like family" at what many claim is their
"favorite North Beach coffee and dessert place" serving perhaps
the "best cappuccino in town"; though it gets "cramped", it's
"perfect for playing hooky from work", "people-watching" or
indulging in "a drop of sambuca" before "spending too much on
an Italian dinner" at one of the many trattorias "on the strip."

Caffe Puccini   18 | 15 | 18 | $6
411 Columbus Ave. (Vallejo St.), 415-989-7033
Listen up as "you might get an Italian aria sung to you by one of
the staff" at what some insist is "the premier North Beach cafe",
with sidewalk seating and "a little bit of glamour" to go with it;
"come for the coffee" or to "watch the world pass by", and hope,
like many do, that no one else "finds out about this little secret."

Caffe Trieste 🚭   22 | 15 | 17 | $6
601 Vallejo St. (Grant Ave.), 415-392-6739; www.caffetrieste.com
"Locals still hang out and argue about philosophy" at this "timeless"
"Beatnik-era" "stronghold" "in the heart of North Beach", its little
sister in Sausalito and latest arrival in Berkeley; serving up the
"best espresso outside Italy" and "great pastries" along with
opera and mandolin music on select Saturdays, they're worth the
"pilgrimage" whether you're an "artist", "poet", "tourist" or just
a javaholic who wants to "discuss Noam Chomsky."

Cama   - | - | - | E
(fka Doctor Bombay's)
3192 16th St. (Guerrero St.), 415-864-5255; www.camasf.com
'Laid-back' takes on new meaning at this revamped Mission
lounge, whose name in Spanish means 'bed', as in the padded,
pillowed perches beckoning parched patrons who order drinks like
the Pillow Talk and the Jet Lag from the overhead cocktail menu;
low lighting and smooth grooves cushion the mood in the main
room while a backyard lounge offers smokers a dreamy respite
from the slumber squad.

Campton Place   24 | 25 | 25 | $12
*Campton Place Hotel, 340 Stockton St. (bet. Post & Sutter Sts.),
415-955-5555; www.camptonplace.com*
"Understated elegance is the key" at this "fine boutique hotel
bar" that "does everything right" from the "sophisticated" new
decor to the "classy cocktails" and "wonderful wines" (17 by
the glass) served by an "attentive but unobtrusive" staff; a "well-
heeled" clientele prizes a "quiet spot" to kick back "after a hard
day of shopping", whether in Chinatown trinket shops or at "the
toniest Union Square stores", both only a short walk away.

C&L   - | - | - | E
(fka Charles Nob Hill)
1250 Jones St. (Clay St.), 415-771-5400; www.aqua-sf.com
Martinis run dry and Manhattans mean, while the wine is fine
inside the clubby lounge of this upscale steakhouse, formerly the
tony Charles Nob Hill and now a meat emporium founded by the
fish-friendly folks behind Aqua; the reborn room still has an old-
school vibe, while the gin in your glass and beef on your plate strike
a nice balance between classic and innovative.

Canvas Cafe/Gallery   23   24   18 $6
1200 Ninth Ave. (Lincoln Way), 415-504-0060; www.thecanvasgallery.com
"You feel cultured just being at" this "exciting" Inner Sunset "coffeehouse/gallery/performance space"/"singles scene" that offers an "eclectic" array of art and events, an "urbane setting for taking" it all in and now a full bar too; connoisseurs can "sit by the fire" "while a DJ spins or band plays" or "bring friends to share insightful comments with", though some prefer "plugging in" and "searching dating sites."

Capp's Corner   20   15   19 $7
1600 Powell St. (Green St.), 415-989-2589
"Some things never change", like this "excellent" restaurant with a "raucous bar to boot", a "great North Beach tradition" that's maintained the "same Italian feel" since opening in 1960 thanks to its memorabilia-covered walls; it's "one of the last true family-style places left", and the "outstanding" service contributes to its status as a "convenient" "gathering place" for a quick drink before *Beach Blanket Babylon*.

Carnelian Room   24   23   21 $10
Bank of America Ctr., 555 California St., 52nd fl. (bet. Kearny & Montgomery Sts.), 415-433-7500
You "can't get any higher (legally) in San Francisco" than this "renowned" restaurant and lounge affording "unbelievable" "views from atop the Bank of America building"; sure, it's a tad "stuffy" for some surveyors, and libations are "expensive", but "on fogless days" the experience is definitely "worth one drink to show out-of-towners", "dates" or "your mom" the "spectacular" cityscapes; N.B. jackets are suggested for men after 5 PM.

Casanova Lounge ⊅   20   17   16 $5
527 Valencia St. (bet. 16th & 17th Sts.), 415-863-9328
"Play pool and listen to rock" on "one of the best jukeboxes in the city" at this "groovy spot" with "comfy seating", "great homemade lamps" and "paintings of skanky nudes"; a "stand-up" vibe, "straightforward drinks" and "far-out DJs" seduce its "cool" clientele most nights, but "weekend warriors" "slumming it in the Mission" raise its "low profile" too high for locals.

Cat Club ⊅   18   10   14 $7
1190 Folsom St. (bet. 7th & 8th Sts.), 415-431-3332
Though it's "not for the faint of heart or the Marina blond", this SoMa dance club "gets it right" by "catering to the freaks, rejects and throwbacks" of the Bay Area, with DJs spinning "punk, mod, Goth, new wave and industrial" along with Tuesdays' Drunken Monkey party, the "super-crowded" 1984 on Thursdays and all-girl Saturdays; drinks are "strong", making it the "perfect pickup joint for a weekend date"; N.B. a post-*Survey* redo outdates the Decor score.

C. Bobby's Owl Tree ⊅   24   25   14 $5
601 Post St. (Taylor St.), 415-776-9344; www.theowltree.com
"An explosion of owls" – stuffed, carved and ceramic – "adorns every corner" of this otherwise "divey" Downtown bar, their "watchful eyes on you" as you munch on complimentary Chex Mix and "sip cheap well drinks"; most admit "grumpy" owner Bobby "doesn't have much of a bedside manner", but "you gotta

love the webcam" and the overall "cuckoo" milieu, 'cuz it's "the kind of place that makes SF great."

Centerfolds ⌐   18 | 12 | 18 | $10
391 Broadway (Montgomery St.), 415-834-0662; www.centerfoldssf.com
"Tattooed and pierced vixens sway to overly loud music" and will give you a grind for the right price at this "average lap-dance establishment" in North Beach; it's "good R-rated entertainment" that's "ok for a bachelor party", but keep in mind you "can't drink" (sodas only), "can't touch" and "you're definitely being watched" ("presidential contenders need not apply").

Cha Cha Cha @ Original McCarthy's   21 | 17 | 18 | $6
2327 Mission St. (bet. 19th & 20th Sts.), 415-648-0504; www.cha3.com
This Cuban-Caribbean tapas lounge "housed in an old Irish" tavern in the "heart of the Mission" "brilliantly captures the melting pot" that is San Francisco and provides a "cool place to hang with friends or celebrate a birthday"; vets advise "definitely get the sangria" ("awesome but deadly"), and try to cop a seat around the "huge" "horseshoe-shaped bar" for some "fun people-watching."

Chaise Lounge   – | – | – | M
(fka Charlie's Club)
309 Cortland Ave. (Bocana St.), 415-401-0952
Female fans mourning the passing of Charlie's Club, the longtime Bernal Heights stomping ground, won't be sorry for long once they kick back at this snazzy, comfortable new lesbian lounger, spruced up with elegant chandeliers and a private make-out room; face-lift aside, the neighborhood vibe remains solidly in place, and so does the vintage mural in the front room; plans are on the drawing board for a glassed-in back area with a fireplace.

Chaya Brasserie   22 | 21 | 19 | $10
132 The Embarcadero (bet. Howard & Mission Sts.), 415-777-8688; www.thechaya.com
When the clock strikes five, a "pretty crowd" in power suits pours in for the "happy-hour drink and sushi specials" at this "trendy", "*très* cool" Los Angeles outpost in the Embarcadero; "innovative cocktails", "comfy furnishings" and "friendly" service are reasons enough for the "small bar area" to "fill up quickly", but the "fantastic views of the Bay Bridge" seal the deal for the "Downtown crowd."

Cherry Bar & Lounge   – | – | – | M
917 Folsom St. (5th St.), 415-974-1585; www.thecherrybar.com
Mariah Hanson, the founder of Palm Springs' popular Dinah Shore Weekend, is the force behind this SoMa lesbian lounge, where women (and depending on the night some men) mix for DJ parties, live music and other happenings; despite a lipstick-red redo, cherry-pickers grr-ripe that it's "still waiting to fulfill its potential."

Chieftain Irish Pub & Restaurant   17 | 16 | 21 | $6
198 Fifth St. (Howard St.), 415-615-0916; www.thechieftain.com
There may be "dozens of Irish bars in San Francisco, but this one gets the mix right", offering "a nice place to sit back and have a few" pints or watch European sports events (opens at 5 AM for major games) on satellite TV with the "super-friendly" SoMa crowd; the pub "feels like it's been around 100 years" thanks to fixtures and furniture shipped over from the Olde Sod, and the "cool" staff and "great" live music are more reasons to say *slainte*.

Cinch Saloon ⇗　　　∇ 16 ｜ 16 ｜ 20 ｜ $5

1723 Polk St. (bet. Clay & Washington Sts.), 415-776-4162;
www.thecinch.com

"Hold onto your hat 'cause it's going to be a wild ride", as this
"always-hopping gay bar" on Polk Street "is a serious drinking
place" and the "reasonable prices" make it a cinch; "funky Western
decor", a "small patio out back" and a "refreshingly unpretentious"
vibe make it "a good place to relax", and though cynics suggest
the cowpokes are perhaps a tad "older and less aesthetically
pleasing than their Castro" counterparts, "they're friendlier" too.

Cip　　　– ｜ – ｜ – ｜ E

(fka My Place)

1225 Folsom St. (8th St.), 415-863-1290

Purse your lips and slowly savor every sip of the many by-the-glass
champagnes or rose, orange and cucumber cocktails populating
the menu at this newly made-over SoMa space; its seedy days as
gay hook-up hot spot My Place have slipped into history, leaving
sleek furnishings and moody lighting that hint at atomic-age chic.

Circolo　　　– ｜ – ｜ – ｜ E

(fka Gordon's House of Fine Eats)

500 Florida St. (Mariposa St.), 415-553-8560; www.circolosf.com

The Mission space housing onetime dot-com mainstay Gordon's
House of Fine Eats is now a multilevel venue designed by co-owner
and local club maven Jon Mayeda; evening meals and late-night
grooves round out the offerings, while behind a cool mesh curtain
in an adjacent lounge, DJs spin for a crowd lubricated by mango
mojitos and lychee gimlets.

Cityscape　　　23 ｜ 22 ｜ 19 ｜ $10

Hilton San Francisco & Towers, 333 O'Farrell St. (Mason St.),
415-923-5002; www.cityscaperestaurant.com

"Get dolled up", as it's "a real treat to have a drink" and gaze upon
the "breathtaking" 360-degree views from this lounge set 46 stories
high atop the Union Square Hilton; "cool your heels between deals"
or make "meaningful conversation on a first date", but don't expect
a "hot spot" or the DJ to play anything that's not "generic";
N.B. there's a cover charge after 10 PM on weekends.

City Tavern　　　15 ｜ 14 ｜ 15 ｜ $6

3200 Fillmore St. (bet. Greenwich & Moulton Sts.), 415-567-0918

You "can't go wrong with $2 Tuesdays" when a couple of bucks will
buy you a beer, well drink or an appetizer that keeps city slickers
returning to this "cornerstone of the Triangle region" in Cow Hollow;
it remains an "unpretentious" place to "gather with friends" or to
"scope out the singles scene" packed with "Marina newbies" (aka
"fish in a barrel"), but be warned: if you're on the other side of 30,
you're "overage" here.

Cliff House　　　20 ｜ 18 ｜ 16 ｜ $8

1090 Point Lobos Ave. (Great Hwy.), 415-386-3330; www.cliffhouse.com

"If the weather cooperates, nothing beats" "having a cocktail
and watching the waves" or a "showstopper sunset" from the
oceanside windows of this "true classic" (the current building
dates to 1909 and the original to 1863) in the Outer Richmond
that's been transformed into a stark white modern setting; don't
expect to be alone, however, as there are usually "loads of

buses parked outside" ("can you say 'tourist'?"); N.B. the recent renovations may outdate the Decor score.

Clooney's Pub ⊄   — | — | — | I

1401 Valencia St. (25th St.), 415-826-4988; www.clooneyspub.com
"You'll meet some good characters" and lots of "real people" at this longtime Mission family-owned joint and its San Carlos offshoot where you can count on snagging a stool despite its proximity to the area's trendiest clubs; it might be "the epitome of a dive bar", however ("*Barfly* could've been filmed here"), so leave your Gucci at home.

Club Deluxe ⊄   19 | 18 | 18 | $6

1509 Haight St. (Ashbury St.), 415-552-6949; www.clubdeluxesf.com
"You must have a martini to feel comfortable" at this "smooth" "retro rockabilly bar" that bestows "a little civility" on the Upper Haight; "hipsters turn out in droves to soak up the Eisenhower-era charm", remembering that "bowler hats and wide ties go well with the hard drinks and entertainment" that ranges from jazz to swing.

Club EZ5   — | — | — | M

682 Commercial St. (Kearny St.), 415-362-9321
"Walk through the inconspicuous door" of this recently renovated Downtown spot on the edge of Chinatown and you are "instantly transported to 1967" via the "orange walls, Scandinavian modular furniture and bean-bag chairs"; DJs get a groove going and "there's room to dance when the bar's not booming", but generally "patrons are more focused on socializing" with each other as well as the "charming" staff and "not messing their spectacular haircuts."

Club Hide   — | — | — | M

280 Seventh St. (bet. Folsom & Howard Sts.), 415-621-1197
Leave your chaps back at the ranch as this SoMa club has shaken the cowboy persona from its past incarnation as Rawhide in favor of a slicker, more contemporary vibe with hip-hop and house on the new sound system; it's still a "big" venue with a "large main dance area" downstairs and a patio upstairs where the weary can hide under the heat lamps; N.B. open Thursday–Saturday.

Club Six   ▽ 17 | 15 | 19 | $7

60 Sixth St. (bet. Market & Mission Sts.), 415-863-1221; www.clubsix1.com
"It doesn't look like much from the outside" and certainly its "rough neighborhood" on a stretch of Sixth Street "may dissuade you", but "consummate young clubbers" consider this SoMa lounge to be "bouncing" with "rockin'" DJs, "great drinks" and a "cool underground vibe"; P.S. those who once fumed about the "poor ventilation" and "grungy" decor just might give it a high-five thanks to its new look, complete with an additional level, loungey feel and live music room.

Cobb's Comedy Club   — | — | — | E

915 Columbus Ave. (Lombard St.), 415-928-4320; www.cobbscomedyclub.com
Its "gorgeous", 8,000-sq.-ft. new digs providing 400 seats in North Beach means this venerable comedy club can accommodate more chuckleheads in the space that was the elite Lido Lounge in the 1920s and later the Bill Graham–run Wolfgang's; it's a showcase for A-list acts and musicians, but keep the two-drink minimum in mind when budgeting your night out.

Columbus Café ✍ 19 10 17 $5
562 Green St. (Columbus Ave.), 415-421-8003
"Leave your attitude at the door" when venturing into this "real man's bar" in North Beach to indulge in what many call "the best happy hour in the city", and the "cheap drinks" are even easier to swallow in the "laid-back atmosphere"; an "older", "friendly" crowd appreciates the "great staff" that's sometimes known to mete out "tough love."

Comet Club 13 10 13 $6
3111 Fillmore St. (Filbert St.), 415-567-5589
"Come late, come soused and bring your dancing shoes" say comet-tators about this "small, popular" Cow Hollow club where "'80s music meets the Top 40"; it's "jammed" with a "young" crowd ("the state should put a college next door"), and naysayers tag it a "sweat factory", but admit "if you can get in the door and you've had at least 10 cocktails, then it rocks."

Connecticut Yankee 21 17 20 $6
100 Connecticut St. (17th St.), 415-552-4440; www.theyankee.com
"The beer always seems colder" at this refreshingly "normal", "friendly sports bar" at the bottom of Potrero Hill, home base for "huge Red Sox fans" and other "New England expatriates" looking to "grab some drinks", eat some "hearty" chowdah and "watch the game" on new plasma TVs; "prices are fair", and the "patio's a great place to chill", making it a "good neighborhood hang."

Cortez – – – E
Hotel Adagio, 550 Geary St. (Taylor St.), 415-292-6360; www.cortezrestaurant.com
"So hip it hurts" say enthusiasts who've explored the drinks, tapas and other delights at this "hot" *hermana* to Chez Nous in the Downtown Hotel Adagio; hearts are conquered by the "amazing decor" featuring Mondrian-ish panels and "lighting from the next century", along with the "unusual", "delicious" cocktails and lots of vinos by the glass served by "knowledgeable bartenders", though a few feel oppressed by the "expensive" offerings.

Cosmopolitan Cafe, The 19 21 18 $9
Rincon Ctr., 121 Spear St. (bet. Howard & Mission Sts.), 415-543-4001; www.thecosmopolitancafe.com
"One of the best happy-hour spots" in SoMa is this restaurant with a "popular bar" that caters to "young professionals" as well as an "older, richer crowd" with "sophisticated decor", "excellent", "strong drinks" and "tasty" small plates; though a few world-weary sorts scorn the after-work "meat market" scene "frequented by predatory lawyers", when it "clears out later" you can "carry on a conversation" or listen to the singer/pianist.

COZMO'S CORNER GRILL 18 18 17 $8
2001 Chestnut St. (Fillmore St.), 415-351-0175; www.cozmoscorner.com
"*The Bachelor* should hold casting" calls at this Marina mecca (Cosmopolitan Cafe's sibling) where "San Francisco yuppie types come, unapologetically, to hook up" with their fellow "beautiful people" in a "stylish" yet "comfortable" setting; sure, it's "noisy" and "squishy", but "well-made" cocktails and "good wines by the glass" along with the "fun-loving crowd" make it "worth a trip."

Crow Bar ⌿   15 | 10 | 16 | $5

401 Broadway (Montgomery St.), 415-788-2769

"Despite its rough location and gruff exterior", this "no-nonsense North Beach bar" boasts the "best beer list in the neighborhood" and a "cavernous" space in which to "drink, shoot pool and hide from the sun"; sure, the crowd's less than "savory", and lotharios lament the lack of "beautiful ladies", but there's also "never an attitude" at this "wonderfully decadent watering hole."

Daddy's ⌿   15 | 13 | 18 | $6

440 Castro St. (bet. 18th & Market Sts.), 415-621-8732;
www.daddysbar.com

"Rougher-looking daddy types congregate" at this longtime leather bar in the Castro, an "edgy" escape from the neighborhood's "sweater bars"; the decor here may be "as old and butch as the clientele" (not exactly a "Tom of Finland fantasy"), but the staffers are as "genuinely nice" as they are "hot", especially when clad in their Calvins on Monday 'Underwear Nights' and half-naked on Wednesday 'Faggot Nights.'

Dalva ⌿   22 | 19 | 19 | $6

3121 16th St. (bet. Albion & Valencia Sts.), 415-252-7740

"If you're not careful, you'll miss" the entrance of this "moody", "transcendent" Mission "fave", "but once inside you'll like the candlelight and intimate surroundings", the DJs who spin Monday through Thursday, plus what many hail as the "hippest jukebox in the city"; the "understated", "dark" and "narrow space" appeals to an "unpretentious crowd" that knows to order some "mean sangria" "before catching a flick at the Roxie next door", but be warned: "it's jammed on weekends."

Dave's   – | – | – | I

29 Third St. (bet. Market & Mission Sts.), 415-495-6726

Located within walking distance of both the Financial District and Yerba Buena Gardens and just a half-block from the BART, this SoMa tavern makes "a perfect after-work happy-hour bar" for stiffs looking to unwind from a long day dodging memos or tourists at the museums; the "drinks are cheap", there's light fare and bar food and the no-frills atmosphere "gives non-snobs a real place to relax."

Delaney's   19 | 11 | 21 | $5

2241 Chestnut St. (bet. Pierce & Scott Sts.), 415-931-8529

"An oasis in the middle" of the "high-maintenance" Marina, this "casual, dive-ish" Irish bar "looks unimpressive" from the outside, but inside you'll partake of "PBR on tap and fresh popcorn" served by a "wonderful" staff in an "unpretentious" atmosphere; the owners who took over a few years ago have changed little but spiffed up the digs a bit.

Delirium Cocktails ⌿   ∇ 17 | 13 | 19 | $5

3139 16th St. (Albion St.), 415-552-5525

"Stiff drinks" mixed by the "friendliest bartenders in the Mission", an "unpretentious crowd", pool tables and free barbecue during weekend game telecasts create an "excellent neighborhood feel" at this "great dive"; the semi-"secret dance floor" in the back room plays host to nightly DJs and "fun parties" like 'Built for Speed', plus chicks cheer a "large male-to-female ratio."

Divas ⍝ | ▽ 15 | 14 | 14 | $6 |
1081 Post St. (Polk St.), 415-474-3482; www.divassf.com
"Don't go searching for damsels in distress" at this "intriguing" tri-level club off Polk Street "unless you're prepared for surprises of the third" kind, 'cause the performers taking the stage three nights a week may be "hotter and friendlier than any other exotic dancers in town", but 'girls' they are not; "tranny-chasers" cheer it as a "must-experience", adding "if you like it, you'll be back, if not, what a story!", and what's more, there's karaoke and burlesque on the bill too.

DNA Lounge ⍝ | 21 | 18 | 17 | $8 |
375 11th St. (Harrison St.), 415-626-1409; www.dnalounge.com
There's "no stupid dress code and no attitude, just the best house music around" at this "SoMa institution" that was a "hot spot back in the 1980s" and is now part of the genetic code of a "large, mixed crowd" of clubbers; the "top sound system", acoustics that are "perfect for bumpin' loud beats" and a multilevel space make it "fabulous for dancing", which on certain nights continues after hours; P.S. you can also "check out the scene" via streaming video on its Web site.

Doc's Clock ⍝ | 20 | 12 | 21 | $5 |
2575 Mission St. (bet. 21st & 22nd Sts.), 415-824-3627
"It's always cocktail time" at this "classic" "dive" whose "friendly", "unpretentious" owners and staff are "far from stingy with the alcohol"; you can meet "Mission hipsters" and "local rockers" at the "long, narrow bar" or "master" shuffleboard in a "very David Lynch" atmosphere "back-lit by neon"; either way, the "strong cocktails" make it a "good place to stagger out of at 2 AM"; N.B. a recent change of hands may impact the above scores.

Dogpatch Saloon ⍝ | – | – | – | I |
2496 Third St. (22nd St.), 415-643-8592
With its "dark" interior and "excellent saloon"-style decor, this "neighborhood bar" in Dogpatch, a former "no-man's land" that's gradually coming into its own, is "great for anonymous dates"; "Sunday afternoon jam sessions" and a location right next to the new MUNI light-rail line signals that this "up and comer" may have arrived.

Dolce | – | – | – | E |
440 Broadway (Montgomery St.), 415-989-3434;
www.dolcesf.com
The movers and shakers behind the nightclubs Sno-Drift and the now-defunct Blind Tiger and production companies Mixed Elements and Latitude 38 also back this swanked-out North Beach party palace; pour some sugar on the 2,500-sq.-ft. dance floor, whisper sweet nothings in the bar or laid-back VIP lounge and indulge in a slice of la dolce vita; N.B. open Wednesday–Saturday.

Dovre Club ⍝ | ▽ 15 | 9 | 18 | $4 |
1498 Valencia St. (26th St.), 415-285-4169
"Makes me long for Dublin" exclaim ex-Pats of this "nifty little" "diamond in the rough" that's "tucked away" in a far corner of the Mission; the crowd's a "mix" of "young, trendy" types and "old-timers", many of whom are here for the pub's "great Guinness pour" and not the "nothing-fancy" digs.

Dubliner, The   19 | 14 | 20 | $5
3838 24th St. (bet. Church & Vicksburg Sts.), 415-826-2279
Though it may be "nothing special" on the outside, "real Irish bartenders and local boozers add a nice touch of authenticity" to this "decent pub in Noe Valley"; a "wide variety" of "glorious beers", "wonderful" staff, "protected patio" for "tobacco fiends" and "great jukebox" are additional assets of this "comfy hangout."

Dylan's   ▽ 25 | 15 | 24 | $4
2301 Folsom St. (19th St.), 415-641-1416
Followers of this Welsh pub in the Mission don't rage against the dying of the light as they welcome the chance to "unwind after work" with the "friendliest people you'd ever want to meet" over a few pints; other rare bits include "good prices", a "favorite quiz night", "great Sunday evening jazz jam sessions" and memorabilia that contributes to the "character" of this "ultimate" "local."

Eagle's Drift In Lounge ⊅   – | – | – | I
1232 Noriega St. (19th Ave.), 415-661-0166
Desperados and others who may or may not have come to their senses commonly take it easy in the confines of this Outer Sunset hangout where dart and pool tournaments are among the main orders of business; it's hardly a trendy place, though, which may incite fast-lane fanatics to drift out.

Eagle Tavern ⊅   22 | 16 | 22 | $5
398 12th St. (Harrison St.), 415-626-0880; www.sfeagle.com
"Don't forget your leathers and mirrored aviators" when dropping by this "hot cruise bar" in SoMa that attracts "a cross-section of the fetish community" especially on Sundays for the "compulsory" charity beer busts ("a true celebration of SF's gayness"); "biker paraphernalia" and "cool art" adorn the interior, while a heated "spacious patio" is perfect for "smoking or sunning"; P.S. "party people of all genders and persuasions" mix it up on Thursdays for live punk, blues and other music shows.

E&O Trading Company   20 | 21 | 18 | $8
314 Sutter St. (bet. Grant & Stockton Sts.), 415-693-0303; www.eotrading.com
"After-workers", "shoppers" and "tourists" converge at this recently refurbished Downtown destination (with a new outpost in Larkspur and a sibling in San Jose) whose "elegant", "spacious" and slightly "funky" interior is always "hopping"; live music three nights a week, "delicious", "creative" "umbrella drinks", "smooth" house ales and "appetizing" Asian fusion fare are the stock in trade, though a few blasé sorts sniff it's "passé" and "overpriced" to boot.

Eastside West   20 | 19 | 18 | $7
3154 Fillmore St. (Greenwich St.), 415-885-4000
With its "jazzy atmosphere", "great food and drinks" and "overall good vibe", this Cow Hollow restaurant and lounge attracts a "mellow" thirtysomething crowd bent on "catching the beats spinning" in the "comfy" back room that features a "mesmerizing aquarium"; on "weeknights you can grab seats at the bar and own the place", but weekends are a "crapshoot", and if you're not into a "bridge-and-tunnel crowd" or "too many people", you're coming up snake eyes.

Edinburgh Castle Pub　　　　18 | 16 | 18 | $5
950 Geary St. (bet. Larkin & Polk Sts.), 415-885-4074;
www.castlenews.com
"Dark and foreboding, just like Scotland", this "unique" "classic
in the middle of the Tenderloin" treats its "eclectic" clan to "great
live music", readings by "good" writers such as Irvine Welsh and
"competitive Tuesday trivia nights" in a large setting filled with
"trappings" from the auld country; throw in darts, a "huge beer
selection" and "fabulous fish 'n' chips" "delivered to your table in
yesterday's paper" and it's all a "proper Anglophile could want."

Eight　　　　– | – | – | E
(fka Up & Down Club)
1151 Folsom St. (7th St.), 415-431-1151; www.eightsf.com
Acid-jazz landmark the Up & Down Club has up and split, and
this two-story SoMa nightclub has taken its place; video screens,
sconces and groovy cocktail tables line the narrow space while
guest promoters set the tone for hot numbers kicking back, getting
jiggy on the dance floor or puffing away between brightly lit palms
out on the patio.

850 Cigar Bar　✳　　　22 | 19 | 21 | $7
850 Montgomery St. (bet. Jackson St. & Pacific Ave.), 415-398-0850;
www.cigarbarandgrill.com
"Classy without being stuffy" affirm aficionados of this "mellow
oasis" Downtown, where a "cool, mixed crowd" lauds "quick",
"friendly" service, "good", "reasonably priced" drinks in a "quaint"
"Cuban"-style setting and the chance to "enjoy a cigar" – but due
to a change of hands, in the "great" courtyard only ("get a table
near the fountain"); P.S. check out the "excellent" and "absolutely
danceable" Latin jazz Wednesday through Saturday.

Elbo Room ⇥　　　19 | 13 | 17 | $6
647 Valencia St. (bet. 17th & 18th Sts.), 415-552-7788; www.elbo.com
The prospect of "fantastic musical acts" upstairs, video games and
"serious pool on the ground floor" and a "cheap" happy hour has
Missionites elbowing their way into this "cool two-story bar"; the
concerts come in varying genres, but you can always "lounge for
the price of a drink downstairs"; even if the "decor feels like your
high school friend's basement" and the name's a "misnomer", you
get "all the mood of a smoky jazz club without the carcinogens" and
a "good time" too.

Eldo's Grill & Brewery　　　19 | 20 | 18 | $6
1326 Ninth Ave. (bet. Irving & Judah Sts.), 415-564-0425
"Amazing seasonal ales", "spectacular" margaritas and "great
appetizers with a south-of-the-border" bent are among the draws at
this Inner Sunset brewpub; "personable bartenders" and "comfy"
seating also elicit *olés,* but bashers boo the beer as "bland", the
decor as "franchise"-like and the service as "slow."

Element Lounge　　　　– | – | – | M
1028 Geary St. (bet. Polk St. & Van Ness Ave.), 415-440-1125;
www.elementlounge.com
Come Tuesday nights, the insolvent and the beautiful are in their
element at this DJ-and-drinking destination just off Van Ness, home
to the weekly 'Broke as F---' party (can't beat that $1 Pabst and $3
shots); but that's not the bar's only glory night, as crowds cavort

nightly under a vaulted ceiling to hip-hop, '80s tunes and house in a setting inspired by fire, water and other elemental substances.

Elite Cafe
18 | 19 | 19 | $8

2049 Fillmore St. (bet. California & Pine Sts.), 415-346-8668
"Chase an oyster with the coldest martini on Fillmore (then put your name on the waiting list for a booth and have another)" at this "upscale" New Orleans–flavored seafooder; though it can get "crowded and loud", it's "wonderful to meet up" with a "date" or a "friend" (it's "good for older singles") at the "super-small bar" to enjoy an "excellent" cocktail and primo "people-watching."

Elixir
– | – | – | M

3200 16th St. (Guerrero St.), 415-552-1633; www.elixirsf.com
Even locals may be surprised at the historic pedigree of this Mission saloon (it's been hawking booze since at least 1907), as most know it for the decent "selection of beer on tap" and Tuesday trivia nights; the "tiny room" has been rejuvenated with a "face-lift", enhancing its Victorian-era patina, but it's just as much "a nice, low-key place" as ever that's "great for a late-night" brew or a Bloody Mary from the build-your-own bar on a Sunday afternoon.

El Rio ∌
23 | 16 | 17 | $5

3158 Mission St. (bet. Cesar Chavez & Valencia St.), 415-282-3325; www.elriosf.com
A "fabulous pansexual crowd" of every "culture, color and preference" "feels at home" at this "unique" Mission "favorite" where the entertainment ranges from the "best salsa night" to "great world beat" bands to "free belly-dancing lessons"; the main attraction, though, is the "sublime", "lush" back patio for "chilling" on a "warm evening" of "diversity and Dos Equis"; P.S. "don't miss free oysters on the half-shell during Friday happy hour."

ENDUP, THE ∌
22 | 15 | 18 | $6

401 Sixth St. (Harrison St.), 415-357-0827; www.theendup.com
"The only after-hours club worth knowing about in the city" may be this SoMa "institution" that's been attracting a "happening" gay and straight "party crowd" for three decades and counting; it's "always a good place" to boogey or hang on the patio that "buzzes with a positive vibe"; other endowments include 'Fag Fridays' that are a "blast" and the 'Sunday T Dances' from 6 AM to 8 PM when you can "worship to the beat of house music."

ENRICO'S SIDEWALK CAFE
23 | 20 | 19 | $8

504 Broadway (Kearny St.), 415-982-6223; www.enricossidewalkcafe.com
With its "large", "atmospheric" outdoor seating area, this 45-year-old "perennial hot spot" "in the heart of North Beach" offers a "classic people-watching" scenario; "the mojitos are famous" ("two make you wobble and three may kill you"), you can order from the small-plates menu and "excellent" "live jazz in the background" only enhances the "romantic" mood; it might be "too popular with tourists and suburbanites to be hip", but even those who "hate to admit" it affirm "it rocks."

Eos Restaurant & Wine Bar
23 | 20 | 22 | $10

901 Cole St. (Carl St.), 415-566-3063; www.eossf.com
This "lively wine bar" and restaurant "in a cool neighborhood" (Cole Valley) is an "excellent place to try new" vintages and labels from

its "outstanding list" of 40 by the glass served by a "knowledgeable but not pushy" staff; the "cool", "industrial"-style setting can get a tad "loud" with a large influx of "yuppie hipsters", so "try going on a weeknight" for a more "mellow vibe."

Equinox   22 | 18 | 18 | $11
Hyatt Regency Hotel, 5 Embarcadero Ctr. (Market St.), 415-291-6619
Expect "good old San Francisco hospitality" along with an Asian-inspired ambiance and "fantastic panoramas of the Bay Bridge and the city" from the windows of this "revolving" circular lounge atop the Hyatt Downtown; it's "a great place for a date" or "a nightcap with out-of-town guests", and while some complain about the "hefty" tabs and "cheesy pseudo-futuristic decor", vista-ficionados retort "you go there for the view, the whole view and nothing but the view"; N.B. renovations are scheduled for 2006.

Esta Noche ⊄   17 | 12 | 16 | $5
3079 16th St. (bet. Rondel Pl. & Valencia St.), 415-861-5757
"Best damn Latin drag anywhere" shout supporters of this home to "over-the-top camp" that's one of the "great secrets of the Mission"; the venue itself is "a bit rough around the edges", but the nightly cross-dressing shows starring lip-synching "lovely ladies" (of a sort) are "a hoot and a holler", and those with "the *cojones* to walk in" are rewarded by a "truly raunchy good time."

Expansion Bar ⊄   – | – | – | I
2124 Market St. (Church St.), 415-863-4041
Those with a hankering for an "honest-to-goodness dive bar" could do worse than this Upper Market shot-and-a-beer emporium; regulars along with a handful of hipsters from nearby Cafe du Nord find ways to expand their horizons among the joint's plain-spoken digs, and when conversations lag there's a "great jukebox."

Factory 525 ⊄   – | – | – | E
525 Harrison St. (1st St.), 415-339-8686; www.sfclubs.com
"There's always a positive vibe goin' on throughout" this multilevel danceteria located "a bit off the beaten path" at the eastern edge of SoMa ("perfect if you don't want to deal with the traffic or parking"); from hip-hop to pop to salsa, the music is as varied as the themed rooms, and since it "welcomes everyone", don't bother "if you don't enjoy a good freak show"; N.B. open Thursday–Saturday.

FARALLON   26 | 28 | 24 | $11
450 Post St. (bet. Mason & Powell Sts.), 415-956-6969;
www.farallonrestaurant.com
"Huge jellyfish chandeliers", tentacled barstools and a curvy, wave-inspired design via Pat Kuleto contribute to the "fun under-the-sea experience" of this "magical" restaurant Downtown; the separate bar up front serves "expensive but perfectly made drinks" and "never seems that crowded", while sit-down diners find themselves "inside what used to be a mosaic-walled indoor swimming pool"; with its "terrific staff" and "transporting" decor, no wonder old salts say it's a "required trip to the briny deep."

Ferry Plaza Wine Merchant   – | – | – | M
Ferry Bldg., 1 Ferry Plaza (Embarcadero St. N.), 415-391-9400;
www.fpwm.com
A dedicated seating area along the inside mall of the restored Ferry Building and an extensive by-the-glass menu (with "great prices" to

boot) lend a lively atmosphere to this stylish Embarcadero bottle shop and wine bar co-owned by bacar's Debbie Zachareas; it fills up after work and opens at 8 on Saturday mornings when browsers from the farmer's market can stop by to sample the wares.

Fiddler's Green
19 | 15 | 18 | $6

1333 Columbus Ave. (Beach St.), 415-441-9758; www.fiddlersgreensf.com
"No matter what mood you're in" expect "a good time" at this "fantastic" double-decker pub with live music that's "convenient to Fisherman's Wharf"; the "mellow bar downstairs" is great for fiddling around over pints with your pals "before getting crazy upstairs in the dance club" (open Friday and Saturday only); maybe you'll be partying with "tons of tourists", but if some of them are "adorable, friendly Irish guys, it's worth checking out."

15 ROMOLO
21 | 18 | 17 | $7

Basque Hotel, 15 Romolo Pl. (Broadway), 415-398-1359
"Trendy people" with "too-cool haircuts" battle locals for booths at this "hidden North Beach spot" tucked away in the Basque Hotel up a "steep", "tiny" side street "in the middle of Smutville"; its rep rests not just on "the cachet of an alley address" but also on "stiff drinks" and a "stylish", "modern" setting, which is why this "not-so-well-kept secret" can get "obnoxiously crowded on weekends", so vets advise "go after work instead."

Fifth Floor
23 | 24 | 25 | $12

Hotel Palomar, 12 Fourth St. (Market St.), 415-348-1555;
www.hotelpalomar.com
"If you're looking for a quiet place to drink" and sample "perfectly crafted delicacies", the expanded "posh lounge" of this "upscale" Downtown restaurant in the Hotel Palomar makes for a "romantic" experience; the bartenders are "surprisingly unpretentious", and "if you're a wine snob, this is the place" to indulge as the 1,400-bottle list (30 by the glass) is "one of the city's finest."

Fillmore, The
24 | 21 | 16 | $7

1805 Geary Blvd. (Fillmore St.), 415-346-3000; www.thefillmore.com
Take a trip to this "classic venue" in the Western Addition and "feel the energy of all the legendary musicians" who've played the stage since Bill Graham first booked shows here in 1965 ("you can still feel his spirit rockin' the house"); "the granddaddy" of concert halls, it's "hosted almost everyone who mattered from the past four decades", and if the combination of the bookings, "great sound, amazing architecture and sheer history" of the place doesn't "make you feel humble", nothing will.

Final Final
15 | 10 | 19 | $5

2990 Baker St. (Lombard St.), 415-931-7800
"Popcorn, cheap brews and a raucous crowd" are the highlights of this "quirky" tavern in an "isolated" corner of the Marina where it's "all sports, all the time" thanks to local teams in for post-game gatherings and others with eyes glued to the nine TVs; expect a few "beer bellies" but also "old-school bartenders" who are "friendly" at this "real-deal" "gathering spot."

Finnegan's Wake ⌿
20 | 10 | 18 | $5

937 Cole St. (bet. Carl St. & Parnassus Ave.), 415-731-6119
"You'll get your fill of brogues and beer" at this "neighborhood watering hole" that provides a "welcoming" way station for those

who make the odyssey to Cole Valley; "it's not much to look at", but it's "homey", with pool tables, pinball machines and a "Ping-Pong table on the back patio that brings many folks outside on a nice day"; a "friendly" staff and a crowd of "locals" help make it "everything a pub should be."

Fireside Bar ⌷   20 | 18 | 20 | $6
603 Irving St. (7th Ave.), 415-731-6433
"Neighborhood people and hipsters" from far afield know to "grab a seat by the fire" at this "cozy, unpretentious bar" that hotheads hail as "the coolest place to drink in the Inner Sunset"; other attractions include a "great jukebox", "nice staff" and "tasty" libations, and though some still mourning the Wishing Well's demise feel this incarnation's "a little too slick", most maintain it "kept the welcoming" vibe.

First Crush   17 | 17 | 18 | $10
101 Cyril Magnin St. (Ellis St.), 415-982-7874; www.firstcrush.com
"Kick back and enjoy some phenomenal wines by the glass" from the "all-California list" at this "stylish" Mexican restaurant/bar that's a "terrific respite" from its "slightly seedy neighborhood" near Union Square; while fans are starry-eyed for the "elegant, glowing decor", others are crushed by "disorganized" service and gripe that in terms of grape "there's nothing to blow anyone away."

Fish Bowl   19 | 14 | 18 | $5
1854 Divisadero St. (bet. Bush & Pine Sts.), 415-775-3630
Though it's "small" and "crowded", this "cozy watering hole" attracts a school of "young" "Pacific Heights locals" with its "warm staff", "excellent" drinks, bar food and "great nightly specials"; a preponderance of "hot guys" can make for "lively conversation" at this "lovable favorite."

540 Club ⌷   ▽ 23 | 21 | 25 | $5
540 Clement St. (bet. 6th & 7th Aves.), 415-752-7276; www.540-club.com
"Pabst!" is a common cry among the assorted "neighborhood types" ("loyal, mature Irish crowd" by day, "young hipsters at night") who "mix seamlessly" at this "friendly punk dive" in the Inner Richmond; maybe it's "not much" on first impression, but inside you'll find "attentive" bartenders, a "kick-ass jukebox" and DJs as well as a "come-as-you-are" attitude and a "great front patio area where you can smoke, drink and watch the foot traffic along Clement Street."

500 Club, The ⌷   20 | 12 | 18 | $4
500 Guerrero St. (17th St.), 415-861-2500
"This place is as 'bar' as bars get" maintains the "mélange of greasers, hipsters and yuppies who congregate" at this "non-trendy" relic of the "pre–dot-com era" that hasn't "succumbed to the gentrification of the Mission"; trademarks include its "gigantic neon martini glass sign", a "friendly" staff, "cheap drinks" and "one of the best jukeboxes" in SF, and the decor's "dingy" "enough to keep out the Marina imposters but clean enough for a blind date."

Florio   22 | 20 | 21 | $8
1915 Fillmore St. (bet. Bush & Pine Sts.), 415-775-4300; www.floriosf.com
"When you're in the mood for a glass of wine and some steak frites", it's hard to beat this "cozy neighborhood bistro" on Upper Fillmore co-owned by Bix's Doug Biederbeck; "great ambiance"

and "excellent food" (if not the "considerate service") leave you "feeling like you're in a Parisian cafe", making it an "impressive date place" with "*votre cheri.*"

Fluid   – | – | – | E
662 Mission St. (bet. New Montgomery & 3rd Sts.), 415-615-6888; www.fluidsf.com
"Spectacular" computer-controlled lights and colors "to fit any mood" offset the "white, gleaming decor" of this sprawling "Miami-like" SoMa sophomore that's been discovered by an "interesting mix of art students, financial types and residents of the nearby Paramount" apartments; the "ultrahip surroundings", fortunately, "don't prevent the staff from providing warm, friendly service."

Fly   21 | 19 | 19 | $6
762 Divisadero St. (Fulton St.), 415-931-4359; www.flybar.com
"Everyone should have a local bar" like this "perfect low-key beer and wine joint" (with sangria and "yummy sake cocktails", too) in the Western Addition that also provides "great value"; its "down-to-earth environment" with a "cheap kind of charm" ensures it's "always packed" with thrifty "hipsters", though a few fly swatters say it's "not worth traveling to."

Fog City Diner   19 | 20 | 19 | $9
1300 Battery St. (The Embarcadero), 415-982-2000; www.fogcitydiner.com
A "retro" setting with "art deco touches" combines with "upscale comfort food" (the sort "you wouldn't find at any diner, past or present") to make this Embarcadero "landmark" the "classiest gin-and-burger joint in town"; it's a "hot spot for hungry escapees" from touristy Pier 39 or those "relaxing after work", but don't fog-get the cocktails are "pricey" and the service can be "so-so."

FOREIGN CINEMA   23 | 23 | 18 | $8
2534 Mission St. (bet. 21st & 22nd Sts.), 415-648-7600; www.foreigncinema.com
With "classic" and "avant-garde" films "playing on the wall" nightly in the heated courtyard, "the scenery is never the same twice" at this "chic, post-industrial watering hole" in the Mission; cinephiles applaud the "cool concept", "sexy" atmosphere, complete with a fireplace, "perfect mojitos", "destination-quality food" and a staff that's a lot more "friendly since the dot-com bubble burst", but it gets a thumbs-down for "overpriced" libations.

Frankie's Bohemian Cafe   18 | 14 | 20 | $6
1862 Divisadero St. (Pine St.), 415-921-4725
Though it's a "secret" to the uninitiated, this "colorful" bar and grill is a "tradition" with Western Addition "locals" who lap up "cheap", "gigantic" brewskies (think 22-oz glasses) and scarf down the "best burgers in town"; sure, seating is "tight" and it can get "loud", but the "friendly crowd", "surly but sweet" staff and "TV tuned to SF sporting events" make it a "great neighborhood joint"; N.B. no hard liquor.

Frisson   – | – | – | E
244 Jackson St. (bet. Battery & Front Sts.), 415-956-3004; www.frissonsf.com
The futuristic digs, complete with a backlit, spaceshiplike dome in the center of the dining area and textured Lucite walls, along with cocktails like Fountain of Youth and Blackberry Burst, create a

frisson indeed for the well-heeled who retreat to this warm-toned Downtown nightspot; with late-night bar bites, DJs and mingling opportunities aplenty, the thrills keep on coming till the wee hours.

Front Room, The   17 | 12 | 17 | $6
1500 California St. (Larkin St.), 415-928-1313; www.thefrontroomsf.com
"Reminds you of your college days" sigh nostalgic sorts of this Nob Hill eatery that some claim to be the "best pizza and beer" spot in town; "there isn't much of a bar to speak of", but it's a "completely comfortable spot" for "excellent" pies and salads at "reasonable prices", catching a game on TV or partaking of a brew or two, pitchers of which are an especially "great deal" ($3.50 all day) on Mondays, Tuesdays and Thursdays.

Fuse   20 | 19 | 18 | $7
493 Broadway (Kearny St.), 415-788-2706; www.fusesf.com
With its "funky", "blue neon"–lit interior, vivid-colored furniture, "hot bartenders" and "awesome" DJs spinning "danceable tunes" from house to hip-hop to rock, this "swank retreat" in North Beach makes for a "fun little bar" (albeit with an "emphasis on little") for "stiff" and altogether "superb cocktails"; it "can get crowded" with a fusion of "hipsters", "locals" and the random "tourist", so vets advise "avoid it when there's a line."

Gallery Lounge   – | – | – | E
510 Brannan St. (4th St.), 415-227-0449; www.thegallerylounge.com
Gallery or cocktail lounge? – that's the question on curious patrons' lips between sips of Chardonnay and peeks at the rotating roster of fine artwork that fills the walls of this sleek and chic SoMa hangout; a well-dressed crowd pulls in for an after-work Cosmo come-down, but it's different strokes for nightcrawlers who come to groove to funk, house and upbeat spins.

GARY DANKO   27 | 26 | 27 | $13
800 N. Point St. (Hyde St.), 415-749-2060; www.garydanko.com
"The ultimate dining spot is also a great place for a drink" declare devotees of this "amazing" "SF institution" near Fisherman's Wharf where "the service alone is inebriating" (and No. 1 in this *Survey*); though the bar area is "small", you can order the "incredible tasting menu" without "waiting for a reservation" while sipping "wonderful wines" poured by a "knowledgeable staff"; the experience is "expensive", yes, but those worshiping at the church of Danko say "no one ever regrets" a visit as it's "worth every penny."

g bar   20 | 23 | 17 | $8
Laurel Inn, 488 Presidio Ave. (California St.), 415-409-4227; www.gbarsf.com
"Metrosexuals meet sexy" chicks shod in "great shoes" at this "superb" 25-year-old "hot spot" near the Laurel Inn located in otherwise "sleepy" Pacific Heights; it's more "laid-back" since its "velvet-rope dot-com days", but it still offers "stylish" "mid-century"–modern decor including a "unique" fireplace, "groovy lounge music" and "creative" cocktails for a "young", "civilized" clientele that considers it "best on weeknights."

Gino & Carlo ⌐   21 | 16 | 22 | $5
548 Green St. (bet. Grant Ave. & Stockton St.), 415-421-0896
"Even when it's crowded there's room to move" reveal regulars of this "low-key", "great family-run establishment" that's been beating

"in the heart of North Beach" since 1942; thanks to its "friendly staff and customers" (along with its 6 AM opening time), it remains "a jewel of a bar" with some of the "best people-watching" in town.

Glas Kat Supper Club, The   14 | 14 | 14 | $8

520 Fourth St. (Bryant St.), 415-495-6620; www.glaskat.com
Curious kats will find lots to explore in this large SoMa space, what with the 1,200-sq.-ft. dance floor, "multiple rooms for hanging" and a glass-enclosed Hawaiian restaurant with Polynesian dinner shows; jaded jet-setters jeer it "tries way too hard to be a big-city club", but a "young mixed crowd" gives kudos to the "great" hip-hop, salsa and live music as well as the popular 'Bondage-a-Go-Go' on Wednesdays and Friday Latin nights.

Glen Park Station 🍴   – | – | – | I

2816 Diamond St. (north of Bosworth St.), 415-333-4633
This "decent, divey boozer" in Glen Park may "look a little grubby" on first impression, "but don't be fooled" because the "friendly" staff shakes up "fantastic cocktails" that supporters swear are "better than most fancy Downtown places"; it's basically a simple "locals' hangout" with weekly dart tournaments, Thin Lizzy on the jukebox and a few "down-and-outers" eager to chat.

Gold Cane 🍴   17 | 7 | 20 | $4

1569 Haight St. (bet. Ashbury & Clayton Sts.), 415-626-1112
"Dependably cheap drinks" are the gold standard at this Upper Haight "diamond in the rough" filled with "friendly patrons" who all "get along" and raise cane, be they "punk, yup, trash or 70-year-old barfly"; "exceptional service", a "cozy" patio for smokers and the fact that "you can always find a seat" help fastidious sorts forgive the "run-down" interior.

Gold Club   22 | 18 | 18 | $11

650 Howard St. (bet. New Montgomery & 3rd Sts.), 415-536-0300; www.goldclubsf.com
"If you're looking to satisfy three cravings – alcohol, food and girls – this is the place" say supporters of this "gentlemen's club–style" strip joint in SoMa; it's "classy" for its genre, the ecdysiasts are "pretty" and it's even "acceptable to take a date."

Gold Dust Lounge, The 🍴   18 | 13 | 19 | $6

247 Powell St. (bet. Geary & O'Farrell Sts.), 415-397-1695
"You've gotta love the faux gold" and "red-velvet upholstery" that bedizens this "wonderful" "haven in the middle of Union Square", where the "bartenders seem to have been there as long as the bar" (1933) and "ancient mariners play" Dixieland jazz; a "mixed" crowd of "tourists", "hipsters" and "scary" regulars champion its "cheap drinks" and "fun vibe."

GORDON BIERSCH   17 | 15 | 16 | $8

2 Harrison St. (The Embarcadero), 415-243-8246; www.gordonbiersch.com
"Go for the beer" and "sit outside under the heat lamps" advise advocates hopped up over the "German-style lagers brewed on the premises" that are the signature creation of this Bay Area–based mini-chain; critics complain it's a "high-priced but low-class meat market", with "noisy" digs, "hit-or-miss" service and plenty of "Polo shirts and khakis", but they're über-ruled by fans of the "excellent" brews and "renowned garlic fries."

Grand Cafe   21 | 24 | 20 | $9
Hotel Monaco, 501 Geary St. (Taylor St.), 415-292-0101;
www.grandcafe-sf.com
With its "art nouveau–meets–*Alice Through the Looking Glass*"
decor, this "dramatic" Downtown "delight" in the former ballroom
of the Hotel Monaco is "perfect for a pre-theater cocktail" or a
"romantic" nightcap; its "large", "comfortable" lounge area offers
a "wonderful" wine list and "inventive" drinks delivered by a
"friendly" staff, and though "expensive", it's decidedly "worth a
visit" for a "beautiful experience."

Grandviews Lounge   23 | 20 | 21 | $12
Grand Hyatt Hotel, 345 Stockton St. (bet. Post & Sutter Sts.),
415-398-1234; www.grandsanfrancisco.hyatt.com
Some of "the best views in SF" can be savored at this "surprisingly
wonderful hotel bar" atop the Grand Hyatt Downtown where the
sights from 36 floors up are "truly spectacular"; even if it's an
"expensive" magnet for "Midwestern tourists", it's frequently
"overlooked" by townies who might appreciate the "uncrowded"
conditions and the chance to fall in love with the "beautiful" city
all over again.

Gravity   18 | 16 | 15 | $7
3251 Scott St. (bet. Chestnut & Lombard Sts.), 415-776-1928;
www.gravityroomsf.com
A "diverse" "twentysomething" clientele feels the pull of this
"energetic" force field that's "the place to bump and grind in the
Marina"; "great DJs" playing hip-hop, R&B and "good pop music",
"friendly bartenders" and "pretty people" are all uplifting, but the
"uncomfortably hot" and "crowded" conditions, "self-important"
attitude and "poor excuse for a dance floor" are definite downers;
P.S. "be prepared to wait in line after 10 PM."

GREAT AMERICAN MUSIC HALL   25 | 24 | 18 | $6
859 O'Farrell St. (bet. Larkin & Polk Sts.), 415-885-0750;
www.musichallsf.com
"Great acoustics" and sightlines, a "solid sound system" and a
"top-notch" slate of "amazing" artists leave groupies gushing that
this "ornate", "gilded beauty" in the Tenderloin is "the best venue
for music in the Bay Area"; an "amazing piece of history", it's "still
decorated like a bordello" (its previous life in the Barbary Coast
days), enabling you to "party like it's 1849", and though "big enough
to attract well-known acts" it's still "small enough to feel intimate."

Greens Sports Bar   20 | 15 | 18 | $5
2239 Polk St. (bet. Green & Vallejo Sts.), 415-775-4287
"Expect a crowd" – and a "loud, boisterous, post-collegiate" one
at that – because this "fun sports bar" is "Polk Street's best for live
televised games" thanks to "tons of TV screens" and "cheap, cold
beer" (18 on tap) served by a "witty" staff; timeouts are taken on
its "open-to-the-street" patio or at the pool table, and though it
doesn't serve food, you can order delivery from the "many eateries
in the area."

Grove, The   23 | 20 | 17 | $6
2250 Chestnut St. (Avila St.), 415-474-4843
If you want to see how "the Marina has grown up", stop by this
"comfy", "quintessential neighborhood cafe" whose "smiling" staff

and "wood-and-leather"–bedecked interior evokes "*Northern
Exposure*"; from "divine" breakfasts to "Scrabble and a glass of
wine" to "late-night lattes", it's a "charming" choice for "hanging
out with family, friends or dates", and "if you can nab one of the
outdoor seats, you've found a little slice of heaven."

Grumpy's Pub   15 | 13 | 19 | $4 |
125 Vallejo St. (bet. Battery & Front Sts.), 415-434-3350
"The staff works hard to cater to the happy-hour crowd" and
maintain the "neighborhood" feel of this "great watering hole"
along the Embarcadero; "the advertising set" and other "local
business" types dig the "casual atmosphere and "fabulous",
"friendly bartenders" and "good pub grub"; P.S. it's closed on
weekends when it becomes a "cheap" party rental option.

Habana   18 | 21 | 19 | $8 |
2080 Van Ness Ave. (Pacific Ave.), 415-441-2822; www.habana1948.com
"You'll wish it were easier to get to" Havana itself after tasting the
"amazing mojitos", house cocktails (a "wonderful variation on the
Manhattan") or the potent Hemingway daiquiris at Sam DuVall's
"Cuban-inspired dream of a restaurant" on Van Ness; the lounge
exudes a "vibrant atmosphere" made all the more festive by tropical
murals and a "great rectangular bar" that encourages mingling.

Ha Ra ⊅   – | – | – | I |
875 Geary Blvd. (bet. Hyde & Larkin Sts.), 415-673-3148
Situated on a grungy Tenderloin block, this circa-1947 "perfect
dive" "may have low visual appeal", but that doesn't deter a lineup
of "Bukowski"-esque locals ("retirees, veterans and wrinkled"
regulars); "smart-ass hipsters with Rolling Stones haircuts" fill
the stools "before the show at the Great American Music Hall"
and play vintage tunes on the "great jukebox"; one caveat: "don't
mess with the bartender, but expect him to mess with you."

Hard Rock Cafe   14 | 18 | 15 | $10 |
*Pier 39 (bet. Beach St. & The Embarcadero), 415-956-2013;
www.hardrock.com*
It's "surprising a place this touristy could be so fun" say fans for
whom this Fisherman's Wharf chain link "truly rocks"; others are
hard-pressed for praise, saying it's "a tired formula" ("didn't it die
in the '80s?"), and while it "may work for teens wanting to feel like
grown-ups in a bar atmosphere", for the rest "there are so many
better places to go in San Francisco."

Harrington's Bar & Grill   17 | 13 | 17 | $6 |
245 Front St. (bet. California & Sacramento Sts.), 415-392-7595
"Financial District worker bees" who'd "rather talk stocks than
sports" swarm this "beautiful" Downtown Irish tavern that's a
"heaving", "5 PM hot spot" every weeknight; "liberal libations",
"lots of beers on tap", "sumptuous snacks" and "great service"
keep the atmosphere "festive" and the "fun porch overflowing
in the summer."

Harris'   22 | 20 | 22 | $10 |
*2100 Van Ness Ave. (Pacific Ave.), 415-673-1888;
www.harrisrestaurant.com*
It may have opened in 1984, but this "upscale steakhouse" and
lounge on Van Ness feels like a blast from the "'60s" with big booths,
a mahogany bar and its "martini-up, stirred-not-shaken crowd"; it's

a "relaxing place to unwind", with the aforementioned cocktails being "ice-cold" and some of the "best in the city", and loyalists "love to come on weekends to listen to live jazz."

Harry Denton's Rouge   16 | 18 | 14 | $9 |
1500 Broadway (Polk St.), 415-346-7683
Those who are smitten with the "awesome red" decor and "people-watching" opportunities at this Polk Street club say it's a "great pickup place", especially on Wednesday nights when its 'Work' parties provide an "excellent break" with dancing and cheap drinks; detractors, however, declare "don't be fooled by the line outside", as the crowd's "lame" and the vibe's "cheesy."

HARRY DENTON'S STARLIGHT ROOM   22 | 22 | 19 | $11 |
Sir Francis Drake Hotel, 450 Powell St. (Sutter St.), 415-395-8595;
www.harrydenton.com
"Delicious" cocktails and "an incredible view of the city at night" stir starry-eyed supporters of this "old-fashioned" dance club on the 21st floor of Downtown's Sir Francis Drake Hotel; sure, it's a bit "Liza Minnelli" ("think sequins and heels"), but there's an "intoxicating atmosphere" ("every night feels like New Year's Eve") that overshadows "the crowds, long waits and high" tabs, and at the very least, you should just "do it once to check it off your list."

Harry's   19 | 18 | 19 | $7 |
2020 Fillmore St. (bet. California & Pine Sts.), 415-921-1000
With its "wonderful" ambiance ranging from "comfortably quiet to pleasantly packed", this "standby on the Fillmore stretch" is "friendly without being a meat market", providing an "inviting" gathering point for "twentysomethings"; with big-screen TVs, movies, a "huge cocktail menu", "good bar grub" and "warm" staff, it's no wonder its cronies can't "say anything negative about it."

Harvey's   19 | 18 | 18 | $6 |
500 Castro St. (18th St.), 415-431-4278
"Relax and people-watch" from the "wall-length windows" of this "great bar for the modern queer" that's conveniently situated "at the Castro's crossroads", making it "the epicenter of the 'hood"; it's "relaxing after work" for a burger and beer or on Monday trivia game nights, plus the bimonthly "drag shows are spectacular", but it's "not cruisy" (more of a "before" kind of place) and the staff "changes faster than the Fab 5 make over a room."

Hawthorne Lane   23 | 24 | 24 | $10 |
22 Hawthorne St. (bet. Folsom & Howard Sts.), 415-777-9779;
www.hawthornelane.com
"Civilized, cultured" and "chic for cocktails", this "upscale" SoMa restaurant is "an excellent choice for a special evening" or just to "escape the hustle and bustle of the city" ("I think I've finally exited the twentysomething crowd"); the staff "sets an example for customer service", and there's "great bar food if you don't feel like committing to dinner", which ain't a bad choice as the prices just might "burn a hole in your wallet."

Hemlock Tavern ⇗   21 | 17 | 19 | $5 |
1131 Polk St. (bet. Post & Sutter Sts.), 415-923-0923;
www.hemlocktavern.com
A "fabulous mix" of "freaks" ("punk, emo, Goth", what have you) hang out in harmony at this "intimate" rock 'n' roll venue on Polk

Street that provides "adventurous live music" in the recently expanded back room with a bigger stage (and "separate door charge"); its "unpretentious" attitude, "strong drinks", "warm peanuts" (go ahead, "throw your shells on the floor"), "enclosed smoking area" and "fantastic" bands have fans philosophizing "if I could keep one bar in the city, this would be it."

HiFi   17 | 13 | 17 | $7

2125 Lombard St. (Fillmore St.), 415-345-8663;
www.maximumproductions.com
Plug into the "fab beats" and you'll feel "you can dance all night" with the "twentysomething crowd" that finds this "little lounge in the Marina" to be a "fun" tweet; even though it's "always jumping", the "lines are short", the "booths are big", the cover charges are "low" and the music runs the gamut from house to hip-hop to '80s eclectic; still, a few foes woof it's "lost its coolness" and "needs an upgrade"; N.B. free on Thursdays, $5 cover charge on Friday and Saturday nights.

Hobson's Choice   22 | 17 | 19 | $6

1601 Haight St. (Clayton St.), 415-621-5859; www.hobsonschoice.com
Consider yourself warned, as the "cheap and delicious punch", premium rums (more than 100 types) as well as "dangerous drink specials" served by a "humorous" staff at this "Victorian-themed bar" in the Upper Haight just might "knock you on your keister"; still, that's a good excuse for its "young", "cute clientele" to lounge on the "nice couches" or choose a "comfy corner to sit in", and its "huge" windows "allow people-watching unequaled in the city."

Hole in the Wall Saloon ⌿   ▽ 25 | 15 | 24 | $4

289 Eighth St. (Folsom St.), 415-431-4695; www.holeinthewallsaloon.com
"If you like it sleazy and dark" then check out this "fun little dive" with a "style all its own" in SoMa where "everyone is warmly welcomed", including "an eclectic mix of gay bikers, neighborhood denizens and assorted other freaks"; "rock 'n' roll rules here, a relief" from "the thud-thud-thud of dance music", and groupies who "guarantee a wild experience" claim "it's not a real visit without at least one naked buckaroo running around."

Horseshoe Tavern ⌿   19 | 11 | 22 | $5

2024 Chestnut St. (bet. Fillmore & Steiner Sts.), 415-346-1430
"Everybody's your friend" at this "down-to-earth" "dive" that "hasn't sold out or caved in to the yuppie boutique scene" in the Marina; "don't expect the Taj Mahal", but it does provide a pool table, "good drink prices" and some of the "funniest bartenders in the city", making it a "breath of fresh air" in "an uptight part of town"; P.S. beware weekends, when it can get "overrun by the drunken ex-frat-boy element."

HÔTEL BIRON   26 | 28 | 23 | $8

45 Rose St. (bet. Gough & Market Sts.), 415-703-0403;
www.hotelbiron.com
"Step back in time" and sail "across the ocean to old-time Paris" via the "fantastic decor" of this "cozy wine bar", a "hard-to-find" but "perfect little hideaway" tucked in an alley behind Zuni Cafe in Hayes Valley; over 30 "yummy" *vins* by the glass, a "good" menu of cheese and chocolate, a "friendly" staff and "great artwork" make it an ideal "second date" destination or "quiet" spot to "chill" with some *amis*; N.B. it's now owned by a former bartender.

Hotel Utah   19 | 14 | 18 | $6
500 Fourth St. (Bryant St.), 415-546-6300; www.thehotelutahsaloon.com
Though under new ownership, this "nothing fancy" "narrow little
bit of a place" in SoMa is still an "institution" to local music fans as
it's "everything a cool San Francisco bar should be"; it's "fantastic"
for just a drink or to "watch local acts" and "up-and-coming"
national artists on the "small stage" that affords "up-close" access
to the bands, though being so "tiny" it's also "hard to get a seat."

House of Shields   17 | 13 | 13 | $6
39 New Montgomery St. (bet. Market & Mission Sts.), 415-975-8651
While the proprietors who took over this reopened circa-1908
"classic" near the Financial District over a year and a half ago have
"polished it up", the "cool art deco lighting fixtures" and other
Victorian touches remain; the "funky ambiance" is complemented
by live jazz on Tuesday and Friday nights and "great local DJs on
weekends", and though some attack it as "past its prime", the
house-bound say "thank god it's back."

Houston's   19 | 18 | 22 | $10
1800 Montgomery St. (The Embarcadero, across from Pier 33),
415-392-9280; www.houstons.com
"Those who can handle the San Francisco chill" will find one of the
"best outdoor fireplaces in the city" on the patio behind this "airy,
upscale" Embarcadero link of a "chain that doesn't feel like a
chain"; "stiff drinks", an "impressive wine selection" and "fantastic
appetizers" make it a "blast with a group", and "great service" and
"decent prices" contribute to its "youthful appeal."

Hush Hush Lounge   22 | 17 | 18 | $5
496 14th St. (Guerrero St.), 415-241-9944; www.hushhushlounge.com
A "diverse crowd" is hip to the "happening" happy hours at this
"hideaway" in an "unassuming corner of the Mission" where
Tuesday nights mean dollar beers and the price of a PBR drops to
a "cheap-ass" two bits on Fridays; with "killer DJs" "kicking out
the jams" and creating an "infernal racket", don't expect this small
club's moniker to "reflect its reality", and "don't be embarrassed
to bust a move on the dance floor, 'cause no one else is."

Il Pirata   – | – | – | M
2007 16th St. (Utah St.), 415-626-2626
"Maybe it's the large amount of space" indoors and out, "vinyl
booths" or the two "awesome" patios (one heated, one not),
but buckos brag this Potrero Hill "dive" is a "great place to hang
out" and "fun for dancing" to booty; though a few arrr-gue it's
"seedy" and "past its prime", a mix of techies and drivers from
nearby UPS applaud it as "appealing" and praise the staff as
the "friendliest around."

Independent   – | – | – | M
628 Divisadero St. (bet. Grove & Hayes Sts.), 415-771-1420;
www.theindependentsf.com
Sweet sounds pour forth from this renovated Western Addition
nightspot that was once the Justice League and, before that,
illustrious dark hole the Kennel Club; indie rock, hip-hop, jazz and
world artists are all lined up to shine in a space that music fans have
called home for three decades and counting; N.B. performances
are for those over-21 only.

Ireland's 32   17 | 13 | 16 | $5
3920 Geary Blvd. (3rd Ave.), 415-386-6173; www.irelands32.com
"They know how to properly pour the black stuff", and for some that's all that matters about this "lively" Inner Richmond pub populated by a "younger" crowd that digs the nightly bands; the walls and ceiling are covered in political posters and other "cool paraphernalia", making it the "best place to catch up on your assassinated Irish freedom fighters" – though it's also just a "great place to watch sports", play pool or tee-off at the golf machine.

Irish Bank   19 | 14 | 18 | $6
10 Mark Ln. (Bush St.), 415-788-7152; www.theirishbank.com
An "energetic" "after-work" Financial District demographic is heavily invested in this "fun little" Downtown "party zone" created by a "cozy", "cool" interior filled with Irish artifacts (including a confessional) and a "lovely outdoor space" in the adjacent alley; the "bartenders are more than charming", the beer selection's "excellent" and the fish 'n' chips are among the "best in the city"; insider tip: "it's packed to the rafters" for Friday happy hour.

Jack Falstaff   – | – | – | E
598 Second St. (Brannan St.), 415-836-9239; www.plumpjack.com
Besides Shakespeare, think Gavin – as in Mayor Newsom, who's a partner in PlumpJack, the wine retailer and restaurant group behind this South Beach destination named (as is the company as a whole) for a jolly Bard character; the sleek bar and dining room are done up in luscious green suede, while dark-brown fabrics and cocktail tables accent the spacious glass-enclosed patio that's warmed up with heat lamps – and by the glow of Giants fans (at least when they're winning).

Jack's Cannery Bar ⊐   ∇ 16 | 15 | 20 | $8
441 Jefferson St. (Leavenworth St.), 415-931-6400
"What's not to like about" an establishment that offers "over 86 beers on tap"? ask ale-and-hearty types of this spacious bar in the thick of Fisherman's Wharf; the brews are "fantastic" and the staff's "hilarious", but some jackhammers jibe it "needs an atmosphere injection" as it's "devoid of any kind of vibe."

JADE BAR   25 | 26 | 22 | $7
650 Gough St. (McAllister St.), 415-869-1900; www.jadebar.com
A "legitimate legend in the making", this "hot" Hayes Valley yearling provides a "small" but "beautiful" three-level setting for "unwinding" replete with "comfy chairs", a 20-ft. "cascading waterfall" and "tiled koi pond"; the crowd's "hip but not annoying", the bartenders are "cool" and even the most jaded are impressed by the "tasty Asian-style" tapas and "superb happy hour" during which "quality" cocktails and "premium" beers are two bucks; P.S. "everyone should take a trip to the men's room" to check out the mirror.

JARDINIÈRE   26 | 28 | 24 | $11
300 Grove St. (Franklin St.), 415-861-5555; www.jardiniere.com
"Stellar decor", a "sleek, refined atmosphere" and "superlative service" – "that's what you pay for" at Pat Kuleto's "sensuous" Hayes Valley supper club "designed for decadent" scenesters and featuring a grand staircase and "stunning" circular bar; with "stylish but unpretentious" wines and an "amazing array of drinks"

served by an "experienced" staff and the chance to sample Traci Des Jardin's "beautiful" Cal-French fare, it's the "perfect pre-opera, post-dot-com spot" and a "great setting in which to catch some wonderful local jazz" duos and trios as well.

Jazz at Pearl's　　　　25 ▎ 18 ▎ 20 ▎ $9 ▎
256 Columbus Ave. (Broadway), 415-291-8255; www.jazzatpearls.com
"Thank goodness it's back" sigh supporters of this "great jazz" supper club, a "local favorite" with Spanish-French food and a 1930s-inspired ambiance in North Beach that was "saved from extinction" and rejuvenated by "wonderful" vocalist Kim Nalley and other owners; a "young, hip crowd" enjoys what some claim is the "best" music in the city, and even though old-timers "miss Pearl", they admit it's "better than ever"; N.B. the redo may not be reflected in the Decor score.

Jelly's　　　　– ▎ – ▎ – ▎ M ▎
295 Terry Francois Blvd. (Pier 50), 415-495-3099
If the mood strikes for "margaritas on a Friday", this nightclub and restaurant in China Basin near SBC Park offers a "great patio" from which to watch the fog rolling in or the sunset across the Bay; during baseball season it's a "post-night-game hot spot", and on Sunday afternoons 'Club Havana' offers "fun salsa lessons" and music that jams hard as your legs turn to jelly.

Jillian's　　　　16 ▎ 16 ▎ 14 ▎ $8 ▎
Sony Metreon Ctr., 101 Fourth St. (Howard St.), 415-369-6100; www.jilliansbilliards.com
The "upbeat atmosphere" and "huge TV wall" with three big screens at this SoMa sports bar in the Metreon will "entertain you even if your date doesn't"; being "chock-full of pool tables and frat boys" out for fun, it's "like a Chuck E. Cheese for adults", though jill-ted types find the vibe very "vanilla" (a "great place if you miss the suburbs"); N.B. a recent refurb may impact the Decor score.

Johnny Foley's　　　　19 ▎ 18 ▎ 19 ▎ $6 ▎
243 O'Farrell St. (bet. Mason & Powell Sts.), 415-954-0777; www.johnnyfoleys.com
"They pour a nice pint" at this "dark, pleasant" Downtown "drinking hole" where the "friendly, open atmosphere", "great staff" and "typical Irish pub decor" make it a logical local for "lots of expats"; some suggest it's "a bit too boomy when there's music" (which is nightly), but a "rowdy", "young crowd" "love, love, loves it."

John's Grill　　　　19 ▎ 16 ▎ 16 ▎ $9 ▎
63 Ellis St. (bet. Powell & Stockton Sts.), 415-986-0069; www.johnsgrill.com
"Old San Francisco character" in spades can be found at this "historic restaurant" Downtown whose cameo in *The Maltese Falcon* is commemorated in the "celebrity paraphernalia" adorning the walls; "not much has changed since 1908, including the staff" – along with "excellent martinis", "great seafood and steaks" and "engaging conversations at the small L-shaped bar."

Julie's Supper Club　　　　17 ▎ 18 ▎ 19 ▎ $9 ▎
1123 Folsom St. (7th St.), 415-861-0707; www.juliessupperclub.com
Those "nostalgic" for a "taste of SF circa 1987" can turn to this SoMa "concept" club which in turn embodies a nostalgia for the '50s with its funky mural, "kitschy" artifacts and "fun" cocktails;

it still has a "great vibe" and attracts a "lively" crowd, but blasé
sorts insist it's "way past its coolness expiration date."

Kan Zaman   20 | 21 | 17 | $7
1793 Haight St. (Shrader St.), 415-751-9656
"Eat, drink, smoke and be merry" at this Middle Eastern eatery in
the Upper Haight where "comfy booths", a "surreal ambiance",
"fantastic" mulled wine and "hookahs make you feel you're in
another land"; the "appeal is in the family-style dining and the
chance to have a woman shake her booty at your plate" (that
would be the belly dancer), but a few who no kan do denounce the
"overcrowded" digs and "rushed" service.

Kate O'Brien's   16 | 12 | 19 | $6
579 Howard St. (bet. 1st & 2nd Sts.), 415-882-7240; www.kateobriens.net
"If you want to sit, get here early" as this "classic Irish pub" in
SoMa is a popular "after-work meeting place" with a local crowd
lining the long bar with a new copper counter or packing the
matching tables upstairs and down (where there's also a DJ); it's a
bit "dark inside" and "can be stuffy in summer", but the selection of
"decently priced" beer (16 Gaelic brews on tap) is right "on target"
with its clientele.

Keane's 3300 Club ⌿   – | – | – | I
3300 Mission St. (29th St.), 415-826-6886; www.3300club.com
"It might well be the last of the *Barfly* bars in the far stretches of
the Mission" muse boozers who are keane on this well-worn,
half-century-old saloon; occasional folk and bluegrass bands and
monthly poetry readings attract fresh blood while a "bevy of
streetwise, friendly, hard-pouring bartenders" keeps everybody
lubricated and in line.

Kelly's Mission Rock   18 | 14 | 14 | $7
817 China Basin Way (Mariposa St.), 415-626-5355;
www.kellysmissionrock.com
"Watch the tide roll away" while "sitting on the dock of the bay"
or at least on the outdoor deck of this "huge" restaurant in China
Basin; burgers and beers on a sunny afternoon "can't be beat",
while after dinner (Thursday–Saturday) it becomes a "great"
indoor/outdoor dance club; however, "standoff-ish" service
leaves some calling it a "wasted opportunity"; N.B. in response to
complaints about noise, the city Entertainment Commission had
suspended its entertainment and late-night hours permits in late
April for at least two months.

Kennedy's Irish Pub & Curry House   18 | 14 | 17 | $5
1040 Columbus Ave. (bet. Chestnut & Francisco Sts.), 415-441-8855
"Get your drink on and enjoy a fine curry too" say buffs of this
"wonderland in the heart of North Beach" that boasts a back porch
for smokers as well as pool, air hockey, the "ultimate jukebox" and
"tons of beers" inside; it's packed with a "down-to-earth crowd
looking to have a good time" during the "cheap" happy hour and
beyond, and while the "decor could use a spruce-up", the Indian
food's "surprisingly good" and the "Guinness pour is great."

Kezar Bar   18 | 14 | 17 | $7
900 Cole St. (Carl St.), 415-681-7678
On a "blustery night" ("do we have those in San Francisco?"), this
"friendly", "upscale neighborhood" spot in Cole Valley has just the

"right weathered pub feel" that enables you to "leave your worries at the door and relax"; there's a "good selection of beers on tap", art from local talent on the walls and the "food's always decent", but vets warn "watch out for rabid sports fans on game nights."

Kezar Pub & Restaurant ⊅   19 | 14 | 17 | $6
770 Stanyan St. (bet. Beulah & Waller Sts.), 415-386-9292
"If it's sports, it's on TV" at this "neighborhood pub" that may be the "best place to watch a game in the Haight" where worldwide matches from "hockey to hurling" are shown on 22 screens; with a "plethora of international beers on tap", "great" grub as well as "excellent service", it's no wonder it's "popular" on a "rainy Sunday afternoon", just "be aware of the colors you are wearing during football season."

Kilowatt ⊅   19 | 14 | 19 | $5
3160 16th St. (bet. Guerrero & Valencia Sts.), 415-861-2595
"Show off your tats and piercings" to other "hipsters and punk-rock types" whose lives are lit up by this "rockin' dive" in the Mission boasting "so many cheap beers on tap" that it behooves you to "live within stumbling distance"; it's "rowdy, dark and loud" inside, but the "excellent jukebox, strong drinks" and "high level of play at the pool tables make it worthwhile."

Kimo's   ▽ 14 | 10 | 20 | $5
1351 Polk St. (Pine St.), 415-885-4535
"Cheap drinks" keep the "cheap crowd" fueled at this bi-level "dive-ola" on Polk Street, where gay and straight regulars stick to their stools on ground level and "usually very drunk" bands kick out the punk rock jams upstairs; despite the attempt at Polynesian decor, it's "no trip to Hawaii", and the "quality of the live acts could improve", but it's "worth a visit" for some kimo-nal "fun."

Knuckles Sports Bar   17 | 14 | 17 | $8
Hyatt at Fisherman's Wharf, 555 N. Point St. (Taylor St.), 415-563-1234;
www.hyatt.com
This pair of "standard sports bars" in Fisherman's Wharf and Palo Alto offers just "what you would expect": "reasonably good", "greasy food", a "friendly staff", gaming area (San Francisco) and, of course, "many TVs"; their Hyatt hotel locations mean they're both "frequented by tourists" and there's "no major scene", but for "hanging with the guys, having a few beers" and watching some ball, they accomplish the goal.

Kokkari Estiatorio   24 | 25 | 24 | $10
200 Jackson St. (Front St.), 415-981-0983; www.kokkari.com
"First class all the way", this "sensational" Downtown Greek restaurant offers "fabulous" wines and "creative" cuisine; the "warm", "rustic" interior is dominated by a "wonderful fireplace", while the "small" but "comfortable bar" up front is populated by a happy-hour crowd vying for the dozen or so stools and chatting up the "cheerful", "outstanding" staff, and "if you're lucky, you might find your Helen of Troy."

La Rondalla ⊅   18 | 17 | 16 | $6
901 Valencia St. (20th St.), 415-647-7474
"It's always Christmas at this Mission District dive" where "ancient ornaments", lights and other "cheesy decorations" "dangle from the ceiling" year-round; a "colorful crowd" orders "stiff margaritas"

and "powerful" sangria to deal with the "roaming mariachi bands", and even if the food's your basic "grease fix", the *"feliz navidad"* vibe's a "hell of a lot of fun."

Larry Flynt's Hustler Club
17 | 12 | 16 | $9

1031 Kearny St. (bet. Broadway & Columbus Ave.), 415-434-1301;
www.hustlerclubsf.com

"Whether you're male or female", *Hustler* honcho's North Beach strip joint/restaurant is "worth checking out" what with two stages, two bars and contemporary decor; expect the usual bevy of "beautiful" ladies and "lots of scary breasts", but since "you can get a real drink here", the trade-off is "the girls don't get fully naked", making for what some feel is a "pricey" and "by nature somewhat frustrating experience."

La Scene Café & Bar
▽ 21 | 21 | 21 | $9

Warwick Regis Hotel, 490 Geary St. (Taylor St.), 415-292-6430;
www.warwickhotels.com

This Downtown Warwick Regis Hotel bar has a "lovely" ambiance, making it a "great place to meet for drinks before or after the theater"; the "charming" staff and "cozy" accommodations don't impress scenesters who sneer it's "stuffy", but discerning drama devotees consider it a "sophisticated" choice and prefer that it remain a "well-kept secret."

Last Day Saloon
17 | 11 | 18 | $6

406 Clement St. (bet. 5th & 6th Aves.), 415-387-6343;
www.lastdaysaloon.com

"Don't confuse the up from the down" at this double-decker Inner Richmond club, as the lower level is more of a "locals' pool bar" with a "fraternity atmosphere", while day-trippers troop upstairs to see "some seriously talented acts" making "great music" in an "intimate" setting; though a few naysayers insist it "needs remodeling", the "low-key" digs have been around since 1973, while its Santa Rosa sibling opened post-*Survey*; N.B. credit cards accepted with a $20 minimum.

Last Supper Club, The
20 | 19 | 19 | $7

1199 Valencia St. (23rd St.), 415-695-1199; www.lastsupperclubsf.com

As its name implies, the "emphasis is on the restaurant", but this "warm", "great-looking" Mission District "up-and-comer", now under new ownership, boasts a "bustling" scene at the "tiny bar"; disciples are passionate about the "fabulous cocktails" "adorned with little plastic monkeys", including "pleasing basil gimlets", a prelude to "excellent" Southern Italian fare; even if the service is "overwhelmed", the staff's "friendly" and the vibe is "welcoming."

La Suite
– | – | – | E

(fka Slanted Door)

100 Brannan St. (The Embarcadero), 415-593-9000;
www.lasuitesf.com

From the deco-style chandeliers and tin ceiling to the retiled floors and dark-wood details, the Chez Papa/Baraka team has worked wonders, adding sophisticated Gallic ambiance to this sweet South Beach space that once housed the Slanted Door; Suite-hearts court romance over cocktails like the seductive French Kiss and fare that would make Parisians proud (hello, cheese cart), but when the Giants are in town the bay-view bar becomes a pitch-perfect point for pre- and post-game tippling.

Laszlo
22 | 23 | 19 | $7

2534 Mission St. (bet. 21st & 22nd Sts.), 415-401-0810;
www.foreigncinema.com

"One of the most New York–feeling" hangouts in town is this "excellent" DJ bar attached to the Foreign Cinema in the Mission; reviewers rave about the "cool" bi-level layout, "chicly modern decor", "low lights", "good-looking people" and the "strange but fascinating movie clips" projected on the wall, though critics sneer about the "snootie-patootie" staff, adding it's "about 15 minutes past its prime."

Latin American Club ♥
20 | 19 | 21 | $5

3286 22nd St. (bet. Mission & Valencia Sts.), 415-647-2732

"Eerie taxidermy" and other "bizarre decorations" that coexist on the walls with rotating selections of artwork attract "interesting" patrons to this Mission District "charmer" that's "too far down for the Marina kids to stumble"; "amazing", "eclectic music" also helps keep it "memorable", while "friendly bartenders" keep it real with "strong", "cheap-ass drinks"; no wonder it's "easy to meet people", especially during Sunday happy hours when you'll rub "elbow, hips and other body parts" with your fellow revelers.

Le Central Bistro
20 | 17 | 21 | $9

453 Bush St. (bet. Grant Ave. & Kearny St.), 415-391-2233

"Sit and sip with the power hitters" at this "reliable" Downtown "old-school bistro"; it "seems like a bit of an 'in' club" to the uninitiated, and there are some "local loudmouths at the bar", but its central assets are the "super food", "good wines", "great cognac list" and a staff that "always remembers your drink"; even those who deem it "dated" admit that's part of its "charm."

LE COLONIAL
24 | 25 | 18 | $10

20 Cosmo Pl. (Taylor St.), 415-931-3600; www.lecolonialsf.com

"Grab a sofa if you can" and chill with an "awesome fresh cocktail" and appetizers in the upstairs "romantic lounge" of this "old-world" French-Vietnamese restaurant Downtown, "a jewel in the heart of the city" that's nearly hidden in a small alley; it's "gorgeous and lush with a tranquil sexy vibe" ("your date will be impressed"), though keep in mind on weekend nights the place is "surprisingly hopping" with DJs spinning "thumping house music."

Left at Albuquerque
15 | 15 | 16 | $7

2140 Union St. (bet. Fillmore & Webster Sts.), 415-749-6700;
www.leftatalb.com

"Tons of different tequilas" ("one for each mood") and "huge" margaritas "rule" at these Southwestern chain links in Cow Hollow and Campbell; "fantastic" happy-hour specials, "great" outdoor seating and an "upbeat atmosphere" help compensate for the paucity of "personality", and even when the "cheesy post-college" crowd descends, the "good drinks and decent food make them hard to bash."

Lefty O'Doul's
15 | 13 | 17 | $6

333 Geary St. (Powell St.), 415-982-8900

"Union Square wouldn't be the same without" this "hofbrau-type" Downtown "institution" that offers "history, tradition, cheap eats and a good selection of beers" all under one roof; opened in 1958 by the eponymous local baseball legend, it's popular with "old-timers" and tourists who dig the "great sports memorabilia" and enjoy "singing with the crowd" at the piano bar.

Levende
– | – | – | E

(fka butterfly)
1710 Mission St. (Duboce Ave.), 415-864-5585; www.levendesf.com
This Mission hipster maintains the club-cum-restaurant ambiance that defined previous tenant butterfly; the young and the trendy lounge around on cushioned couches and chairs, milking their martinis and specialty cocktails, while DJs beg attention with down-tempo, hip-hop, funk and lounge sounds; rich brown walls, a cement floor and an open-beamed ceiling create a vibe that's one part industrial-chic cool and one part bachelor-pad casual.

Lexington Club ⌀
– | – | – | M

3464 19th St. (Valencia St.), 415-863-2052; www.lexingtonclub.com
"Girls who like girls and boys who used to be girls who like girls" are gaga for the "last [full-time] lesbian bar in town" marked by its distinctive pink neon sign in the heart of the Mission; even those with "too many Y chromosomes" think it's a "great spot" (though they can only go if accompanied by an XX), and the "tattooed and pierced crowd" agrees, saying "may it live forever!"

Liberties, The
18 | 17 | 20 | $5

998 Guerrero St. (22nd St.), 415-282-6789; www.theliberties.com
Like the Guinness it pours, this "authentic Dublin-style Irish pub" in the Mission boasts a "dark" but "hearty" soul that attracts a "slightly older crowd" for a "good, quiet pint" and "comfort food" that "should not be missed"; "friendly bartenders", a "cozy" setting that includes sidewalk seating and a "relaxing" atmosphere help make it "extraordinary in its ordinariness."

Liberty Cafe & Bakery
21 | 21 | 21 | $10

410 Cortland Ave. (Bennington St.), 415-695-8777
"The great wine bar hidden behind" this "excellent" Bernal Heights restaurant offers a "homey", "intimate" cottage setting in which to throw your "dough" at the "best fresh bread" (it's a bakery by day) or "chat and sip" "good, eclectic" vinos (Thursday–Saturday nights); it may "not be a place to find love or lust", but it's certainly "comfortable" for a "pre-dinner" rendezvous.

Lime
– | – | – | E

2247 Market St. (bet. Noe & Sanchez Sts.), 415-621-5256;
www.lime-sf.com
Tart at times but never sour, this bi-level Castro mod pod attracts well-dressed space-age travelers with its *Jetson*-tastic '60s-driven decor and groovy pop soundtrack; relax in a curvy white booth, take in the pendant lamps and blue-and-fuchsia glow, and dig the inventive cocktails and small plates of fish tacos and mini burgers made for picking; N.B. the tiny TVs embedded in the bar and bathrooms are sure to be icebreakers during conversational lulls.

Lingba Lounge
20 | 20 | 15 | $7

1469 18th St. (bet. Arkansas & Connecticut Sts.), 415-355-0001;
www.lingba.com
For "a really good example of tropical done right, not tacky", check out this "hip corner bar" in Potrero Hill where a "cool crowd" quaffs "delicious", "insane" cocktails and "watches retro surf reels" in a "dark, sexy" interior that evokes the "beaches of Thailand";

"groovy down-tempo beats" and live entertainment create a "relaxed" mood that seems to extend to the "slow service."

LION PUB, THE ⊄   23 | 21 | 18 | $7
(aka Lion, The)
2062 Divisadero St. (Sacramento St.), 415-567-6565
Though it "used to be a gay bar", this Pacific Heights "gem" now draws a "typical SF mélange of homo-, hetero- and metrosexuals"; it's "somewhat difficult to find" as there's "no sign", but once inside, the "dark, intimate interior" offers a fireplace, "plenty of small, cozy tables", "complimentary snacks" and bartenders concocting "fantastic greyhounds" with freshly squeezed pink grapefruit juice (perhaps that's why the "drinks are as expensive as the real estate" in the neighborhood).

Li Po ⊄   20 | 14 | 17 | $6
916 Grant Ave. (Washington St.), 415-982-0072
It's "easy to fall into a lost weekend binge" at this "mysterious" Chinatown "landmark" where "locals", "hipsters" and bemused "tourists" explore an "alternative reality" kindled by "cheap, strong drinks"; the "dark", "1940s-noir" setting with "private red booths" and a "divey underground space" is just made for "trysts" ("who was that girl and what did we do?").

Lit Lounge   – | – | – | M
101 Sixth St. (Mission St.), 415-278-0940
The PlayStations and Japanimation decor of previous tenant Pow! are long gone, and the mood at this SoMa spot is instead set now by whims of the DJs who spin hip-hop, house, soul and techno under the fractured glow of a mirror ball in the small back room; up front is an antique bar, red walls and frayed vintage furniture, and with a happy hour running later than average, expect to get plenty lit.

Little Shamrock ⊄   22 | 19 | 20 | $5
807 Lincoln Way (bet. 9th & 10th Aves.), 415-661-0060
Lucky enough to have survived since 1893, this "endearing" Irish pub in the Inner Sunset has "character and charm galore" thanks to its "great fireplace" and "friendly bartenders"; it's "packed" with "longtime loyal" "locals" who come to "play backgammon" and "shoot some pool" or "kick it on broken-in" couches with a pint from the "fantastic beer selection" as they "talk about back in the day."

Liverpool Lil's   20 | 16 | 20 | $6
2942 Lyon St. (bet. Greenwich & Lombard Sts.), 415-921-6664
"The perfect neighborhood bar" just might be this "cordial" and "cozy" "faux-English pub" that's "off the beaten path" from the area's busy singles scene; "a good place to go in the cold" or to "watch a game" and "eat a burger" (food is served until 1 AM), it attracts "convivial patrons" who appreciate the "great selection of beers" and "well-made drinks."

Loading Dock   – | – | – | M
1525 Mission St. (bet. 11th St. & S. Van Ness Ave.), 415-864-1525
Depending on which dress code is in force, you'll find loads of men in denim, leather, latex or a specific uniform docked at this "fun fetish club" "given over to the darker pursuits" in a "fantastic space" in SoMa; scaredy cats cry "don't go unless you know what you're getting into", however, old hands retort it "not nearly as fierce as it's made out to be", and in fact, it's "rather friendly."

Lobby Lounge   ▽ 24 | 25 | 24 | $10

Renaissance Stanford Court Hotel, 905 California St. (Powell St.), 415-989-3500

"Although not as heavily trafficked as other Nob Hill bars", this "enjoyable", "peaceful oasis" in the Renaissance Stanford Court Hotel is "as comfortable as your favorite easy chair", making it a "quietly elegant" spot for afternoon tea or evening cocktails; the wood trim, player piano and 19th-century paintings enhance the "relaxed, classic atmosphere."

LOBBY LOUNGE AT RITZ-CARLTON   26 | 26 | 27 | $13

Ritz-Carlton, 600 Stockton St. (Pine St.), 415-296-7465; www.ritzcarlton.com

"One never knows who might" walk through the doors of this "posh", "gorgeous", "dignified" Nob Hill lounge in the Ritz-Carlton, but "rock stars" and "power" players have been "sighted" sipping "great champagne" and "well-prepared cocktails" while listening to "relaxing" piano music; though prices are "not modest", you do "get what you pay for", including "impeccable" service, "terrific" hors d'oeuvres and sushi, plus the chance to warm your well-manicured hands by the "cozy fireplace."

Loft 11   ▽ 19 | 20 | 15 | $9

316 11th St. (bet. Folsom & Harrison Sts.), 415-701-8111; www.loft11sf.com

This spacious SoMa spot "was once a favorite brewpub" (20 Tank) and "has been reincarnated" as a nightclub and restaurant serving "great" Pacific Rim small plates before the dancing kicks off on the newly installed glass floor; it's "a beautiful space with tall ceilings", a second-floor loft, booth seating and a "friendly" young crowd, though bashers boo the "lines at the bar" and a vibe that "can be cool or not"; N.B. a recent refurb may impact the Decor score.

London Wine Bar   18 | 17 | 21 | $8

415 Sansome St. (bet. Clay & Sacramento Sts.), 415-788-4811

Considered "the oldest wine bar in America", this "dark, cozy" Downtowner provides a "comfortable" retreat "after work" or on a "cold evening" to sample from its "interesting", "strong list" of 1,000-plus bottles; a "good selection of appetizers" and a "helpful" staff are equally "impressive", though the "drab" decor "leaves a lot to be desired."

Lone Palm   22 | 19 | 20 | $5

3394 22nd St. (Guerrero St.), 415-648-0109

"Rat Pack glamour" meets "down-to-earth prices" at this "dark", "little gin joint" in the Mission, where "committed drinkers" and "couples on dates" dig the "art deco" scene as they "fill their tanks" with what some call the "best Manhattans in the city"; "super-friendly service" abets the "sophisticated-without-being-uppity" vibe, and the fact that it "doesn't try too hard" helps it "succeed where others have failed."

Lone Star Saloon ⊄   – | – | – | I

1354 Harrison St. (9th St.), 415-863-9999

"If you like your men big and hairy", this SoMa saloon "should be your first stop in San Francisco", as it's considered "bear heaven for the gay community"; even when the "great space" is "packed belly to butt" (it's a "full", er, den on Sundays), "the 'paunch 'n' raunch' is still the friendliest, furriest place to be."

Lou's Pier 47   22 | 16 | 22 | $13
300 Jefferson St. (Jones St.), 415-771-5687; www.louspier47.com
A favorite of tourists and locals alike, this "casual venue" in
Fisherman's Wharf offers "live blues for boomers who love to rock";
in addition to the "great entertainment", it's "pleasant" to "dine
under the awning along the boardwalk" on New Orleans–accented
fare, and all in all, it offers "good value for the area."

Lucky 13 ⌐   20 | 16 | 17 | $5
2140 Market St. (Church St.), 415-487-1313
"Those who try too hard need not apply" to this "down-home"
"punk rock bar" on Upper Market where "friendly" "pierced
zeitgeist types" bond over the "killer jukebox" that's "heavy on
the heavy sounds"; an "excellent beer selection", pool, pinball and
"free popcorn" as well as a "secret patio" make it a "dependable
dive" for "freaks" to "be themselves" over "good, stiff drinks."

Luella   – | – | – | E
1896 Hyde St. (Green St.), 415-674-4343; www.luellasf.com
It's easy to wind up sipping Pinot Noir and getting friendly with your
neighbors at this new Russian Hill wine haven (founded by the
folks behind Andalu), as the bar area's sized just right for cozy
conversations; split a small plate of Mediterranean nibbles, sip a
Bellini or just concentrate on the well-conceived, approachable
and affordable list of reds and whites by the bottle or glass.

Luna Lounge   ∇ 18 | 17 | 20 | $7
1192 Folsom St. (8th St.), 415-626-6043; www.lunalounge-sf.com
This "beautiful", "funky" dance destination in SoMa doubles as a
"perfect after-work happy-hour" spot with "cheap" beverages and
several separate lounges providing a "cool atmosphere"; those
harboring an "aversion toward frat boys" are less than moon-eyed,
but buffs howl "it's out of this world."

Luna Park   22 | 20 | 19 | $7
694 Valencia St. (18th St.), 415-553-8584; www.lunaparksf.com
"Lively to a fault", this "hopping Mission hangout" hasn't waned
in "popularity" thanks to the "infamous" cocktails ("one word:
mojito") and "amazing", shareable dishes such as goat-cheese
fondue at "wallet-friendly" prices; it's "comfy" and "romantic" ("try
for one of the curtained booths"), and the "entertaining bartenders"
and "friendly, helpful" staff contribute to the "great vibe."

Lush Lounge ⌐   22 | 21 | 23 | $7
1092 Post St. (Polk St.), 415-771-2022; www.thelushlounge.com
"All sorts of funky people" – "gay, straight, it's all good" – converge
on this Polk Street "pickup scene for the alternately oriented"
known for its "creative" cocktails as well as a clientele that appears
to have come from a "Diane Arbus shoot"; though it's no longer a
piano bar, the "people-watching" is still primo or you can "check
out the autographs on the walls" of the "cool space."

Lusty Lady ⌐   ∇ 19 | 7 | 18 | $6
1033 Kearny St. (Broadway), 415-391-3991;
www.thelustylady.com
"Power to the workers" proclaim PC porn enthusiasts of this North
Beach emporium that's the nation's first "employee-owned" and
union-organized strip club; it's actually a "traditional peep show"
where spy holes "look onto a big dance floor" inhabited by "diverse,

sexy" "nudies", and though it provides "no drinks", "where else can you see a naked girl for 25 cents?" P.S. "don't wear sandals" here.

MacArthur Park | 17 | 17 | 18 | $9 |
607 Front St. (bet. Jackson St. & Pacific Ave.), 415-398-5700; www.macpark.com
"The happy-hour buffet is a nice touch" and the chief attraction for many of the Financial District denizens who descend upon this longtime Downtown "after-work rib house", now under new management; "when there's a full crowd" it gets "quite noisy" with lots of "action at the bar", leading some to decry it as a "meat market" and others to sniff it's "old news" and at its core just a "way overrated burger joint"; N.B. the Palo Alto branch is unrated.

Mad Dog in the Fog ⊽ | 19 | 13 | 18 | $5 |
530 Haight St. (Fillmore St.), 415-626-7279
The "excellent" "bartenders move at the speed of light" to pull pints of Boddington's and other "great" ales for thirsty "British expats" at this "hugely popular" Lower Haight pub that's the "best place to watch soccer in the city"; though the "focus is on futbol", it's also known for its "lively trivia nights" where the doggedly determined players are "serious"; N.B. beer and wine only.

Madrone Lounge | – | – | – | M |
500 Divisadero St. (Fell St.), 415-241-0202; www.madronelounge.com
Hidden inside a vintage Victorian (and former pharmacy) in the Western Addition is this comfortable, couch-strewn art and DJ lounge; when not perusing the paintings or big-screen videos that fill the tall blue walls, scope out the articulate list of wines by the glass and bottle or down a vodka shot infused with seasonal delights like cucumber and ginger; N.B. happy hour Hot Boy specials (a Tall Boy and a Hot Pocket) are an indie-crowd staple.

Magnolia Pub & Brewery | 19 | 17 | 19 | $5 |
1398 Haight St. (Masonic Ave.), 415-864-7468; www.magnoliapub.com
With its rotating roster of "unique" cask-conditioned ales and other "super-fresh" varieties all "made on the premises", this "hoppin' little brewpub" in the Upper Haight is "a quirky can't-miss for anyone who loves great beer"; there's not one but two happy hours each evening (except Tuesdays when pints are $2.50 all day), and its "tattooed" groupies are grateful for their "neighborhood comfort place" that feels "a little like Berkeley."

Make-Out Room ⊽ | 21 | 17 | 18 | $6 |
3225 22nd St. (bet. Mission & Valencia Sts.), 415-647-2888; www.makeoutroom.com
"Slightly glamorous" and "slightly divey" but "perennially cool", this "cavernous" Mission "classic" is "good for an intimate night with your favorite local" and national live acts or DJs; the "giddy" atmosphere, "fantasy setting" complete with disco ball and "stiff drinks" will "make you automatically love the band", and while the changing artwork is "always interesting" to peruse, the room's "dark enough to do just what its name says" if the mood strikes.

MANDARIN LOUNGE | 26 | 24 | 26 | $15 |
Mandarin Oriental Hotel, 222 Sansome St. (bet. California & Pine Sts.), 415-276-9888; www.mandarinoriental.com
This "beautiful lounge" on the bottom of the sky-high Mandarin Oriental Hotel Downtown is undeniably "great for a business drink"

and a "delicious appetizer" but also a super-"swanky", "perfect place for a relaxed rendezvous" to the strains of piano music; keep in mind "the tabs could bankrupt a tai-pan", but sometimes "superlative service" and a "quiet, discreet location" are well worth paying for.

Mario's Bohemian Cigar Store Cafe　20 │ 15 │ 19 │ $6 │
566 Columbus Ave. (Union St.), 415-362-0536; www.mariosbohemian.com
You can no longer buy or smoke cigars inside this "tiny" North Beach cafe, but you can indulge in the "affordable wines" "served Italian-style in glasses" and "awesome focaccia" sandwiches and panini "from the baker's oven"; it's "perfect to start an evening" of bar hopping or simply "lingering over coffee" as its "low-key" vibe's "conducive" to "good conversation."

MarketBar　19 │ 19 │ 17 │ $8 │
1 Ferry Bldg. (bet. Market & Mission Sts.), 415-434-1100
While it "feels like a bistro in Paris", this "beautiful" find from BIX's Doug Biederbeck has a much more convenient location in the historic Ferry Building along the Embarcadero; sidewalk seating offers "great views of the Downtown skyline" while you quaff an "outstanding cocktail", though the "wait for a drink" can be "ridiculous" during happy hour.

Marlena's ⊅　– │ – │ – │ M │
488 Hayes St. (Octavia Blvd.), 415-864-6672
"Drag is never a drag" declare divas who've fallen in love again with this long-running gay watering hole in Hayes Valley that's a "blast for the karaoke acts" on select Saturdays; while admittedly not everyone's cup of tea, the bartenders provide "good pours" and it's a sure bet "your open-minded out-of-town guests will get a kick out of it."

Mars Bar　18 │ 15 │ 19 │ $6 │
798 Brannan St. (7th St.), 415-621-6277; www.marsbarsf.com
Though it's "no longer as packed as during the glory days of the boom", this "little corner spot" in SoMa is still worth exploring for its "upbeat" vibe, bartenders who "treat their regulars well", "cheap drinks" and "great" snacks; a few rovers rail that despite its "popularity with young people", it's "long in the tooth", but vets advise it's "fun on the patio when the weather's nice"; N.B. a recent change of hands may impact the above scores.

Martuni's　23 │ 18 │ 20 │ $8 │
4 Valencia St. (Market St.), 415-241-0205
It's worth "braving the crowds" at this "wonderful piano bar" near the Civic Center for "stellar martinis", "fabulous girlie drinks" and the "crew" of "drag queens" and "breeders" belting out show tunes "in a unifying lovefest"; "don't think this is karaoke" as the "regular sirens" "take their singing seriously", but the atmosphere's "convivial", the service is "excellent" and it's the "perfect place for a gay man to take his mom."

Mas Sake Freestyle Sushi　18 │ 16 │ 14 │ $8 │
2030 Lombard St. (bet. Fillmore & Webster Sts.), 415-440-1505; www.massake.com
"Bodacious sushi" and a "hottie" staff attract a "boisterous", equally "beautiful" crowd to this Cow Hollow "pickup scene", aka "the set of *90210*"; "don't expect to have a quiet conversation",

but it's "great for groups" clamoring for "the best sake bombs around", and if the Japanese fare's "pricey" and merely "decent", the "eye-candy" waitresses provide the "special sauce."

MATRIXFILLMORE   20 | 25 | 15 | $9
3138 Fillmore St. (bet. Filbert & Greenwich Sts.), 415-563-4180;
www.matrixfillmore.com
Mayor Gavin Newsom's "ultralounge" in Cow Hollow "caters to people like himself – young, rich and pretty", and it does so in "beautiful" style, with "plush, purple" decor, "cocktail tables that spell out 'S-E-X'", TVs in the loos and DJs every night; once a "psychedelic club for acid-crazed hippies", it's now "packed" with "single gals" in search of "amazing, delicious" drinks and "single guys to pick up the tab" (meaning 'bill'); naysayers, however, suggest "not even Neo would be cool enough" for this *Zoolander* of bars" that "wishes it were in LA."

Mauna Loa ⌿   17 | 10 | 17 | $5
3009 Fillmore St. (Union St.), 415-563-5137
Perhaps the "only unpretentious place" left in "ritzy" Cow Hollow is this "comfortable", "kick-ass dive" with "all the booze and none of the fuss" of other Triangle bars; there's "lots of stuff for big kids to do", including foosball, high-definition TVs, "fun hoops in the back" and a "fantastic jukebox", and though the "narrow space" gets "crowded" with "aging frat boys" on weekends, it's by and large "mellow."

Max's Opera Cafe   16 | 14 | 16 | $8
Opera Plaza, 601 Van Ness Ave. (Golden Gate Ave.), 415-771-7300;
www.maxsworld.com
If you're inclined to swig your gin in an "East Coast Jewish-style deli", this restaurant and bar on Van Ness near the Opera House and Civic Center "is as close as you'll get"; the "portions are enormous" and there's "free entertainment" in the form of servers who take the stage "to sing Broadway show tunes", but critics carp it "could be anywhere in the U.S. and you wouldn't know the difference" at all; N.B. its Burlingame and PA offshoots are more eatery than nightlife.

Maya   21 | 21 | 20 | $9
303 Second St. (bet. Beach & Larkin Sts.), 415-543-2928;
www.mayasf.net
"Not your usual taqueria", this "upscale" SoMa Mexican with a Manhattan sibling attracts amigos with "superb" food, "excellent" margaritas, "professional" service and "beautiful", "stylish" decor including a "comfy" lounge and outdoor seating; although the guacamole just might be "the most expensive you've ever had", it's "like that $5 milkshake in *Pulp Fiction* – so worth it" (and it offers "great happy-hour specials", too).

McCormick & Kuleto's   21 | 21 | 20 | $9
Ghirardelli Sq., 900 N. Point St. (bet. Beach & Larkin Sts.),
415-929-1730; www.mccormickandkuletos.com
"The view people move to San Francisco for" is right outside the windows of this "spacious", "mellow" chain outpost "overlooking the Bay" in Fisherman's Wharf; the "spectacular" scenery is "a must-see even on a misty day", and while the potables are "pricey" and the place itself is "way too oriented toward onetime visitors", the service is "excellent" and it makes for a "romantic" rendezvous.

Mecca　　　　　　　　　　24　24　21　$10

2029 Market St. (bet. Church & Dolores Sts.), 415-621-7000;
www.sfmecca.com
"Label queens and fashionistas rule" the "dark interior" of this
"swanky", "Manhattan-y bar" and restaurant on Upper Market;
"the scene's mostly gay" but not exclusively so, as a "mixed
crowd" admires the "awesome food", "creative" cocktails like the
frozen Bellini and "seductive" ambiance; P.S. loyalists also "love"
the drag shows.

Men's Room ⊽　　　　　▽ 13　11　19　$6

3988 18th St. (bet. Noe & Sanchez Sts.), 415-861-1310
"You can guess from the name what the vibe is" at this gay
"hangout" in the Castro filled with "all sorts" of man-kind catching
a game on TV; "friendly, knowledgeable bartenders kick it way up",
though unimpressed passersby say there's "no reason to walk in
the door" as the "neighborhood has lots of popular pubs."

Metro City Bar　　　　　　－　－　－　M

3600 16th St. (Market St.), 415-703-9751
"Love the balcony" laud looky-loos of this Castro cafe that affords
"good street views" and "great people-watching" from its second-
floor perch; the owners who took over a few years ago have
updated its image, including adding marble floors and a Spanish
tapas menu, but it's still popular for after-work and late-night
hanging, and from the staff to customers, the folks "are as
friendly" as ever.

Metronome Dance Center　　▽ 22　17　20　$6
(fka Metronome Ballroom)

1830 17th St. (De Haro St.), 415-252-9000; www.metronomeballroom.com
"Dust off those moves or come to learn new ones" at this "good
ballroom dancing venue" in Potrero Hill, "one of the few places in
the city that's social without being a meat market"; there's "no food
or drink here" but "lots of space" to pick up tips and techniques on
salsa, swing, tango and other styles, and the "warm environment"
is "great for singles and couples, straight or gay."

Mezzanine　　　　　　　24　20　20　$7

444 Jessie St. (bet. Mint & 6th Sts.), 415-820-9669; www.mezzaninesf.com
An "open space" with "lots of room" that's "designed for partying"
is how merrymakers depict this popular SoMa dance club in a
"renovated warehouse" with "wack-ass '90s South Beach" decor;
the weekend dance parties are a magnet for an "unpretentiously
attractive" gay/straight clientele and are "fabulous fun if you love
house or techno" spun by "cutting-edge DJs" and "sweaty hunks"
who come to shake it like a Polaroid on Saturday nights ("it's like
Club Universe never ended").

Michael Mina　　　　　　－　－　－　E
(fka Compass Rose)

Westin St. Francis, 335 Powell St. (bet. Geary & Post Sts.),
415-397-9222; www.michaelmina.net
After overhauling Downtown mainstay the Compass Rose, dressing
it in cream-colored drapes and celadon green chairs, former Aqua
chef Michael Mina's magnificent space quickly became the talk of
the town, as much for its signature look as its inventive entrees; the
dining room overlooks the massive lobby of the historic Westin St.

Francis, while the lounge tucked to the rear offers a posh crowd plush comfort just right for sipping ginger-pomegranate Cosmos or indulging in a bottle from the impressive wine list.

Michael's Octavia Lounge   – | – | – | M |
1772 Market St. (Octavia Blvd.), 415-863-3516; www.octavialounge.com
Boasting easy-on-the-wallet dinner-and-a-show packages, this gay-friendly Hayes Valley supper club brings cabaret, comedy, jazz and drag shows to an area that may, once nearby Octavia Boulevard opens, become a bustling Lower Castro crossroads; the acts add sass to an atmosphere lacking in flash.

Midnight Sun ⊄   17 | 14 | 18 | $6 |
4067 18th St. (Castro St.), 415-861-4186; www.midnightsunsf.com
In the unlikely event that you're "behind on your queer TV, stop by for a show" at this "archetypal video bar" in the Castro featuring "more monitors and screens than Liza's had face-lifts" with "100 strangers providing the laugh track"; "cute preppies" and other "all-American types" "surreptitiously" cruise and bond over *Will & Grace,* especially during the "good happy hours", but those who've seen the other side of midnight moan "boys watching television – why did we come out again?"

Mighty ⊄   – | – | – | E |
119 Utah St. (15th St.), 415-626-7001; www.mighty119.com
Done up with glass chandeliers, steel countertops and exposed-brick walls covered with artwork, this monstrous space in an industrial corner of Potrero Hill offers room to move – 6000-sq.-ft. worth, in fact; serious spins from world-class DJs cement its growing status as a dancers' mecca of Mighty fine proportions.

Milk Bar   21 | 19 | 19 | $7 |
1840 Haight St. (Stanyan St.), 415-387-6455; www.milksf.com
Fans are fired up that there's "finally a cool club in the Upper Haight" where you can "bust out your Puma gear" and "listen to phat beats"; it's "not for the decibel intolerant", but if "dancing your ass off" in the "intimate" space or lounging in a "white vinyl booth while drinking Red Stripes" or drinks "poured with a heavy hand" seem like a good time, then it sounds like you've "got milk."

Millennium   ▽ 22 | 18 | 22 | $9 |
Savoy Hotel, 580 Geary St. (Jones St.), 415-345-3900;
www.millenniumrestaurant.com
If you're "dating a vegan you'll all but live" at this Downtown restaurant serving the "most creative" and "tasty" meat- and dairy-free cuisine around accompanied by "great elixirs" both alcoholic and non; the "friendly staff" can help "decipher" the all-organic wine list, and since relocating to the Savoy Hotel, the now-larger bar area is even better for a "delightful evening."

Mint Karaoke Lounge, The ⊄   22 | 13 | 18 | $6 |
1942 Market St. (Duboce St.), 415-626-4726; www.themint.net
"Sing your heart out" at this "fun" karaoke club on Upper Market where you're "guaranteed to come out smiling"; the room's a bit "tacky", but the bartenders are "wonderful" and the KJ sports a "huge selection of songs from Abba to Zappa", and while many of the chosen titles "are predictable, the performers are not"; be warned, though, that "this is the top of the circuit", and the budding Idols here are likely "practicing at home."

Mitchell Brothers O'Farrell Theatre   24 14 19 $11
895 O'Farrell St. (Polk St.), 415-776-6686
"The crème de la crème (and then some) of strip clubs" is "not for prudes", as the "hot" dancers at this Tenderloin flesh parlor writhe and grind in the altogether and "go out of their way to make you feel relaxed"; never mind the "steep cover charge", this "landmark" purveys "sleazy San Francisco entertainment at its finest", though some critics complain it's "a shadow of its former self" noting the "high level of hustle."

Mix ⊅   ▽ 18 12 18 $5
4086 18th St. (Castro St.), 415-431-8616
While "the name may have changed" at this Castro gay bar long known as Uncle Bert's Place, "the low-key, neighborhood feel thankfully remains the same", with many a favorite nephew and a few nieces still parked on a stool or mingling on the "wonderful back patio"; some note with skepticism that "it's now supposedly hip", though most maintain it's still the "best place" around "to watch the game and chug a cold brew."

Moby Dick ⊅   18 14 20 $6
4049 18th St. (bet. Castro & Noe Sts.), no phone; www.mobydicksf.com
A "loyal regular crowd" of "cute" gay men and the "attractive straight women who love them" make Ahab-it of this "shimmy-up-to-the-bar-and-chat place" that's the "Castro equivalent of comfort food"; the "friendly" staff, "great slushy girlie drinks", "decent pool table" and a "giant" conversation-starter aquarium help create a "happy vibe" in the "small", "homey" space.

Molotov ⊅   18 16 18 $5
582 Haight St. (Steiner St.), 415-558-8019
The objective at this "wonderful bar" is to "get hammered", as it's "one of the few places in the Lower Haight" that serves liquor; some are soured by the "scary industrial interior" and "hard-edged" clientele, but if your idea of an explosive evening is "challenging your neighbor to a chugging contest" and "being loud and irritating", you just might find it "a fun hangout."

MoMo's   19 18 16 $9
760 Second St. (The Embarcadero), 415-227-8660; www.sfmomos.com
"Everyone's favorite tailgate spot has them hanging off the rafters before and after Giants games" largely because this "happening" South Beach eatery–cum–"meat market" is so close to SBC Park that "you can hear the crowd roar"; naturally, procuring your "pricey" but "unbeatable Bloody Mary" is "difficult" when it's "insanely packed", but if you can "set up shop on the patio", it's "worth a visit."

Monkey Club   20 24 20 $7
2730 21st St. (Bryant St.), 415-647-2144; www.themonkeyclubsf.com
Its "isolated" site "on the outskirts of the Mission" notwithstanding, this "swanky" "little" lounge provides a "perfect hangout" with "cool" decor and "comfy couches" complemented by DJs spinning "smooth music with a kick"; admirers also go ape for the "first-class drinks" served "quickly" and the "diverse", "eye-candy" crowd, adding "if you're shopping for meat, this is your market."

Moose's
24 | 23 | 23 | $9

1652 Stockton St. (bet. Filbert & Union Sts.), 415-989-7800;
www.mooses.com
"Ed Moose has buffed and polished his namesake establishment
to a fine sheen", and it shows not only in the "beautiful peach
walls and dark wood" of this North Beach "institution" but in the
"excellent", "consistent service" and "tasty" cuisine as well; it
also serves as a "sophisticated sports bar", and the "highbrow
clientele" of local "celebrities" and "terrific" nightly piano jazz
make it a de facto "shrine to Herb Caen."

Movida Lounge ⏁
23 | 20 | 20 | $6

200 Fillmore St. (Waller St.), 415-934-8637
"Sipping sangria and counting tattoos" is a local pastime at this
"dimly lit" Lower Haight lounge where "you can actually carry on
a conversation" in a "pleasant, mellow atmosphere" enhanced by
"cool art on the walls"; the beer, wine and "delicious soju and sake
cocktails" will have you "livin' Movida loca" in no time, or at least
"bumpin'" in your seat to some "smoothly spun vinyl."

Mr. Bing's ⏁
16 | 10 | 22 | $4

201 Columbus Ave. (Pacific Ave.), 415-362-1545
"Cheap drinks and awesome service" are the calling cards of this
"minuscule landmark" between Chinatown and North Beach that
may be the "ultimate dive" despite the fact "you're likely to find
tuxes as well as ripped jeans" donning the "mixed crowd" that may
embody "entropy"; if nothing "quirky's happening", you can check
out the "phenomenal jukebox" or "have a beer and watch the
mah-jongg game."

Mucky Duck ⏁
12 | 9 | 16 | $5

1315 Ninth Ave. (Irving St.), 415-661-4340
Dive devotees duck into this Inner Sunset haunt to "play pool, have
a few with friends" and soak up the "positive energy" that makes it
"a great retreat from everyday life"; but others make quacks about
its "lack of character" and "less-than-appetizing clientele", adding
"I wouldn't go back if you paid me."

Murio's Trophy Room ⏁
16 | 14 | 18 | $5

1811 Haight St. (bet. Shrader & Stanyan Sts.), 415-752-2971
"Weird people" from "all walks of life" are winners at this "old-time
Haight Street spot" that may be "seedy" but remains "one of the
best rockers' bars" in town (the "key is the pool table and good
jukebox"); "make sure you're wanting a wild night" as it's "never
a dull moment" here, and take note that "if you're wearing Prada,
don't think you'll be getting in on" the billiards game "anytime soon."

Myth
– | – | – | E

(fka MC2)
470 Pacific Ave. (Montgomery St.), 415-677-8986; www.mythsf.com
Tasteful sophistication and moneyed hipness combine head on at
this Downtown legend-in-the-making tucked away on a quiet street
near North Beach and run by restaurateur Tom Duffy and chef Sean
O'Brien (a Gary Danko alum); intriguing menu aside, the mood,
crowd, groovy music, affordable wines and even the modern
setting, with a marble bar and spacious seating, make this Myth
a story worth sharing; N.B. cocktails are served, plus a line of
signature libations is now in the works.

City of San Francisco A | D | S | C

Nectar Wine Lounge — | — | — | E
3330 Steiner St. (Lombard St.), 415-345-1377;
www.nectarwinelounge.com
Young oenophiles seeking solace from the crowded Marina scene outside slake their thirst with some 45 *vins* by the glass and a sophisticated small-plates menu at this airy mecca for all things grape; imbibers saddle up stools at the glass-and-stainless-steel bar and sink into plush armchairs, while those intent on expanding their expertise partake in the semi-regular wine dinners.

Nickie's BBQ 22 | 15 | 17 | $6
460 Haight St. (bet. Fillmore & Webster Sts.), 415-621-6508;
www.nickies.com
It may "get hot" and "crazy-crowded on weekends", but the "fabulous" "DJs know what they're spinning" (from hip-hop to funk to reggae) at this "small but thumpin'" Lower Haight "hole-in-the-wall"; if you "enjoy being pressed up against while grooving to '70s staples (and who doesn't?)", "the scene is always fun" and the setting for "many memorable nights", even if no BBQ is served; N.B. no cover before 10 PM, except Tuesdays.

Noc Noc 22 | 24 | 18 | $6
557 Haight St. (bet. Fillmore & Steiner Sts.), 415-861-5811
"One of the strangest bars anywhere" may well be this "boho Lower Haight hangout" with its "must-see" interior that evokes "*Mad Max*", a "David Lynch movie" and an "alien's cave"; who's there? equally "interesting" folks who relish the chance of "drinking inside a Goth sci-fi novel" as they sit on "weird, sculpted furniture" or "scruffy floor cushions"; the "owner's the best", the music "rocks" and though there are no cocktails, it offers "hearty" microbrews, wine and sake.

Noe's ⊘ 15 | 12 | 19 | $5
1199 Church St. (24th St.), 415-282-4007
"Plenty of regulars" pile into this "inviting" "neighborhood hangout" in Noe Valley that "doubles as a sports bar"; sure, there's "not much character" and it "badly needs a face-lift", but that's the appeal to "locals" who can "relax" with their fellow "rowdy" patrons in the "blue-collar" ambiance and watch satellite TV.

Noe Valley Ministry ⊘ — | — | — | I
1021 Sanchez St. (23rd St.), 415-454-5238;
www.noevalleymusicseries.com
"Hidden away in Noe Valley", this "low-key" venue is a Unitarian Church by day, but on select weekend evenings it turns into an "intimate", "fabulous place" to enjoy acoustic folk, jazz, country or indie rock acts; watching from the pews and drinking a beer (sold at intermission) may seem sacrilegious, but "if you consider some musicians to be gods, there's no better place to see them"; N.B. those tired of circling the block will sing hosannas over the paid parking facility.

North Star Cafe 20 | 12 | 20 | $6
1560 Powell St. (Green St.), 415-397-0577
"Free popcorn" and a "homey pool room" make this "unassuming joint" in North Beach a "good meeting place for an easy night"; the bar's been around for over a century and is "not much to look at", though that hasn't stopped the "under-30 crowd" from packing

74 subscribe to zagat.com

in on weekends when "post-college binge drinking" is in effect and you're sure to "see more than one backwards baseball cap."

N'Touch ⌂   16 | 10 | 16 | $6

1548 Polk St. (Sacramento St.), 415-441-8413; www.ntouchsf.com
"The only full-time gay club catering to the Asian crowd", this "older-than-the-hills" Polk Street vet's "more popular than ever" thanks to "great bartenders", "fabulous karaoke nights" and "sexy go-go dancers" on Fridays and Saturdays; in fact the "narrow space" is "overstuffed on weekends."

Occidental Cigar Club   ▽ 21 | 18 | 22 | $8

471 Pine St. (bet. Kearny & Montgomery Sts.), 415-834-0485; www.occidentalcigarclub.com
If you're keen to "relax after work with a drink" and a stogie, this "great traditional bar" Downtown is your "smoker's haven in a smoker-hating city"; let the "witty and knowledgeable" staff help you navigate the single-malt menu, then "join in a game of dice", puff on a cigar and the "evening will drift away."

Odeon   24 | 19 | 21 | $5

3223 Mission St. (28th St.), 415-550-6994; www.odeonbar.com
"'Quirky' is an understatement for this outrageous alt-theater" bar "on the outskirts of the Mission" where "you're guaranteed to see an interesting show" including "weird cabaret acts", "wacky bands", "burlesque" and other "wonderful oddities" booked by owner and "longtime promoter Chicken John"; you'll "rub elbows with Burning Man celebrities" as you cultivate "the next morning's hangover" (bonus: it's this *Survey*'s Best Buy), and though it's "not for everyone, if it's for you, it's heaven."

Old Rogue, The ⌂   – | – | – | I

2319 Taraval St. (33rd Ave.), 415-566-9122
Old-timers and former rascals and roustabouts hold court during the day, but come nightfall this "nice little local hangout in the Outer Sunset" sees an influx of whippersnappers for darts, booze and live music; it's Irish in spirit but "nothing spectacular" in decor, though thanks to new ownership, that assessment may be outdated.

Olive Bar & Restaurant   21 | 21 | 20 | $7

743 Larkin St. (O'Farrell St.), 415-776-9814; www.olive743.com
A "surprise in the 'Loin", this "great little find" is "easy to miss 'cause it has no windows" but worth seeking out for "super martinis" and "tasty" tapas-style dishes ("wild mushroom pizza = yum") served by "good folks" till the wee hours; the "chilled", "cool" interior features booths and low tables, and "great music" provides a "funky" vibe that "appeals to the overly hip crowd."

111 MINNA   22 | 23 | 16 | $8

111 Minna St. (bet. New Montgomery & 2nd Sts.), 415-974-1719; www.111minnagallery.com
"How could you not like a gallery that serves liquor?" and Cali-style organic eats query minna-malists "crowding" this "ultrahip" SoMa bar featuring "art and music in one happy space" where "fierce DJs" spin "cutting-edge" tunes amid "amazing installations"; no wonder it attracts a "see-and-be-seen" mix of "students", "effete" techies, "fashionistas" and "trendy professionals", though critics cavil "it's a scene, and the staff has the scowls to prove it"; P.S. habitués hail the "happening" Wednesday night 'qool' parties.

One Market
20 | 21 | 20 | $11

1 Market St. (Steuart St.), 415-777-5577; www.onemarket.com
A "good place to take clients for cocktails" or "meet an MBA",
this "elegant" bar and restaurant on the Embarcadero offers a
"subdued" but "airy" atmosphere and a "comfortable" setting;
while "good after-work specials" and "excellent" wines by
the glass are valuable commodities, the "pricey" potables and
somewhat "stuffy" surroundings make it a hard sell as a "hot spot
for trendy types."

Oola
– | – | – | E

860 Folsom St. (5th St.), 415-995-2061; www.oola-sf.com
Revelers with a case of the late-night hungrys find plenty to ooh-
la-la about at this narrow, split-level SoMa lounge and bistro;
tasty as the food is, those who frequent the white barstools of this
snazzy space know the draw's not all about the cuisine, as a
buzzing bar crowd and creative cocktails like the Ginger Snap and
watermelon Cosmo keep the joint jumping until the wee hours.

Orbit Room Cafe, The ⊽
20 | 17 | 17 | $6

1900 Market St. (Laguna St.), 415-252-9525
"Coffee in the sun on the sidewalk by day, swank cocktails by night"
is how space cadets revolve around this "comfortable, relaxed"
Upper Market cafe; the "drinks are tall and tasty", the staff's
"wacky and wonderful", the decor "fun and modern" and the "big
windows ideal for cruising the scene", though ground control
complains that "stone seats", no matter how "interesting", "make
for cold butts."

O'Reilly's Irish Pub & Restaurant
22 | 20 | 18 | $6

622 Green St. (Columbus Ave.), 415-989-6222; www.oreillysirish.com
With its "real Irish bartenders, decor and wolfhound", you'd
"better bring your real Irish drinking abilities" to this "authentic
pub" in North Beach with "lots of imported beers on tap" and
"murals of famous poets on the walls" for inspiration; it's "always
full" with a "young", "friendly crowd", but you can "usually find a
good corner in which to snuggle with your pint", and if you can
"grab a sidewalk table on a sunny day, you'll be loving that Guinness
even more"; N.B. plans are underway to open a sibling called
O'Reilly's Holy Grail on Polk Street.

Original Joe's
17 | 12 | 20 | $7

144 Taylor St. (bet. Eddy & Turk Sts.), 415-775-4877
"Some surprisingly good dishes" can be found on "the copious
menu" at this "timeless" Tenderloin "old-school grill" with large
leather booths that have seen their share of local luminaries'
derrieres; "the bar is a great place to escape" the neighborhood
or the rest of your day, and while it "hasn't changed" since opening
in 1937, it really has "no reason to."

Oxygen Bar
– | – | – | M

795 Valencia St. (19th St.), 415-255-2102; www.oxygensf.com
"Takes you to a different world" sigh supporters of this "great
alternative" in the Mission that makes a main course out of oxygen
("choose a flavor" and "get inflated"); cynics who snort it's "much
ado about – literally – nothing" should be walking on air over its
post-*Survey* transformation to a sushi and sake lounge featuring
beer and organic wines.

OZUMO
24 | 26 | 19 | $10

161 Steuart St. (bet. Howard & Mission Sts.), 415-882-1333;
www.ozumo.com
"Stylish people" and "business types" pack into the "happening lounge" of this "modern Japanese" along the Embarcadero where the "gorgeous space", "groovy music" (DJs every night) and "wonderful views of the Bay Bridge" are anything but lost in translation; "you could go broke and not even care" with such "delicious" sake, "creative" cocktails and "awesome sushi", though it does offer "great happy-hour specials."

Padovani's Restaurant & Wine Bar
– | – | – | E

Hotel Milano, 55 Fifth St. (Market St.), 415-543-7600;
www.padovanirestaurants.com
The 'Cruvinet' that keeps open bottles airtight for weeks makes the wine bar (which offers several dozen by the glass) a highlight of this upscale SoMa outpost of a Honolulu favorite run by French chef Philippe Padovani; both the front lounge and back dining room are spacious, the martinis are professionally crafted, the *vins* unique and the menu inviting and hardly typical.

Palomino
19 | 19 | 18 | $9

345 Spear St. (bet. Folsom & Harrison Sts.), 415-512-7400;
www.palominosf.com
The "affluent over-35 crowd" and "young preppies" alike stampede this "popular" "happy-hour watering hole" on the Embarcadero with a "long bar" and "great patio" that affords "stellar" sightlines of the Bay Bridge over "excellent" cocktails; a few foes yawn it's a "bland" franchise and bridle at ponying up for the "overpriced" offerings, but admit it's a "pleasant" "standby."

Papa Toby's Revolution Café
– | – | – | I

3248 22nd St. (Bartlett St.), 415-642-0474
You can't help but "feel very European" at this "charming, hip cafe" in the Mission, the kind of "mellow", "neat little place" where you can "catch up with a friend" over beer and wine; there's "live music a few nights a week", and the windows and doors opening onto the heated patio make it a "great place to people-watch and be with like-minded bums."

Paradise Lounge
19 | 18 | 19 | $7

1501 Folsom St. (11th St.), 415-621-1911;
www.paradiseloungesf.com
For years local bands and indie touring acts ruled the multiple rooms and stages of this SoMa rock 'n' roll staple, but after a closure, "a terrific makeover" and a reopening in 2003, it's become a dressed-up house and hip-hop venue "on par with many of the larger clubs" in the area, with "nice lounges upstairs" and "fine dance floors"; N.B. open Thursday–Saturday.

Paragon Restaurant & Bar
19 | 19 | 17 | $9

701 Second St. (Townsend St.), 415-537-9020;
www.paragonrestaurant.com
"A great selection of vodkas" (some 60 from around the world), "infused liquors" and "unique" "comfort food" have patrons praising this pair of "upscale" bistros; the SoMa location attracts Giants fans for beers and "tasty burgers before the ballgame", while in the Claremont Resort in Berkeley, a "sunset cocktail" on

the deck enhances "Marin to Peninsula" views that encompass the Golden Gate; one quibble: the crowd's not a paragon of "cool."

Pendulum ⌷   16 | 7 | 16 | $5
4146 18th St. (Collingwood St.), 415-863-4441
"If you like meeting and mingling" with Latino and "African-American men and their admirers", this "butch" Castro gay club offers a "friendly", "diverse crowd in an otherwise monotone" neighborhood scene; there's "good music", a "small dance floor", a drag show and go-go boys on Tuesday 'La Cantina' nights and a "great patio", though some swingers "wish the owners would invest more in the decor", as it badly "needs a makeover."

Perry's   17 | 15 | 20 | $7
Galleria Park Hotel, 185 Sutter St. (bet. Kearny & Montgomery Sts.), 415-989-6895
1944 Union St. (bet. Buchanan & Laguna Sts.), 415-922-9022
www.perrysusa.com
This Cow Hollow "icon" and its Downtown counterpart are local "standbys" "for a casual dinner and a beer" alongside "familiar faces" and a "cast of characters" in a space that "never seems to age"; some call them "sophisticated places for adults to drink" and watch sports, though foes parry they're "fern bars" "for the many-times-divorced crowd" sporting "ill-fitting Banana Republic khakis (the horror, the horror)."

Phoenix   ▽ 17 | 14 | 19 | $5
811 Valencia St. (19th St.), 415-695-1811; www.phoenixirishbar.com
When you're looking for "nice" and "easy", this "cozy" local Irish pub in the Mission fits the bill for a pint of the black stuff or "above-average food"; ale hounds hail the range of European beers, and it sure gets popular during happy hour and with young 'uns as the clock ticks toward midnight; however, taciturn types insist "it's a bar, it's fine and that's all you can say."

Phone Booth ⌷   ▽ 20 | 11 | 18 | $5
1398 S. Van Ness Ave. (25th St.), 415-648-4683
A "happy", "flirty", "mixed crowd" of "hipsters" with a "sense of Mission style" heeds the call of this "tiny" "dive worth swimming in"; with its "campy" decor, a "great jukebox", a "fun pool table" and "good, quick service", it's a "laid-back" "drinker's paradise" where you can be "loud and stupid" in "flip-flops and jeans."

PIED PIPER BAR   25 | 26 | 19 | $10
Palace Hotel, 2 New Montgomery St. (Market St.), 415-512-1111; www.sfpalace.com
An "eventual must-do for every Bay area socialite", this "dark" Downtown bar is a "hidden treasure" tucked inside "one of the most beautiful hotels in the city", the circa-1875 Palace; the "grand", "historic" interior is dominated by the "great" eponymous Maxfield Parrish mural, and even if your fellow art lovers are "suits staring into their dirty martinis", it's definitely "worth a visit."

Pier 23 Cafe   21 | 11 | 14 | $6
Pier 23, The Embarcadero (Battery St.), 415-362-5125; www.pier23cafe.com
You "can't beat the views in the summer" say sun-worshipers and their peers about this waterfront "destination" along the Embarcadero that's a "fabulous place for happy hour on a hot

day" (and "the whole city knows it"); the "fun, relaxed Jimmy Buffett atmosphere" doesn't change attitudes in the evening when "great live reggae and other music" and "strong margaritas" keep the dance floor "insanely crowded."

Pig & Whistle   19 | 14 | 19 | $6

2801 Geary Blvd. (Wood St.), 415-885-4779; www.pig-and-whistle.com
"English and Irish accents" surround you at this "British pub transported to the edge of the Inner Richmond" that's a "great place to watch the World Cup with a bunch of trashed" expats; the "best selection of UK beers on tap" (and now hard liquor too), "good grub" and live music on weekends, plus a pool table, darts and jukebox make it a "fun place to hang with friends" or meet some "surprisingly attractive women."

Pilsner Inn ⌖   20 | 16 | 21 | $6

225 Church St. (Market St.), 415-621-7058
Providing "a model for friendly gay bars worldwide", this "down-to-earth" Upper Market local attracts a "cool" crowd that "ranges from Abercrombie to alternative" with "one thing in common: cuteness"; the "hot guys know how to party and play pool", the "jukebox rules" and in summer, "it's all about the beer garden"; P.S. it's also "welcoming to straight folk."

Pink   – | – | – | E

2925 16th St. (bet. Mission St. & S. Van Ness Ave.), 415-431-8889; www.pinksf.com
Walls of bright fuchsia set the tone for this stylish and oh-so-über-hip Mission destination; the lounge went through a major overhaul in 2004 and as a result is a mix of old-fashioned (candles, chandeliers, ornate mirrors) and thoroughly modern (white bench seating, smooth metallic bar), with booming house, Brazilian and soul beats, courtesy of top DJs like Franky Boissy.

Place Pigalle   20 | 14 | 21 | $5

520 Hayes St. (bet. Laguna St. & Octavia Blvd.), 415-552-2671; www.place-pigalle.com
You'll find "mainly locals" hugging the bar, "making out" on the couches or playing pool in the "clubby" back room of this "dark" "punk-rock beer" boîte that's an escape from the "pretension" of Hayes Valley; "cool art exhibits", an "impressive selection" of draft brews and "huge goblets" of "decent wines" ensure that loyalists "always leave happily wrecked" and then come back for more.

Plouf   20 | 18 | 19 | $9

40 Belden Pl. (bet. Bush & Pine Sts.), 415-986-6491; www.ploufsf.com
Order an "interesting house drink" or "impressive" bottle of wine with a bucket of "awesome mussels", plunk yourself at a table in the "cute", "hidden alley" and savor that Parisian "streetside cafe feeling" that exudes from this Downtown bistro; it's all so "authentic" that the "flirty" French waiters "dressed like sailors" just might "steal your girl if you're not careful."

Plough and Stars, The   20 | 13 | 22 | $5

116 Clement St. (2nd Ave.), 415-751-1122; www.theploughandstars.com
It's "the pot of gold at the end of the rainbow" rave starry-eyed admirers of this "friendly" "Inner Richmond neighborhood pub" that's "as real as it gets considering Ireland is thousands of miles away"; the weekly calendar "features good, traditional Irish music"

mixed with bluegrass and pool night on Tuesday, and while the interior's "basic", with 15 beers on tap it "out-Celts" the competition as a place to get plowed.

PLUSH ROOM 27 | 23 | 24 | $12
York Hotel, 940 Sutter St. (bet. Hyde & Leavenworth Sts.), 415-885-2800; www.plushroom.com
The "finest cabaret in SF" is found in a "former speakeasy" "hidden" in the York Hotel Downtown where the "beautiful and acoustically perfect" space and "superb sound system" attract "exceptional jazz programming" and the "best" singers as well as "delightful" comedy acts; other plush touches including "cocktails made with care" and "very good service" make it a "super place for a date."

Ponzu 21 | 22 | 17 | $9
Serrano Hotel, 401 Taylor St. (bet. Geary & O'Farrell Sts.), 415-775-7979
"Groovy", "wonderful" cocktails like the sake-infused Blushing Geisha and "tasty" Asian-inspired small plates await those who venture to this "beautiful" Downtown "jewel" in the Serrano Hotel; it's a "relaxing bar for the thirtysomething crowd", and even though it's "pricey" and may see more than its share of "tourists" and "dorky office workers", it's "all in all a great place to get pissed" especially during the "good happy hour."

Postrio 22 | 23 | 20 | $11
Prescott Hotel, 545 Post St. (bet. Mason & Taylor Sts.), 415-776-7825; www.postrio.com
Wolfgang Puck's "remarkable" Downtown restaurant in the Prescott Hotel also boasts a "sophisticated", "established bar scene" with a "wonderful late-night menu" of its own; the "modern" space is "comfortable" with "small booths", the drinks are "good" and "hearty" and the staff has "lots of personality", and though postmodernists pout it's "getting long in the tooth", the wolf pack proclaims it "the place to take people you want to impress."

Pound-SF ⊘ – | – | – | I
Pier 96, 100 Cargo Way (bet. Cesar Chavez & Evans St.), 415-826-5009; www.poundsf.com
There's just "a small stage" and "one black room", but this "total metal dive" in Bayview is "perfectly suited for enjoying your favorite local" and occasional national punk and hard-rock bands; "the one drawback" is it's "out in the middle of nowhere on an industrial pier" (96) and is "tough to find", but that doesn't stop "more people than you'd expect" from showing up.

Power Exchange ⊘ 19 | 16 | 15 | $5
74 Otis St. (Gough St.), 415-487-9944; www.powerexchange.com
"Know what you're getting into before visiting" this SoMa "sex club extraordinaire" that straight/gay/bi fetishists feel is the "best spot to get kinky" and "play out your darkest fantasies"; power rangers note there are often "more voyeurs than performers" ("beware of the single guys"), but even so it's "not for the faint of heart", and if you need liquid courage, remember there's "no liquor served here."

Powerhouse ⊘ ∇ 23 | 18 | 22 | $6
1347 Folsom St. (Dore St.), 415-552-8689; www.powerhouse-sf.com
It's "nirvana for bears", the "hard-core leather crowd" and the "men who love them" at this "fabulous", "frisky" tavern that's

"one of the cruisiest bars in SoMa"; the back room has enough "energy and heat to make your beer sizzle", helped along by touches of erotica on the walls, those "big butch daddies" and the "fun theme nights" like Wrasslin' Wednesdays.

Prive Lounge   – | – | – | E |
Roe Restaurant, 651 Howard St. (Hawthorne St.), 415-227-0288;
www.privesf.com
Part the tiger-print curtains and enter a plush world of couches, velvety fabrics and private booths at this high-end DJ lounge upstairs from SoMa restaurant Roe; hoof it on the hardwood floor or relax with a tropical delight under the sparkle of the spinning mirror ball; N.B. Prive is open Thursday–Saturday only, though Roe has cocktails, DJs and live combos Tuesday–Saturday.

Public, The   24 | 23 | 21 | $9 |
1489 Folsom St. (11th St.), 415-552-3065; www.thepublicsf.com
The general public praises this "New York–style" SoMa lounge and restaurant that resembles the "beatnik pad of the millennium"; with its "funky, loft"-like space, "low lights" and "unmatched", "faded-elegance couches", it has all the "makings of a very cool spot"; "sexy guests" sip "excellent" cocktails served by a "sweet", "pierced" staff, and the earthy Italian "food's equally great."

Puerto Alegre   22 | 12 | 19 | $5 |
546 Valencia St. (16th St.), 415-255-8201
"Damn those margaritas are good" announce amigos of this "awesome" "hole-in-the-wall" Mission mainstay, and "boy do they get you drunk"; besides the "unbelievable" drinks, the "bad-for-you" Mexican food is "great" and the atmosphere's "welcoming"; sure, it's "divey" and the lines are "horrendous", but the "crowds keep coming back" for pitchers of that "rocket fuel."

Punchline Comedy Club   23 | 17 | 19 | $8 |
444 Battery St. (bet. Clay & Washington Sts.), 415-397-7573;
www.punchlinecomedyclub.com
Punch-drunk partisans claim the "comedians never disappoint" at this "intimate" Downtown club that's been making people laugh for nearly a quarter century and provides an "especially good activity when the world's so gloomy"; wisecrackers hail the "top national acts" as well as the up-and-comers, and while you won't find "a bad seat in the house", do come thirsty as there's a "two-drink minimum and they hold you to it."

Purple Onion   – | – | – | M |
140 Columbus Ave. (bet. Jackson & Kearny Sts.), 415-956-1653;
www.caffemacaroni.com
Woody Allen, Phyllis Diller and the Smothers Brothers were among the famed folks who kvetched and crooned on this legendary North Beach club's stage during its heyday in the '50s and '60s; shuttered after a more recent stint as a punk-rock stomping ground, it was re-revived by the owners of local favorite Caffe Macaroni as an outlet for an eclectic array of comedy, cabaret and live music.

Ramblas   24 | 22 | 23 | $7 |
557 Valencia St. (bet. 16th & 17th Sts.), 415-565-0207;
www.ramblastapas.com
"Delicious traditional Spanish tapas", "excellent" margaritas, "yummy sangria" and fresh beer from brewpub sibling Thirsty

Bear bolster the "lively environment" at this "centrally located Mission favorite"; its "reasonably priced" small plates and "cozy" setting make it a "fabulous choice" for groups, and the "cute bartenders" and "attractive crowd" of "locals night after night" contribute to a "fun evening" overall.

Ramp, The   22 | 13 | 15 | $6 |
855 Terry Francois St. (Mariposa St.), 415-621-2378;
www.ramprestaurant.com
"One of the great outdoor places in San Francisco" is this "end-of-the-road" restaurant out in China Basin that's the "ideal" destination for a "lazy Sunday afternoon" enjoying "amazing views" and a few "delicious Bloody Marys"; even if "it's not known for its cuisine", you can "take your mom for brunch, the boys for a wild night or your date to dance" to live music from May through October.

Rasselas Jazz Club &   20 | 16 | 20 | $8 |
Ethiopian Restaurant
1534 Fillmore St. (Geary Blvd.), 415-346-8696;
www.rasselasjazzclub.com
"Get down with the locals" at this "cozy, intimate" "jazz joint" in the Western Addition along a stretch of Fillmore that once housed many music clubs; the "mellow setting" makes it a "great neighborhood spot to take in" some "fantastic" sounds including blues, Latin, R&B and Brazilian bands as well as the classic stylings of the house regular Robert Stewart; N.B. there's a cover charge on Friday and Saturday nights.

R Bar   21 | 16 | 26 | $6 |
1176 Sutter St. (Polk St.), 415-567-7441
Folks in the restaurant industry can be found after their shifts "letting loose" at this "awesome" hangout (that was previously An Sibin) just off Polk Street, lured by the "low-key" vibe, high "energy" of the "cool", "outstanding owner" and "friendly" staff; the "young" crowd of civilians is equally "hip", "there's room for dancing" and regulars can only "hope it won't get trendy."

Red Devil Lounge   23 | 18 | 18 | $7 |
1695 Polk St. (Clay St.), 415-921-1695;
www.reddevillounge.com
With its "Gothic", "*Phantom of the Opera*" feel, this "cathedral-esque club" and local music venue on Polk Street is a helluva "great place to check out bands" ranging from alternative to pop to "'80s cover" acts; if the "tight crowds" are bedeviling, you can trek "upstairs for comfortable surroundings with a view" over a "strong drink" and some mingling with a "mix" of "trendy" "Marina- and Missionites."

Red Eye Lounge   – | – | – | E |
1337 Mission St. (bet. 9th & 10th Sts.), 415-437-1337;
www.theredeyelounge.com
No need to pack the Visine on your trip to this SoMa oasis, as the young, mixed, dance-friendly crowd is more urban-chic than red-eyed and rowdy; chill on the couches and take in the laser-light show, groove to late-night spins of hip-hop, techno and house, and if you're one of the privileged, scope out the saltwater aquarium in the VIP lounge; N.B. bottle service waives the admission fee for parties of four.

Red Jack Saloon   ▽ 18 | 15 | 22 | M
131 Bay St. (Stockton St.), 415-989-0700
This "local hangout" is one of the only close-to-home taverns for those residing in (or passing through) the no-man's land between North Beach and Fisherman's Wharf; it's nothing fancy or flashy, just "a nice neighborhood bar to stop in after work, watch a game, shoot some darts" and have a drink during the "great happy hour."

Red Room   23 | 25 | 19 | $8
Commodore Hotel, 827 Sutter St. (bet. Jones & Leavenworth Sts.), 415-346-7666; www.jdvhospitality.com
"Lusciously red in all the right ways", this "beautiful", "womblike" lounge in the Commodore Hotel near Nob Hill and the Tenderloin provides "cool lighting" that makes "everything look great" and "massive", "delicious" drinks that make everybody feel "good"; the "down-tempo" music agrees with the "eclectic", "easygoing crowd", and even if it's so "tiny" it's "impossible to find space" on weekends, the "sexy" setting is room-ored to "inspire trysts."

REDWOOD ROOM   24 | 27 | 17 | $11
Clift Hotel, 495 Geary St. (Taylor St.), 415-775-4700; www.clifthotel.com
It's "eye-candy heaven" with "young, beautiful people" (and a few "crusty millionaires") crammed in every nook of this "dazzling" Downtown Clift Hotel lounge transmuted by Philippe Starck into a "surreal dreamscape" of "floor-to-ceiling redwood paneling, lush draperies" and digital "portraits that pay more attention than you might think"; you bet it's "trendy beyond trendy" – it's this *Survey*'s Most Popular – so "you'd better wear your Prada" and remember that if you're not a Trump you might need to "take out a second mortgage just to pay your bill."

Restaurant LuLu   20 | 20 | 19 | $9
816 Folsom St. (bet. 4th & 5th Sts.), 415-495-5775; www.restaurantlulu.com
"One of the best martinis in the city" (not to "mention over 70 wines by the glass" and 300 by the bottle) awaits the "executive set" at the "spacious" bar of this "beautiful" restaurant in SoMa; the lulu-gubrious insist it's "way too noisy" and the decor's like "time travel to 1999", but lulu-natics laud the "enjoyable" atmosphere and "great service", insisting it's still a "fun place to meet friends."

Rica   – | – | – | E
(fka Charlie's)
1838 Union St. (Octavia Blvd.), 415-474-3773
Come for the tapas but stay for the cocktails and the respectable tequila selection at this Cow Hollow magnet that's owned by Michael Schwab, who also owned its former incarnation, the upscale bar Charlie's; you can pretend San Francisco has a real summer on the outdoor patio, but when the fog rolls in, chances are you'll find the sleek, chic indoor surroundings – zinc bar, plasma TVs – just as inviting.

Rick's   18 | 14 | 20 | $9
1940 Taraval St. (bet. 29th & 30th Aves.), 415-731-8900
"Tucked away by the beach" in the Outer Sunset, this Hawaiian-themed restaurant is a "nice little hangout for locals" craving mai tais "who don't want to venture" beyond the 'hood; except on monthly Luau Platter nights, the menu's more about "comfort food than anything Polynesian" ("great pot roast"), but the "festive"

"cruise-ship" decor, live music Tuesday through Saturday and "friendly staff" help ensure a "pleasant time."

Rickshaw Stop   – | – | – | I
155 Fell St. (bet. Franklin St. & Van Ness Ave.), 415-861-2011; www.rickshawstop.com
Park your cart at this Civic Center welcome wagon, then relax with a cocktail and a corn dog or a plate of noodles in the red velvet–swathed space; punk bands and fund-raisers dot the entertainment schedule, with DJs spinning indie rock, electronica and hip-hop; N.B. open Wednesday–Saturday.

Riptide ⌒   – | – | – | M
3639 Taraval St. (bet. 47th & 48th Aves.), 415-681-8433; www.riptidesf.com
Rustic is the byword at this circa-1941 Outer Sunset tavern where a recent renovation uncovered all the trappings of a Tahoe-type lodge, including walls made of knotty pine, high ceilings and brick floors; cozy up by the fireplace listening to DJs on Fridays and live bluegrass, country or jazz on Saturdays, or catch a glimpse of the Pacific tide rolling away from the streetside seats.

Rite Spot Cafe   ▽ 20 | 13 | 19 | $5
2099 Folsom St. (17th St.), 415-552-6066; www.ritespotcafe.net
"No apple martinis or sex-on-the-whatever", cuz "real drinks" are the way to go at this "right-on", "surprisingly cool" dive "in the middle of nowhere" (aka the Mission) that's a "great little place to enjoy eccentric but catchy" live music acts; dating from 1950, it "feels very retro" from the "dark" decor and "decent Italian" food (served until 11) to the "friendly, accommodating" bartenders.

Roccapulco   ▽ 21 | 14 | 16 | $6
3140 Mission St. (Cesar Chavez), 415-648-6611; www.roccapulco.com
"Dress up and shake it" to "hot music" from the "well-known Latin artists" who "perform almost every weekend" at this "salsa heaven" in the Mission where you can take lessons; never mind that the name "sounds like a bad *Flintstones* episode" because "the dance floor and stage are huge", and if hoofing's not your thing there are tables upstairs and down "so the uncoordinated can hang"; N.B. open to the public Wednesday–Sunday.

Rogue Ales Public House   ▽ 18 | 15 | 21 | $5
673 Union St. (Columbus Ave.), 415-362-7880; www.rogue.com
Toss off a Dead Guy (ale, that is) or a Chocolate Stout at this two-year-old North Beach outpost of an "amazing Oregon brewery" that's been around some 15 years; suds-ologists agree it's "a great place to try the excellent" offerings, of which some two dozen are on tap here (along with 16 non-Rogues), and its "anti-corporate vibe" and "excellent bartenders" keep its rogues' gallery going.

RoHan Lounge   20 | 19 | 22 | $7
3809 Geary Blvd. (2nd Ave.), 415-221-5095; www.rohanlounge.com
There aren't too many "sleek spots" in the "pub-ridden" Inner Richmond, which is why this "chic and chill" Korean lounge is a "true treasure" and "nice change of pace for the neighborhood"; cocktails made with soju may be "everywhere now", but they're especially "delicious" and "unusual" paired up with "zippy"

Asian-style tapas in a "pretty, plush" setting "spiced up" by DJs; N.B. aside from the aforementioned liquor, it's beer and wine only.

Rose Pistola | 21 | 21 | 20 | $9 |
532 Columbus Ave. (bet. Green & Union Sts.), 415-399-0499
"Lots of atmosphere" pervades Laurie Thomas' "lovely" Italian restaurant that makes for a "sophisticated stop on the North Beach circuit"; avoid "the cramped seating in the middle" and instead "sit at the bar and have dinner" or a glass of "great" wine selected by the "knowledgeable" staff; you can "catch some jazz" (Thursday–Sunday), or "grab a seat outside and watch the peeps go by" as it's "quite a show."

Rosewood | 21 | 23 | 17 | $7 |
732 Broadway (bet. Powell & Stockton Sts.), 415-951-4886;
www.rosewoodbar.com
"Blink and you'll miss" this "hidden treat" on "busy Broadway", but it's worth keeping your eyes peeled for this "stylish spot" in North Beach that feels like "a new planet"; the "cool retro decor" is "done all in rosewood (go figure)", and from Wednesday through Saturday, the "great revolving DJs" spin everything from hip-hop to plain old "hip music"; even when it gets "packed with the Marina crowd" it's "still seductive", though the "cost of your haircut (or your bra size)" may affect how soon you can get a drink"; N.B. there's a new private room and glass-walled VIP area.

Route 101 ⊭ | – | – | – | I |
1332 Van Ness Ave. (bet. Bush & Sutter Sts.), 415-474-6092
Those hankering for a cocktail before or after an action epic can find respite at this "great dive bar right on Van Ness", as it's just blocks away from a couple of big movie houses; "stop in to play some pool" or quaff a "good martini", but "stay to people-watch", as the latest Tarantino has nothing on the characters haunting this "interesting place."

Royale | ▽ 17 | 18 | 18 | $6 |
1326 Grant Ave. (bet. Green & Vallejo Sts.), 415-433-4247
Its blue palette, 17 TVs and "small, swanky" interior make this North Beach lounge "perfect for hanging out with trendsetters" on "comfortable velvet couches" or "shaking your groove thang" to DJs spinning "great hip-hop beats" and other sounds (Wednesday–Saturday only); renegades regard the "too-crowded" weekend nights as a royale pain, but the "great atmosphere" still rules.

Royal Exchange, The | 17 | 13 | 15 | $6 |
301 Sacramento St. (Front St.), 415-956-1710
If you're a "Financial District professional" who "still has a job", you're likely to be found wearing your "banker blues" at this Downtown pub during the "crazy" happy hours with "one thing in mind: getting blotto"; "honest drinks" and an "excellent selection" of 32 beers don't hurt, and its "mainly masculine environment" makes it prime "spying" territory for "single ladies."

Royal Oak ⊭ | 19 | 20 | 14 | $6 |
2201 Polk St. (Vallejo St.), 415-928-2303
"Cushy antique couches" and "lots of foliage" evoke a "'70s fern bar" at this "old standby" on Polk Street, and that's just fine by fans who find it "cozy" and "relaxing" after work; however, it's "too loud on weekends" and "tough to get a drink", but that doesn't deter a

veritable "East Coast invasion sporting khakis, Oxford shirts and Topsiders" there to ogle the famously "zowie waitresses"; N.B. a recent refurb may impact the Decor score.

Roy's   22 | 22 | 23 | $11
575 Mission St. (2nd St.), 415-777-0277; www.roysrestaurant.com
"Attentive service, creative drinks" like the Hawaiian martini and a "trendy ambiance" keep this "upscale bar" and dining room busy day and night; the SoMa outpost of Roy Yamaguchi's archipelago is "the gated community of restaurants", meaning "everything is pretty, manicured and well-tended", and even if it's "extremely expensive" and "a little touristy", it's still "wonderful"; N.B. the Pebble Beach branch is unrated.

Rubicon   21 | 21 | 23 | $11
558 Sacramento St. (bet. Montgomery & Sansome Sts.), 415-434-4100; www.sfrubicon.com
This "high-class" Downtowner offers "superior dining for the corporate crowd", but with bars upstairs and down it also doubles as a "great post-work hangout" for "good-looking" folks to "unwind with a glass of wine" (some 30 to choose from); the list "resembles an encyclopedia", but cognoscenti know the go-to man is Larry Stone, the "delightful", "down-to-earth master sommelier" who makes "superb" recommendations.

RUBY SKYE   20 | 21 | 15 | $10
420 Mason St. (bet. Geary & Post Sts.), 415-693-0777; www.rubyskye.com
"Beaux arts meets the Internet age" at this "hot" "converted theater"–turned–"ultra-luxe club" Downtown, a "huge, bi-level", "energy-packed" palace featuring "fab decor" and "world-class DJs"; skywatchers acclaim its "sexy go-go dancers" and "young, black-wearing" "beautiful-people" patrons, though rebels who see red revile it as "plastic", with "pricey" drinks and a "cover charge that keeps the cool kids away"; N.B. open Thursday–Saturday.

RX Gallery ⊅   – | – | – | E
132 Eddy St. (Mason St.), 415-474-7973; www.rxgallery.com
The live electronic musicians, DJs and rotating art exhibitions at this contemporary Tenderloin hipster haven run by local concert promoters Blasthaus are just what the doctor ordered for a night of cool grooves; nurse your sake, soju cocktails and Belgian ale in the minimalist downstairs space or while soaking up the sounds from the cozy upstairs lounge; N.B. beer and wine only.

Sadie's Flying Elephant ⊅   – | – | – | M
491 Potrero Ave. (Mariposa St.), 415-551-7988; www.flyingelephant.com
Sure, "it's not much to look at", but this "hidden" Potrero Hill "hangout" is "one of the best dives in town" according to its herd that also admires its "grunge on steroids" decor and "excellent", "cheap drinks"; the "welcoming" staff "loves to make people mingle" over "fun" rounds of bingo or trivia games, and there's occasional live music and now independent films too.

Sake Lab   18 | 23 | 18 | $8
498 Broadway (Kearny St.), 415-837-0228; www.sakelab.com
"You'll feel like you're in the *Jetsons'* living room" at this "chic", "blue neon–accented" North Beach newcomer with "interesting", "futuristic" furniture; technicians extol the "excellent sake selection" (over 50 varieties), "fancy" but "reasonably priced"

drinks and "must-do" sashimi, though control groups predict this "cool concept" is an experiment that "probably won't last."

Saloon, The ⌐   15 | 9 | 12 | $5 |
1232 Grant Ave. (Columbus Ave.), 415-989-7666
Combine "German tourists and conventioneers" with locals who "haven't left their stools in 40 years", throw in "lots of alcohol" and you've got the "Fellini"-esque mix that makes this "old-time dirty blues" joint in North Beach such a "great dive"; the tavern's the longest running in town, so nobody's knocking the decor that "hasn't changed" since 1861.

San Francisco Brewing Company   17 | 14 | 17 | $6 |
155 Columbus Ave. (Pacific Ave.), 415-434-3344;
www.sfbrewing.com
Housed in a 1907 saloon, this "authentic brewpub" manages to maintain its "historical charm" as well as "survive and thrive in the high-rent district" of North Beach; assessments of the "fresh beer" range from "excellent" to "skunky", but the "solid happy hour" (offering cocktails too), live jazz and "interesting people-watching" from a sidewalk seat make it "relaxing after work."

Sauce   – | – | – | E |
131 Gough St. (Lily St.), 415-252-1369; www.saucesf.com
Order your sauce on a plate or in a glass from a smiling bartender at this new Hayes Valley bistro for comfort food and cocktails; the cozy back bar is occasionally open for dancing, while the narrow front room is perfect for pre- and post-symphony refreshments or for just a low-key evening out; N.B. live music is in the works.

Savanna Jazz   – | – | – | M |
2937 Mission St. (bet. 25th & 26th Sts.), 415-285-3369;
www.savannajazz.com
This "great music venue" and restaurant that formerly housed rock and sushi club Voodoo Lounge in the Mission provides a comfortable home for jazz bands and their fans, contributing to the mini-renaissance of live performance that's taking place all across town; expect nightly shows and a reasonable food menu in a rejuvenated space.

Savoy Tivoli ⌐   18 | 15 | 16 | $6 |
1434 Grant Ave. (bet. Green & Union Sts.), 415-362-7023
There's "never a dull moment" at this "old standby" in North Beach, a "hipster hangout in the beatnik era" and the original home to *Beach Blanket Babylon* in 1974; it's still "hopping" with a "lively" crowd that appreciates lots of "space to move around" and shoot pool and lauds the "great" heated patio, though a few are put off by the "heavy-drinking", "frat-house" element that materializes late in the evening.

Scala's Bistro   21 | 21 | 21 | $9 |
Sir Francis Drake Hotel, 432 Powell St. (bet. Post & Sutter Sts.),
415-395-8555; www.scalasbistro.com
"Centrally located Downtown" next door to the Sir Francis Drake Hotel, this "superbly decorated" restaurant with a "cozy" bar "caters to the Union Square crowd" and makes a convenient "stop for a glass of wine when you need a break from the shopping and tourist scene"; though it can be operatically "noisy", it makes for "fun people-watching."

SEASONS BAR
25 | 25 | 26 | $13

Four Seasons Hotel, 757 Market St. (bet. O'Farrell & Stockton Sts.), 415-633-3737; www.fourseasons.com

"Cocktail hour doesn't get any better than" at this "bastion of sophistication" Downtown, a "well-kept secret" that's tucked inside the Four Seasons and "hidden from conventioneers and tourists"; "posh" but "comfortable", the lounge and piano bar are decked in "muted tones" and the service is "impeccable and gracious"; the "superb" drinks may be "frighteningly expensive", though mavens maintain it's "worth it" for such a "lovely, civilized" experience.

1751 Social Club
13 | 13 | 14 | $7

1751 Fulton St. (Masonic Ave.), 415-441-1751; www.1751socialclub.com

"Oddly appealing" is how supportive socialites rate this "fun, laid-back" music venue that took over the old Storyville space in the Western Addition and supplied a "much-needed face-lift"; the remodeling hasn't won over diehards, though, who say it "hasn't found its groove yet" and yearn for the return of the "real jazz club", but boosters insist it's a "great place to dance" to hip-hop, soul and pop tunes.

Shanghai Kelly's
18 | 14 | 20 | $5

2064 Polk St. (Broadway), 415-771-3300

"Nobody takes themselves too seriously at" this "classic old-time" sports-oriented tavern situated on a "good people-watching corner" of Polk Street; it "appeals to the 'dude' crowd" so "expect to watch snowboarding" on the four TVs, but the "friendly" staff "welcomes all" and "won't let your glass go empty" according to "lots of loaded" loyalists ("I left my liver in San Francisco").

Shanghai 1930
21 | 22 | 18 | $10

133 Steuart St. (bet. Howard & Mission Sts.), 415-896-5600; www.shanghai1930.com

"Walk down the stairs" and you're instantly whisked "back to the '30s" by the "sexy atmosphere" of this "stylish", "decadent", "subterranean jazz" lounge and restaurant on the Embarcadero; "bring a secret lover" for the "delectable", "high-class Chinese food" and "sultry" nightly grooves, and you'll see why the "beautiful people" proclaim an "overpriced" "cocktail never tasted so good"; N.B. the attached Guanxi Lounge is a members-only cigar club.

Simple Pleasures Cafe ⊄
▽ 16 | 12 | 18 | $5

3434 Balboa St. (bet. 35th & 36th Aves.), 415-387-4022

"Thank goodness" for this "nice, neighborly" cafe in the Outer Richmond that multitasks as a "great spot to have a beer, read a book, watch live music" or "discuss philosophy" over coffee and wine with a "casual crowd"; its funky interior even "makes the fog seem warm and comforting", and nostalgic sorts note it's "like time-traveling back to college."

Skylark ⊄
18 | 15 | 17 | $6

3089 16th St. (Valencia St.), 415-621-9294; www.skylarkbar.com

A "hip" but "comfortable" setting that even includes a waterslide and a wading pool, "great" DJs who "keep it bumpin' all night" and a "super-cool staff" ensure this "old-school lounge in a bustling part of the Mission" is "hopping most nights"; drinks are "good" and the clientele's generally "cute", but a few locals sneer it's often filled with "self-consciously slumming" "Marina types", and the "small dance floor" in the back gets too "crowded" with "nowhere to escape."

Slanted Door, The　　　　　– | – | – | E
Ferry Bldg., 1 Ferry Plaza (Market St.), 415-861-8032;
www.slanteddoor.com
Previously a hit restaurant in the Mission and South Beach, Charles Phan's Vietnamese phenom moved to these expanded digs in the Embarcadero's Ferry Building in 2004; the incredible view of the Bay and the aquatic slant of the decor create a relaxing aura for sipping house cocktails like ginger-kaffir limeade or the lemongrass-infused Phantasm, each made with local vodka Hanger One.

Slim's　　　　　21 | 13 | 16 | $6
333 11th St. (bet. Folsom & Harrison Sts.), 415-255-0333;
www.slims-sf.com
"The band is the star" at this SoMa nightclub, a "simple room that resonates" with the sound of "music taken seriously" and features "some of the best bookings" in town of "amazing" rock, blues, country and R&B artists; the space itself is "garage-y" and "can get stuffy", "but don't be put off" as it's a "prime place" to check out both established artists and "up-and-comers"; N.B. make dinner reservations to guarantee yourself a table.

SLOW CLUB　　　　　25 | 23 | 24 | $8
2501 Mariposa St. (Hampshire St.), 415-241-9390; www.slowclub.com
"Candles light the black and steel interior" of this "excellent hidden gem" in the outer reaches of the Mission that provides a "warm", "cosmopolitan" space that's "always filled with locals"; it's mainly a restaurant, but the "friendly" staff at the "colorful", "bustling back bar" also serves "outstanding food" ("be sure to have a burger with your beer") along with "delish martinis" and other "sexy drinks."

Sno-Drift　　　　　17 | 20 | 14 | $9
1830 Third St. (16th St.), 415-431-4766; www.sno-drift.com
"A cool version of Superman's fortress of solitude", this China Basin "chalet"-like club offers a "fun ski-lodge atmosphere" with "two rooms for dancing", a fireplace and "strong drinks"; "good DJs" keep things "pumpin'" with "beautiful" "twentysomethings" "hooking up left and right", but the "uncomfortably hot" digs and onslaught of "folks from the 'burbs" is kryptonite to critics who add "it used to be the place to be but just isn't anymore."

Soluna　　　　　– | – | – | E
272 McAllister St. (Larkin St.), 415-621-2200; www.solunasf.com
Once the day's dining tables are cleared, the staff at this Civic Center staple pushes them aside and turns their attention from the menu to mojitos; DJs spin salsa, R&B, worldbeat and house music to an energetic crowd that's as colorful as the artwork and decor from Tuesday through Saturday, plus Thursday is also 'Twilight' night, a dinner theater of sorts with music and visual surprises.

Space 550 ⌿　　　　　18 | 17 | 16 | $6
550 Barneveld Ave. (bet. Industrial St. & Oakdale Ave.), 415-550-8286;
www.space550.com
Despite being "located on the other side of the solar system" in the boondocks of Bayview, this 15,000-sq.-ft. dance club "rules the circuit galaxy" with "great" hip-hop, house, trance and Sunday's

'Sundance Saloon' when "hundreds of gay men and women two-step the night away" and "the smile-per-capita ratio is" sky-high; overall "lines aren't bad", and space cadets dig the "big room where you can see the people in action", though the fun "depends on the party being thrown."

SPECS BAR ⇗
25 | 22 | 21 | $5

12 William Saroyan Pl. (bet. Broadway & Columbus Ave.), 415-421-4112
"Buccaneers, beats and bastards have all gotten plastered" at this "drinking man's museum" that's the "embodiment of North Beach" with a "profusion of sailor curiosities on walls" that "haven't changed in 40 years"; it's "unassuming down to the cheese and Ritz crackers" and "stiff drinks", and for spectator sport you can watch the "salty dog regulars sneer at the button-downs"; its clientele of "reprobates" agrees that it's "tough to find, but oh-so worth it."

Steps of Rome ⇗
22 | 16 | 19 | $7

348 Columbus Ave. (bet. Grant Ave. & Vallejo St.), 415-397-0435
"Watch your date" as the "adorable waiters" at this "late-night cafe in North Beach" "are a bit aggressive" as they "break into song and dance" and "grab patrons to share in the fun" (though "no one seems to mind"); it's "always buzzing" with a "young crowd sipping espresso and Pinot Grigio" and eating "munchies" to a soundtrack of "loud Italian" pop songs, a scenario that's both "cheesy" and utterly "charming."

Stud, The ⇗
21 | 12 | 15 | $6

399 Ninth St. (Harrison St.), 415-863-6623; www.studsf.com
It's "stud heaven" at this SoMa "landmark" that dates from 1966 and is still "filled with shirtless, sweaty Chelsea men pumping and grinding the night away" to "killer house" and appreciating "great theme nights" like Tuesday's "mind-bending" Trannyshack; it's "one of the less intimidating gay clubs in the scene", "attracting a broad spectrum of people" including women who "want to dance with sexy" dudes "who have no interest in taking them home."

Studio Z
– | – | – | M

314 11th St. (Folsom St.), 415-252-7666; www.studioz.tv
"An interesting and eclectic array of entertainment" from gallery events to film screenings to concerts and dance parties takes place inside this "fantastic" SoMa performance space with a mezzanine and multiple bars; when the music's right it's "great for getting your groove on", though Z-nophobes zap it as a "huge empty square room" with "nothing in the way of decor."

Sublounge
∇ 20 | 16 | 21 | $5

628 20th St. (3rd St.), 415-552-3603; www.sublounge.com
"Chill out, dance or play video games in the airplane seats", a "funky" touch that keeps the "mostly local" crowd grounded at this "soulful" but "no-stress" Dogpatch lounge; other "first-class" features include "some of the best DJs in SF (without having to go to a megaclub)", a "cool staff" and a "super-fun" atmosphere abetted by 2-for-1 cocktails from 6–7 PM.

Suede
– | – | – | E

383 Bay St. (Mason St.), 415-399-9555; www.suedesf.com
Earth tones, luxurious fabrics, curved banquettes and clean modern lines define the upstairs rooms of this upscale (with a cover charge to prove it) lounge on the far end of North Beach near Fisherman's

Wharf; below is a spacious dance palace with five rooms, a 20-ft.-long bar, high ceilings and booming house; N.B. an enforced dress code requires chic threads.

SUITE ONE8ONE   25 | 23 | 18 | $9 |
181 Eddy St. (bet. Mason & Taylor Sts.), 415-345-9900; www.suite181.com
"An A-list atmosphere" awaits those who brave the "shady" Tenderloin, "wait in line" and crack the "fully enforced door policy" at this "cushy" "hot spot" that "has it all" including a "hip Manhattan vibe", three "large dance" floors, a patio and a new VIP lounge; others report a less-than-"suite experience" due to "attitude" on the part of the staff and "hit-or-miss music", but the majority maintains the DJs are "great" and insist it's "*the* place to be right now"; N.B. open Thursday–Saturday.

Suppenküche   22 | 16 | 22 | $6 |
601 Hayes St. (Laguna St.), 415-252-9289; www.suppenkuche.com
"It's odd to see hipsters chowing down on potato pancakes" and sucking down Spaten, but "the food delivers" and there's an "unsurpassed selection of imported beers" on tap and in the bottle at this "trip to Deutschland" in Hayes Valley; the "small" space has a "stark", "Euro-modernist feel" with "white walls", "wood floors" and "communal tables", but *achtung*, baby, as it's *sehr* "loud" and more of a "restaurant than nightlife scene."

Sushi Groove South   22 | 20 | 19 | $9 |
1516 Folsom St. (bet. 11th & 12th Sts.), 415-503-1950
"Wear black and be beautiful to fit in" at this "edgy" SoMa lounge that attracts "scenesters galore" with its "awesome bar" serving "funky sake cocktails" as much as its "incredible" edibles; DJs spin "sexy techno and house" in the "chic" interior, making it "great for impressing a date", but be warned: it's "not the sort of place you'd go for just a drink because the sushi is toooo good!"

Swig   – | – | – | E |
(fka Blue Lamp)
561 Geary St. (Taylor St.), 415-543-2282; www.swigbar.com
Dark and musty Tenderloin denizen Blue Lamp has been dusted off, scrubbed up and transformed into a swanky, cosmopolitan lounge; previously defined by its fading velvet curtains and crusty, graying clientele, it's now decked out with a new fireplace, modern furniture and slick hardwood floors, a setting just right for the young cocktailers who come to swig signature libations and dance to the DJs and live bands; N.B. check out the blues jam every Sunday and open mike on Monday nights.

Tadich Grill   21 | 18 | 20 | $8 |
240 California St. (bet. Battery & Front Sts.), 415-391-1849
"It doesn't get more old San Francisco" than this "landmark" seafood joint "in the heart of the Financial District" that was established in 1849 and today is the longest-running in town ("it's the Wrigley Field" of local restaurants); it's "standing only" at the small front bar, but the lack of stools is soon forgotten as "those guys know how to make a martini"; N.B. closing time is 9:30 PM.

Ten 15 Club ∉   19 | 15 | 13 | $8 |
1015 Folsom St. (6th St.), 415-431-1200; www.1015.com
"If you like techno on a large sound system", this "cavernous" late-night club in SoMa is "the West Coast mecca for world-class

DJs"; it "doesn't have much in the way of decor, but it does offer a gigantic", 16,000-sq.-ft. arena spread over three floors for "young" "party people to get together"; while it's "great for dancing" till the wee hours (open Friday–Sunday), you'll have to get past doormen who can be "jerks" and vie with the "writhing" masses first.

Thee Parkside   19 | 9 | 17 | $6 |
1600 17th St. (Wisconsin St.), 415-503-0393; www.theeparkside.com
"The new home of your old-school rock fan", this "punk-rock" "Potrero Hill hideaway" provides a "sweet, dingy" space for watching "great shows by up-and-coming bands and a rad back patio" for smoking and Sunday afternoon hot dogs and chili; "don't expect luxury", but it's "chock-full of local atmosphere", and with "good drinks", an "eclectic crowd" and occasional drop-ins by "headline" acts, "you can't go wrong hanging out here."

Thirsty Bear Brewing Company   17 | 16 | 16 | $7 |
661 Howard St. (bet. New Montgomery & 3rd Sts.), 415-974-0905; www.thirstybear.com
"Thank god the dot-commers have left the city" as "now you can get a table" say parched partisans of this SoMa brewpub that serves "delicious" tapas along with "excellent home-brewed beers"; the "warehouselike" space is "ideal for large parties", but grouches growl it's "loud" and "overcrowded."

13 Views Lounge   19 | 17 | 15 | $10 |
Hyatt Regency Hotel, 5 Embarcadero Ctr. (Market St.), 415-788-1234; www.hyatt.com
Just as the name promises, the lounge in this towering atrium of the Embarcadero's Hyatt Regency offers 13 "enjoyable window views" of the surrounding scenery from Justin Herman Plaza to the San Francisco Bay ("on a clear day"); detractors denounce it as a "boring hotel bar in a dated setting" with service that "could be improved", but View-masters opine that the "open space" means it "never gets loud" or "crowded."

330 Ritch   19 | 15 | 16 | $7 |
330 Ritch St. (bet. Brannan & Townsend Sts.), 415-541-9574
"Exposed brick and brushed steel" create an "airy loft feel" at this "cool little" South Beach restaurant; "decently priced drinks" make it a "good after-work meeting spot" even though it's "off the beaten path", and late nights the "wide array of music" brings in a dancing crowd, especially the 18-and-over Popscene on Thursdays ("new wavers, mods, geeks, Poindexters, they're all here"); N.B. open Wednesday–Sunday.

TK's ⊘   – | – | – | I |
328 W. Portal Ave. (14th Ave.), 415-566-9444
Laid-back sorts savor this "small", "old-style neighborhood" tavern in sleepy West Portal that's a "locals' dive" and a "drinker's bar" through and through; sure, it gets "pretty rowdy", and sadder-but-wiser types warn "beware the serious dart players", but the staff at this "survivor" "makes it all worthwhile."

Tokyo Go Go   22 | 22 | 19 | $8 |
3174 16th St. (bet. Guerrero & Valencia Sts.), 415-864-2288; www.tokyogogo.com
This "adorably retro" Mission "hangout" with a "Pan Am–mod" feel is "the loudest sushi place you'll find east of Tokyo" though

that doesn't stop girls and boys on the go-go from flying in for its "tasty" food and "excellent sake selection"; sure, it's totally "trendy" ("the crowd is way too cool for me"), and you "pay for the ambiance", but with fish this "fabulous" and service this "fantastic" nobody's minding too much.

Tommy's Joynt ⊅
16 | 14 | 18 | $5

1101 Geary Blvd. (Van Ness Ave.), 415-775-4216; www.tommysjoynt.com
"Unbelievably cheap" "brewskis" (100 from all over the world) and "great old-time grub" ("BBQ brisket's the draw") are "what everyone goes for" at this circa-1947 hofbrau off Van Ness; with walls covered in "eclectic artifacts", it was "kitschy before kitsch existed", but it's "funky", "comfy" and always "worth a visit."

Tommy's Mexican Restaurant
21 | 16 | 21 | $8

5929 Geary Blvd. (bet. 23rd & 24th Aves.), 415-387-4747; www.tommystequila.com
With its "phenomenal selection" of some 260 top-shelf (100-percent blue agave) tequilas curated by "sommelier" Julio Bermejo, this Richmond "treasure" provides both an education and a "fun" night out; naturally, the margaritas are "heavenly", but the Mexican fare's also "delicious", the "atmosphere's great" and even if it's "standing room only", it's "worth the wait" for "the real thing."

Tonga Room
21 | 24 | 17 | $10

Fairmont Hotel, 950 Mason St. (California St.), 415-772-5278; www.tongaroom.com
"It's *Pirates of the Caribbean* for grown-ups" at this "tiki paradise" replete with "fake rain shower" in Nob Hill's "infamous" Fairmont; "anyone who's ever loved a Martin Denny record" will dig the "lousy lounge music sung from a floating raft", "fun umbrella drinks" (albeit "at hotel prices") and "fab '50s-style South Pacific decor"; those "inclined toward camp" will be in heaven, and "the scorpion bowl will bring even boring souls to life."

Tongue & Groove
16 | 16 | 18 | $7

2513 Van Ness Ave. (Union St.), 415-928-0404; www.tongueandgroovesf.com
"Good" local bands and DJs draw groovers to the bar of this Van Ness club that's "a great space for a small concert" with a "cool staff" and "reasonable prices" to boot; those wanting privacy can "nab the couches" in the "small but comfortable" back lounge.

Tonic
20 | 18 | 18 | $7

2360 Polk St. (Union St.), 415-771-5535; www.tonic-bar.com
Come for the "free Gummi Bears" that line the bar of this "loungey local haunt" in Russian Hill and stay for the "friendly, low-key" vibe emanating from the "small" but "stylish" room; patrons can be "trendy", but with "great DJs", afternoon wine tastings and a "swanky" setting it's also a spot "where the uncool can feel cool", and though it's "packed" on weekends, it's a "good alternative" for "meeting people."

Tonno Rosso by Faz
- | - | - | E

Hotel Griffon, 155 Steuart St. (bet. Howard & Mission Sts.), 415-495-6500
Blond wood, an open-hearth fireplace and golden-orange lighting keep the mood bright and glowing at the spacious streetside lounge of this Italian eatery just off the Embarcadero inside the Hotel Griffon; while the gleaming mirror behind the bar offers

opportunities for reflection, the best view is actually across the dining room – squint and you just might glimpse the Bay Bridge.

TONY NIK'S
25 | 22 | 22 | $6

1534 Stockton St. (bet. Green & Union Sts.), 415-693-0990

To tony types the "best atmosphere for a martini" in town is this "glamorous" "hidden gem" in North Beach with a "romantic" setting featuring "beautiful wall tiles and a vinyl bar"; even though it's "tiny", its "slightly off-the-beaten-path" location ensures it's rarely "too crowded", and when you factor in the "friendly staff" and "great" cocktails, it's practically "perfect for a first date."

TOP OF THE MARK
26 | 23 | 21 | $12

Mark Hopkins InterContinental Hotel, 1 Nob Hill, 19th fl. (bet. California & Mason Sts.), 415-616-6916; www.markhopkins.net

"A multitude of martinis" (over 100 versions) and "intoxicating" 360-degree views "overlooking the city" await those who make it up to this "true SF landmark" atop Nob Hill's circa-1926 Mark Hopkins Hotel; it's a "romantic" "tourist place that's worthy of a resident" ("don't forget to dress up" as "dancing is a must"), and even though there's a "high-dollar cover charge" on weekends, it's "worth it to sit by a window with your honey."

Toronado ∌
21 | 13 | 19 | $5

547 Haight St. (bet. Fillmore & Steiner Sts.), 415-863-2276; www.toronado.com

This Lower Haight pub is "the holy grail for beer aficionados" thanks to its "stunning selection" of "microbrews from around the world", including over 50 on draft and 100 bottles, many of them "hard-to-find" brands; you're welcome to bring in food so "get a sausage from Rosamunde next door" and groove to the "kick-booty" rock 'n' roll jukebox with a "cool", "mixed crowd" – just don't let the "gruff" bartenders get you hopping mad.

Tosca Cafe ∌
23 | 20 | 21 | $7

242 Columbus Ave. (Broadway), 415-986-9651

"It never ages" say mavens of this "North Beach mainstay" that's "a step back in time" to at least 1919 and remains "so retro it's avant-garde"; arias drift out of the "great Italian opera jukebox" as bartenders line up the "world-famous brandy cappuccinos" and "indie film celebrities" duck into the "secret back room"; even if it's a bit "dark and dingy", that's exactly "the way the regulars like it."

Town Hall
– | – | – | E

342 Howard St. (bet. Beale & Fremont Sts.), 415-908-3647; www.townhallsf.com

Vintage chandeliers, exposed-brick walls and cool artwork set the mood at this "hip SoMa" restaurant situated inside the 1907 Marine Electric Building; the elegant yet homey decor is reflected in the cuisine (courtesy of ex-Postrio chefs Mitchell and Steven Rosenthal), which can be enjoyed along with cocktails like the Mitcharita or the Dorothy Parker at the long bar.

Trader Vic's
– | – | – | E

(fka Stars)
555 Golden Gate Ave. (Van Ness Ave.), 415-775-6300; www.tradervics.com

Fans of Hawaiian shirts raise mai tais, the fruity libation first created by Victor Bergeron, the founding owner of this Polynesian palace,

to toast the Bay Area original's new branch, set in the Civic Center–
area spot previously home to Stars; island tunes and a 32-ft.
outrigger fill a room trimmed in tiki masks and nautical paintings,
while a massive mirrored bar trades in rum and tropical delights;
N.B. there are also outposts in Emeryville and Palo Alto.

Trad'r Sam's ⬀   20 | 19 | 17 | $7
6150 Geary Blvd. (25th Ave.), 415-221-0773
"Tacky tiki decor" and "delicious volcano" libations attract a
"democratic crowd" of "barflies, students and professionals" to
this "bizarre" taste of "the tropics in the middle of the Richmond
District"; perhaps it "looks like a dump", but so would you if you'd
"been around forever" (since 1939), and regulars recommend that
you "plan on calling in sick to work the next day" cuz that "mean
scorpion bowl" will almost certainly "bite you on the ass."

Trax   ▽ 18 | 14 | 20 | $5
1437 Haight St. (bet. Ashbury St. & Masonic Ave.), 415-864-4213;
www.traxsf.com
"Daily and nightly drink specials" have a "mixed crowd" of gays
and straights making trax for this Upper Haight longtimer that's also
known for "cute bartenders" and "great music" from the owners'
collection; sure, it's "a little seedy" but it's "comfortable" for
"conversation" and watching sports on TV, and if you nab a seat
by the window there are always "interesting people walking by."

Treat Street Cocktails ⬀   – | – | – | I
3050 24th St. (Treat Ave.), 415-824-5954
"Friendly natives and cheap" booze supply an antidote to "the
somewhat intimidating" location of this "Mission dive"; perhaps
there are a few too many "permanent stains on the floor", "local
punks hogging" the pool table and pinball machines and "dead
heads" adorning the walls ("think Ted Nugent" not Jerry Garcia),
but the jukebox is "A+" and having "plenty of space to drink and
fall face down without anyone noticing" is a real treat.

Tunnel Top ⬀   22 | 16 | 20 | $6
601 Bush St. (Stockton St.), 415-986-8900; www.tunneltop.com
"Escape the corporate Downtown scene" at this "happening"
"little" lounge located directly above the Stockton Tunnel where
an "interesting crowd" of "hipsters" "lets it all hang out" in a
"divey" bi-level space that's "dimly lit" by the "best chandelier"
fashioned from wine bottles; "great DJs" spin "cool beats" but
the bartenders also "rock", serving up "cheap" "killer mojitos."

12 Galaxies   – | – | – | M
2565 Mission St. (21st St.), 415-970-9777; www.12galaxies.com
Live music is enjoying a resurgence in the Mission thanks in good
part to the efforts of this double-storied, 6000-sq.-ft. venue in the
former Galia space; alternative bands from this solar system and
beyond achieve lift-off on the ground-floor stage, and galactic
travelers needing a break can escape to the 360-degree balcony
that affords prime views of the action below.

21st Amendment Brewery Cafe   19 | 15 | 18 | $6
563 Second St. (bet. Brannan & Bryant Sts.), 415-369-0900;
www.21st-amendment.com
There's "no Prohibition going on" inside this aptly monikered South
Beach brewpub that serves "nothing-fancy" food alongside "solid",

"small-batch" microbrews featuring "delicious seasonals"; the "wood-paneled interior is homey and warm", making it a "pleasant" destination for "down-to-earth people who like good beer" – and baseball, as it's "within walking distance" of SBC Park and "tends to overflow" when the Giants are in town.

2223 Restaurant & Bar　　23 | 21 | 22 | $8
2223 Market St. (bet. Noe & Sanchez Sts.), 415-431-0692
"Perky servers", "imaginative cocktails" and a "polished" vibe keep the "A-list gay crowd" coming back to this "small and noisy" but "always accommodating" Castro bar and restaurant; it's "great for a casual night out" ("meet for a drink and stay for" the "reliably excellent food"), and don't mind the "tight table spacing", as that just leads to "fun conversations" (its name may be "just a number", but "be prepared to hand out yours").

Twin Peaks Tavern ⊅　　16 | 15 | 20 | $6
401 Castro St. (Market St.), 415-864-9470
This "charming little saloon" is "one of the Castro's venerable institutions" as it was "the first gay bar with full-length windows"; today it offers a "pleasant" if "non-edgy environment" as well as "excellent people-watching" on the "busiest corner" in the neighborhood, and remains a "favorite among the 50-plus" set.

222 Club ⊅　　– | – | – | M
222 Hyde St. (bet. Eddy & Turk Sts.), 415-440-0222
A laid-back crowd braves seedy Tenderloin surroundings to gather over beer, wine, sangria and soju cocktails (no hard liquor) at this inviting new venue; plunk down your greens (cash only) for a hearty European red with a housemade pizza (the limited menu is available until midnight) at the comfortable bar, or shake it on the dance floor in the back room; N.B. closed Mondays.

Underground SF　　– | – | – | E
(fka The Top DJ Bar)
424 Haight St. (Webster St.), 415-864-7386; www.undergroundsf.com
Previously known as The Top DJ Bar, this Lower Haight disco inferno now operates under a new name, though it still aims to keep the dance floor packed, grooving and sweaty with cutting-edge spins and theme nights like 'Strangelove', 'Lowrider' and 'Drunk and Horny'; N.B. owner S. 'Cip' Cipriano also runs Cip, a SoMa newcomer.

Uptown ⊅　　▽ 24 | 17 | 24 | $5
200 Capp St. (17th St.), 415-861-8231
As long as you can "avoid weekend pub-crawling idiots" and negotiate your way past the ladies "doing the Capp Street stroll outside", you'll find a "serious local scene" at this "reliable little dive" in the Mission; an "unpretentious staff and clientele" make it a "gem" for a low-key hang or "to end your night with that last pint you know you shouldn't have ordered."

Varnish Fine Art & Wine Bar　　– | – | – | I
77 Natoma St. (bet. 1st & 2nd Sts.), 415-222-6131;
www.varnishfineart.com
Aesthetes who enjoy perusing paintings and sculpture with glasses in hand will love this loftlike SoMa spot featuring upmarket wine, soju, beer and sake in its permanent collection; you can sit at the tiny bar in the back or roam the airy room filled with works from

emerging artists, and its opening parties lay it on thick with live jazz, rock and other performances.

Velvet Lounge, The   18 | 16 | 17 | $7
443 Broadway (bet. Kearny & Montgomery Sts.), 415-788-0228; www.thevelvetlounge.com
"You can always count on meeting someone new" at this North Beach "hot spot" where "the dance floor is vast" and "great" DJs in two rooms spin "everything from '80s to hip-hop" to techno; if detractors deem it "a bridge-and-tunnel" destination with "cheesy" decor ("ah, the Velveeta Lounge"), more consider it a "fun place to party"; N.B. no sneakers or athletic wear.

Vesuvio ⌦   23 | 24 | 18 | $6
255 Columbus Ave. (Broadway), 415-362-3370; www.vesuvio.com
"Many of the writers you idolized as a college scruff bent their elbows at this wonderful" circa-1948 "North Beach institution" that "takes you back to the heady days of Kerouac" and is "fancifully decorated" with memorabilia from "its illustrious past"; though the exterior was recently restored, it's still loaded with "working-class character" from the "surly barkeep" to the poetasters "brooding in the corner" with a tome from the "legendary City Lights bookstore next door."

View Lounge   23 | 18 | 17 | $10
Marriott Hotel, 55 Fourth St. (bet. Market & Mission Sts.), 415-896-1600; www.marriott.com
"Breathtaking" vistas of "Alcatraz and beyond" have re-viewers raving about this 39th-story lounge atop Downtown's Marriott that's a "must-see for visitors and locals alike"; the space is "relaxing", the seating's "comfortable", the drinks are "sophisticated" (albeit "expensive") and if the fog rolls in you can always amuse yourself "eavesdropping on the conventioneers."

VinoVenue   – | – | – | M
686 Mission St. (3rd St.), 415-341-1930; www.vinovenue.net
Oenophiles who like to try before they buy find no reason to whine at this self-serve SoMa *vin*-ery, which offers 104 varieties from California and around the world; buy a tasting card, insert it into one of the automated stations placed throughout the room and treat yourself to a one-ounce tasting; shop for bottles or relax in the lounge with a glass or a flight (cost varies but runs as little as a buck a pour).

Voda   – | – | – | M
56 Belden Pl. (bet. Bush & Pine Sts.), 415-677-9242
"Bright white and neon"-lit decor and DJs help make this vodka-themed lounge a "cool new hot spot" amid the French bistros on Downtown's pedestrian-friendly Belden Place; it's a small, simple space with low banquettes in the back and bar shelves lined with some 70 "diverse" brands along with "tempting" infused versions of its signature liquor.

Warfield, The   22 | 21 | 14 | $8
982 Market St. (bet. 5th & 6th Sts.), 415-775-7722
Like its sister the Fillmore (both were run by the late Bill Graham), this circa-1922 Downtown "classic" has a "rich history" and is "one of the country's premier music venues" hosting a "wide variety" of "great acts"; originally a vaudeville theater, it's still

"wonderfully ornate" from the balcony to its "beautiful stage", and groupies suggest you "get there early to get up close, as Bay Area fans are some of the most fervent."

Washington Square Bar & Grill   21 | 19 | 20 | $9
1707 Powell St. (Union St.), 415-982-8123
"The old standby" in North Beach is "reincarnated and looking good" say supporters of this "classic" "upscale joint" known as the 'Washbag'; the "legendary bartenders", "cozy" quarters, "great food" and "smooth jazz" lure the "coat-and-tie crowd" as well as the "SF fixtures" who "power lunch" here, though "Herb Caen is sorely missed."

Whiskey Lounge   23 | 22 | 21 | $9
(aka Red Grill)
4063 18th St. (bet. Castro & Hartford Sts.), 415-255-2733; www.flavorsyoucrave.com
"An oasis of serenity in a sea of gay insanity", this "clubby" bar above the Red Grill is "dark" and "inviting", providing the "perfect hideout for a blind date without the whole Castro knowing"; the staff is "excellent", the cocktails are a "treat" and you can order "great" food from the restaurant downstairs to eat while being "entertained by the to and fro of guppies with their girlfriends."

Whiskey Thieves ⊘   – | – | – | M
(fka Julip)
839 Geary St. (Larkin St.), 415-409-2063
You don't have to steal away for a puff at this Tenderloin tavern as it's owner-operated, which means that you can legally light up from your perch at the bar while sipping a scotch or bourbon from the inviting selection; expect no frills from this local hang – though do expect breathing room thanks to a top-notch ventilation system.

Whisper   17 | 16 | 15 | $9
535 Florida St. (bet. 18th & Mariposa Sts.), 415-356-9800
There's "plenty of space [in which] to wander, dance or people-watch" throughout the multiple floors, recently renovated rooms and outdoor areas of this "true mega-club" with a new sound system on the edge of the Mission; it "caters to different crowds on different nights" with Latin, pop and hip-hop parties, and while the "great decor" and "trendy drinks add to the appeal", some hiss that it's "trying too hard" and was "better as the Potrero Hill Brewing Company" several years ago; N.B. open Wednesday–Saturday.

Wilde Oscar's   – | – | – | M
1900 Folsom St. (15th St.), 415-621-7145
Not just another run-of-the-mill Irish pub, this "wonderful" SoMa hangout is distinguished by "funky Wilde quotes on the walls", "smooth", "attentive service" and an ambiance that's "cool enough for local scenesters"; "good food", well-poured Guinness and a long happy hour make it "one of the best drinking bars in the area."

Wild Side West ⊘   23 | 21 | 21 | $5
424 Cortland Ave. (Wool St.), 415-647-3099
When thirsty comes calling, cowgirls and -boys alike hitch up to this "straight-friendly lesbian bar in the heart of Bernal Heights", a "local hangout" known for its interior strewn with "antiques-cum-junk"; be prepared to "get your ass kicked in pool" or just kick it by the "inviting fireplace" and in the "beautiful" "Sapphic

oasis" of a garden; judging by its "happy patrons" and staff, "gay is more than just an orientation here."

Winterland   – | – | – | E
(fka Julia)
2101 Sutter St. (Steiner St.), 415-563-5025
The ghost of rock 'n' roll's past is plenty present inside this hip Japantown lounge and restaurant that bears the name of the legendary arena where promoter Bill Graham presented the Rolling Stones, the Band and the Grateful Dead (who played the closing show in 1978), and is located on the venue's former site; red walls and orange stools set the stage for inventive cocktails like the Swedish Sunrise, and to go-with, affordable bar bites like mac 'n' cheese or pappadam.

Wish   23 | 21 | 21 | $7
1539 Folsom St. (bet. 11th & 12th Sts.), 415-278-9474; www.wishsf.com
"SoMa comfort and NYC style" merge at this "sweet spot" where the "dark", "intimate", "elegantly minimalist" interior and "tasty cocktails made by the best-looking bartenders in town" create a "fabulous atmosphere"; whether you "chill with friends" during the "great happy hour" or boogey on the "small dance floor" to "bumping house beats" spun by "excellent" DJs, you'll see why "it remains hip without trying too hard"; N.B. now open on Sunday too.

Would You Believe . . . Cocktails ⊅   – | – | – | I
4652 Geary Blvd. (bet. 10th & 11th Aves.), 415-752-7444
"Wonderfully strong drinks", "pretty" bartenders and "great" service are reason enough, but true believers say "you gotta go just for the name" to this "strange" Inner Richmond "sleeper"; its "regular crowd" of Asian twentysomethings makes newcomers "feel welcome", and sports on TV keep this "hangout" hopping.

XYZ   24 | 25 | 19 | $11
W Hotel, 181 Third St. (Howard St.), 415-817-7836; www.xyz-sf.com
"Metrosexuals", "Paris Hilton clones", "swank locals" and "out-of-town business" types "looking to get lucky" hang at this "happening" lounge in SoMa's W Hotel where the "color-changing bar", "plush sofas", "warm" lighting and "pulsating music" create an "ultra-sexy" vibe; sure, "you pay for the ambiance", but the drinks are "divine", the crowd's "beautiful" and the experience is "as chic as it gets", making it a "godsend every night of the week."

Yancy's ⊅   16 | 13 | 16 | $5
734 Irving St. (bet. 8th & 9th Aves.), 415-665-6551
"Bring your darts and best friends" to this "cavernous" but "comfortable" Inner Sunset pub with a "big-screen TV", "strong drinks", "fun games" and a new digital jukebox; it's a bit "musty" for some ("reminds me of a frat house the morning after a kegger"), but it's "good for the 'hood" on a "mellow Friday night" and as a spot to "have a beer while you wait for a table" at PJ's Oyster Bar across the street.

Zam Zam ⊅   23 | 24 | 19 | $7
1633 Haight St. (Clayton St.), 415-861-2545
"Bogey and Bacall might have had their first date" at this "film-noir" longtimer in the "gritty Haight" with a "beautiful half-moon bar", "Middle Eastern"–meets–*Swingers* decor and "esoteric" tunes on the jukebox; nostalgic sorts miss "infamous" "martini

nazi" Bruno Mooshei who's gone to his reward, but at least "you don't have to look over your shoulder anymore" and fear getting "kicked out for ordering the wrong drink" (and "props to the owners", who took over a few years ago "and have kept all but the prices" as it was).

ZEITGEIST ⊅　　　　24 | 14 | 20 | $4
199 Valencia St. (Duboce Ave.), 415-255-7505
Grab a "cheap" pitcher and settle into the "enormous beer garden" out back at this "rough and real" "biker bar with heart" that some feel is the "last bastion of the pre-dot-com rebel artist/messenger/skater set" in the Mission; essentially a bunch of "old park benches on a dirt lot", it's "like drinking in a junkyard (glorious!)" that boasts a "fantastic selection" of drafts, "great greasy food", "punk rock blasting" from an "unrivaled jukebox" and "lots of surly attitude."

Zeke's Sports Bar & Grill　　　　18 | 11 | 19 | $6
600 Third St. (Brannan St.), 415-392-5311
Located within walking distance from the ballpark, this "small" SoMa saloon is "a real sports bar without the trappings" that's just the ticket for fans who elect to "escape from over-sophistication" and the "suit-and-tie crowd"; "cheap beverages", "generous tavern fare" and "tons of TVs" make it "great for games", whether pre, post or during.

ZUNI CAFE　　　　24 | 22 | 22 | $9
1658 Market St. (bet. Franklin & Gough Sts.), 415-552-2522
Even after over 25 years, "nothing compares to the buzz" of this "beautiful, huge-windowed" "late-night staple" near Hayes Valley where you can "belly up to the copper bar" for an "impulse drink" including the "chunkalicious Bloody Mary" or a "great glass of wine"; the "super-friendly staff", "amazing" appetizers (including the "freshest oysters") and that "wonderful urban setting" continue to attract an "upscale", "diverse" crowd that "would go back even if the prices were raised."

East of San Francisco

Acme Bar ⌷   ▽ 18 | 18 | 18 | $7

2115 San Pablo Ave. (bet. Addison & Cowper Sts.), Berkeley,
510-644-2226

Loyalists laud this "no-frills bar" in Berkeley as the "perfect spot"
for a pint and an "after-work oasis"; it boasts "one of the best
jukeboxes around", along with "kitschy decor, stiff drinks, pinball"
and "occasional DJs" and theme nights – with all that behind those
swinging doors, life just "doesn't get much better."

Albany Bowl   ▽ 14 | 11 | 15 | $4

540 San Pablo Ave. (Clay St.), Albany, 510-526-8818;
www.albanybowl.com

"Keep ordering pitchers until no one even knows the score"
advise advocates of this "basic alley" in Albany, where rock 'n'
bowl nights, "beer, good music" and a "friendly vibe" add up
to a night of "kitschy fun", whether it's knocking down pins or
knocking 'em back in the "hidden gem" of a cocktail lounge; as it
also boasts a video arcade, pool hall and Thai-food diner, it's no
wonder it remains "popular with everyone from middle-schoolers
to their grandparents."

ALBATROSS PUB ⌷   25 | 18 | 20 | $5

1822 San Pablo Ave. (bet. Delaware St. & Hearst Ave.), Berkeley,
510-843-2473; www.albatrosspub.com

"Hippies, students and professors join together" at this "cozy",
"adorable" "pub-goers' dream" (a fixture in Berkeley since 1964)
to face off over "great" trivia nights, darts, pool and "truckloads"
of board games, drink "world-class beers" and chomp from
"bottomless bowls" of popcorn; the "strange flea-market decor
somehow works", and the "low-key atmosphere" is conducive to
"excellent conversation"; be warned: "bring the party with you",
as it's "a place to congregate" more than a hot "pickup" spot.

Alley, The ⌷   24 | 17 | 17 | $5

3325 Grand Ave. (Lake Park Ave.), Oakland, 510-444-8505

"Get yer sing on at this" "great neighborhood dive" ("bring your
scuba tanks") and piano bar, where Oakland "fixture" Rod Dibble
works the keys and takes requests for "old standards" as he has
for decades; it's "everything a karaoke bar aspires to be", and
when you throw in the "dingy", "business card–covered walls",
"cheap drinks" and the chance to warble with "your eight new
best friends", it's obviously "an institution that you must not miss."

Ashkenaz   20 | 15 | 13 | $7

1317 San Pablo Ave. (Gilman St.), Berkeley, 510-525-5054;
www.ashkenaz.com

The "vibe's tie-dye, tofu and Birkenstock", but "if you like world
music", this "Berkeley institution" run by a nonprofit organization
is a "rock-star joint", with 30-plus years' experience in showcasing
"great" bands and serving as a magnet for "uninhibited" "folk and
ethnic dancers"; "families", "students", "lefties, greenies and old

hippies" come together at this "funky" "barn of a nightclub"; N.B. no credit cards accepted for performances.

At Seventeenth — | — | — | E
510 17th St. (Telegraph Ave.), Oakland, 510-433-0577; www.at17th.com
Leave your jeans and sneakers behind if you want to shake your groove thang to fresh funk, house, hip-hop and R&B on the classy new floor of this 8000-sq.-ft. palace in Downtown Oakland; the luxe space channels its past life as a 1920s cabaret while tuning into the 21st century via futuristic furnishings, moody lighting in candy-cool colors, comfy booths with bottle service and a cigar parlor.

Beckett's Irish Pub 20 | 19 | 18 | $7
2271 Shattuck Ave. (bet. Bancroft Way & Kittredge St.), Berkeley, 510-647-1790; www.beckettsirishpub.com
Those seeking a "cozy fireplace on a rainy night" or just a "nice, traditional" hangout will want to Godot to this "charming", "Irish-style pub" in Downtown Berkeley; decked out in "lovely dark wood" and "low lighting", it's "more upscale than most" college bars, with "grad students" and "adults" enjoying "decent" food and "appealing beers", even though some Endgamers groan it's "Disneyfied"; P.S. Nicole the Human Jukebox performs twice a week and "does an amazing Johnny Cash impression."

Ben & Nick's 20 | 16 | 19 | $6
5612 College Ave. (bet. Keith Ave. & Ocean View Dr.), Oakland, 510-923-0327; www.mrcato.com
"An impressive array" of "obscure beers" is still the main draw of this "friendly" sister to Cato's Ale House, but its boosters also benefit from its location "near the BART" in Oakland's Rockridge district and "laid-back atmosphere that encourages lingering"; "a mixed clientele" of "well-heeled hippies", "frat boys", "tattooed bikers" and even the "stroller" set rallies to "recommend" this "real neighborhood watering hole."

Bench and Bar — | — | — | E
2111 Franklin St. (21st St.), Oakland, 510-444-2266; www.bench-and-bar.com
Hunks, cowboys and other burly types pack the floor at this newly relocated gay dance club in Oakland; the flavor's now decidedly Latin, with theme nights ranging from 'Latin Explosion' Fridays to the studded cowboy-themed '*Lo Bota Loca*' on Saturdays; N.B. ladies get down too on Thursday 'Coochielicious' nights.

Blakes on Telegraph 16 | 11 | 14 | $6
2367 Telegraph Ave. (Durant Ave.), Berkeley, 510-848-0886; www.blakesontelegraph.com
"The drinks are cheap and the crowd is ready to party" at this "typical college hangout" in central Berkeley, located a block from the UC campus; you can "grab a bite to eat upstairs" in the bar or check out the "good range" of live music in the "low-lit, low-roofed" nightclub below; gripers call it "cheesy", advising "just say no", while sympathizers say "they try, bless their hearts."

Café Rouge 20 | 19 | 17 | $8
Market Plaza, 1782 Fourth St. (bet. Hearst Ave. & Virginia St.), Berkeley, 510-525-1440; www.caferouge.net
"Escape the college atmosphere" in Berkeley at this "attractive" restaurant with a "large bar" that's "great for a drink after shopping

on Fourth Street" (or a fix of "well-prepared" indulgences such as oysters and charcuterie); although foes see red over "hit-or-miss service" and "pricey" offerings, the "people-watching's a plus" and most report an "enjoyable experience."

Cafe Van Kleef   – | – | – | M
1621 Telegraph Ave. (bet. 16th & 17th Sts.), Oakland, 510-763-7711; www.cafevankleef.com
"Local music celebs" and "arty types" mix with blue-collar locals and the "charismatic owner" at this quirky Downtown Oakland cafe, gallery and performance venue; acts range from bluegrass to vaudeville, and if the bands don't capture your attention, its eccentric display of memorabilia (boxing gloves, an Oscar statue) will keep you occupied for hours; N.B. closed on Sunday.

Caffe Trieste   22 | 15 | 17 | $6
2500 San Pablo Ave. (Dwight Way), Berkeley, 510-548-5198; www.caffetrieste.com
See review in City of San Francisco Directory.

Cato's Ale House   19 | 16 | 18 | $6
3891 Piedmont Ave. (Montell St.), Oakland, 510-655-3349; www.mrcato.com
"Hang out and relax with your mates" at this "funky" "watering hole par excellence" (sister to Berkeley's Ben & Nick's) in Oakland's Piedmont neighborhood; it was "once a well-kept secret" but is now "increasingly more crowded", and given its "great selection of beers" (23 taps) and "better-than-average bar food", "good mix of people" and "live music most nights", it's little wonder why.

César   23 | 21 | 21 | $9
1515 Shattuck Ave. (bet. Cedar & Vine Sts.), Berkeley, 510-883-0222; www.barcesar.com
"Neighbors and swanksters rub shoulders" at this "irresistible Iberian salon" next door to Chez Panisse in North Berkeley, where "killer" wines and a "superb selection of liquors" are "paired with delicious tapas" that keep you from "getting too sloshed"; the "beautiful people" at "communal tables" keep the "inviting" interior "bustling" "at all hours" with the sounds of "festive chatter", and if it's "not the cheapest bar in town", it's still a "locals' favorite."

Club Mallard   21 | 18 | 22 | $5
752 San Pablo Ave. (Washington Ave.), Albany, 510-524-8450; www.clubmallard.com
"It's always a party" at this "busy" Albany institution that supplies "everything all wrapped into a two-story" building replete with "Midwest hunting lodge" decor and a "large", "purposefully chintzy" tiki-themed outdoor lounge; the "great" bartenders "will make you anything (despite their better judgment)", and there's a "good assortment of drafts" as well; throw in "multiple pool tables" and "you can't go wrong."

Conga Lounge   – | – | – | M
5422 College Ave. (Manila St.), Oakland, 510-463-2681; www.congalounge.com
"Bring your sense of humor" to this "tiny" but "fabuloso tiki bar" in Oakland, as it's loaded with "enough camp to make it feel like summer all over again"; conga-scenti line up for 40 "yummy" cocktails (some served in the requisite "volcano-

shaped" vessels), "Elvis movies on the TVs" and "special events" like monthly 'Hot Hawaiian Night' with a funky acoustic quartet; N.B. open Wednesday–Saturday.

downtown   20 | 18 | 19 | $10 |

2102 Shattuck Ave. (Addison St.), Berkeley, 510-649-3810; www.downtownrestaurant.com

"One of the few sophisticated" establishments in Berkeley, this "good pre-theater" destination offers "heavenly", "swanky drinks" and "great small plates" at the "long bar"; the "accommodating", "knowledgeable" and "positive" staff will help you select a "nice" if "pricey" bottle of wine, and live jazz later in the evening (except on Sunday) adds to the "speakeasy style."

Elephant Bar & Restaurant   18 | 19 | 16 | $8 |

1225 Willow Pass Rd. (Diamond Blvd.), Concord, 925-671-0119
39233 Fremont Blvd. (Gateway Dr.), Fremont, 510-742-6221
www.elephantbar.com

See review in South of San Francisco Directory.

Fat Lady   24 | 24 | 24 | $8 |

201 Washington St. (2nd St.), Oakland, 510-465-4996; www.thefatladyrestaurant.com

"Experience a brothel without committing the sin" at this "small, quaint", "bordello-style bar" just north of Oakland's Jack London Square; the Victorian decor is a "throwback to the days of the Barbary Coast" to match the tall tale of the illustrious madam who allegedly plied her trade here, and the "super-charming staff and fun regulars" make it "perfect for a pop when going to a movie" nearby or for simply catching "a quiet drink."

5th Amendment ⊄   ∇ 18 | 11 | 21 | $7 |

3255 Lakeshore Ave. (bet. Lake Park Ave. & Mandana Blvd.), Oakland, 510-832-3242; www.5thamendment.com

It's a "good mixed crowd" that makes for a "fun scene" at this "funky local bar" in Oakland's Lake Merritt area that's "hopping every night of the week"; admittedly, "the linoleum and fluorescent lighting does nothing" for the establishment, nevertheless "what it lacks in physical ambiance it more than makes up for with a soulful, musical atmosphere."

FREIGHT & SALVAGE ⊄   26 | 12 | 20 | $4 |

1111 Addison St. (San Pablo Ave.), Berkeley, 510-548-1761; www.freightandsalvage.com

"A Berkeley tradition for decades", this "warehouse"-like but "comfortable" coffeehouse lures "knowledgeable fans" with its "exceptional programming" of folk, bluegrass, country and acoustic acts from "unknowns" to "stars"; true, there's "no booze" (java and sodas are available) and "no table service", but it' a "superb" venue for getting "up close and personal with your favorite artists."

Golden Bull   – | – | – | M |

412 14th St. (Franklin St.), Oakland, 510-893-0803

The East Bay is home to a solid punk-rock scene and this unadorned Oakland venue has taken up the cause, offering hard-core buckos a down-to-earth place to see a steady stable of local bands cut loose live; grab this Bull by the horns and ride it straight into the night.

Heinold's First and Last Chance Saloon ⌂
▽ 26 | 19 | 21 | $6

Jack London Sq., 48 Webster St. (Embarcadero W.), Oakland, 510-839-6761; www.heinoldsfirstandlastchance.com

Sure, it's "worn, but then it always has been" say champions who've chanced upon this "wonderful", small "old shack on Jack London Square" (and haunt of the writer himself) that's one of "Oakland's treasures"; dating from 1883, it's crammed with artifacts from the "amusing signs" and photos on the walls to the "slanted floor" (a memento of the earthquake of '06) that may "disrupt your equilibrium" and have you "stumbling before you get to the bar."

Hotsy Totsy ⌂
– | – | – | I

601 San Pablo Ave. (Garfield Ave.), Albany, 510-525-9964

"Never had a bad time and never left sober" mumble mavens of this "down-home" "dirtbag dive" in Albany that's been in the booze biz since 1951; it's "scary but fun" from the eye-catching neon sign to the "old drunkards" within; hot to trot or not, make sure you've got a designated driver as "the drinks are ridiculously strong."

Ivy Room, The ⌂
17 | 11 | 16 | $5

860 San Pablo Ave. (Solano Ave.), Albany, 510-524-9220; www.ivyroom.com

"An amazing array" of "eccentric regulars" lined up at the bar and an "exceptional jukebox" full of vintage 45s are just part of the draw at this "curiously appealing" "old-time neighborhood dive" in Albany; the "eclectic mix" of entertainment includes shuffleboard, pool and live blues, rock and country bands on weekends, and the staff "actively takes care of customers"; P.S. it's surprisingly "safe for single women, as the troll factor is fairly low."

JUPITER
23 | 19 | 18 | $6

2181 Shattuck Ave. (Center St.), Berkeley, 510-843-8277; www.jupiterbeer.com

"Enjoy a great microbrew and California-style pizza" around the fire pit on the "huge", "fabulous outdoor deck" of this "comfortable beer parlor" in Berkeley, a "favorite for students of all ages"; it's "a laid-back place to drink with friends", but "arrive early if you want a table" when one of the "eclectic bands" is playing; either way, the "stellar selection of ales" will "put you in orbit."

Kimball's East
▽ 20 | 19 | 19 | $11

6005 Shellmound St. (Powell St.), Emeryville, 510-658-2555; www.kimballs.com

The "sexy, sophisticated vibe" of this Emeryville supper club and concert venue is "largely due to the well-dressed, classy clientele" tempted by "top" R&B, jazz, pop and other performers as well as comedy acts; an evening out is enhanced by the "excellent selection" of cocktails and a "multicultural" dinner menu served at the tables, which have clear sightlines of the stage.

Kingman's Lucky Lounge
▽ 21 | 23 | 18 | $6

3332 Grand Ave. (bet. Mandana Blvd. & Santa Clara Ave.), Oakland, 510-465-5464

"This happenin' little conversation spot is one of the best-kept secrets in the East Bay" boast lucky loyalists of this "swanky neighborhood bar" whose "fabulously diverse clientele" reflects all "ages, ethnicities, sexual orientations and economic" situations from the "melting pot of Oakland"; "red walls" and "shabby-chic sofas" provide an "inviting" backdrop for "fancy-schmancy" cocktails and the "down-tempo grooves" courtesy of nightly DJs.

La Peña Cultural Center ⌐   – | – | – | I |
3105 Shattuck Ave. (Prince St.), Berkeley, 510-849-2568;
www.lapena.org
Come to "hear some of the world's best Latin musicians" or "learn" a few steps yourself on the dance floor of this politically and socially minded music club and meeting house in Berkeley; from South American bands to Wednesday poetry readings, the roster celebrates multiculturalism while the cafe serves some "great sangria" to keep your evening lubricated and lively.

Left Bank   21 | 21 | 19 | $9 |
60 Crescent Dr. (Contra Costa Blvd.), Pleasant Hill, 925-288-1222;
www.leftbank.com
See review in North of San Francisco Directory.

Lost Weekend Lounge ⌐   – | – | – | M |
2320 Santa Clara Ave. (Park St.), Alameda, 510-523-4700
"Tipsy hipsters drink the night away" at this Alameda watering hole, dubbed a 'lava lounge' for the iconic psychedelic lamps that spice up the decor; happy-hour specials, a healthy jukebox and thrice-weekly DJs (Thursday, Friday and Saturday) spinning punk rock and '60s beats keep East Bay barflies buzzing.

Luka's Taproom & Lounge   – | – | – | M |
2221 Broadway (W. Grand Ave.), Oakland, 510-451-4677;
www.lukasoakland.com
A working crowd rules during lunchtime and at happy hour at this suds emporium on the edge of a revitalized Downtown Oakland, but come nightfall, drafts (some 16 on tap), DJs, and pinball and pool in the adjacent lounge are the main draw; the down-home decor and neighborly atmosphere nod to the space's past as a hofbrau – in other words, check your urban pretensions at the door.

924 Gilman   ▽ 22 | 9 | 11 | $4 |
924 Gilman St. (8th St.), Berkeley, 510-525-9926;
www.924gilman.org
This all-ages "youth-oriented cooperative" remains "a landmark in the indie-rock community" for the "hundreds of bands" ("of widely varying quality") that pass through "trying to appeal to the Berkeley alternative scene" of "gutter punks" and "suburban high-schoolers"; it may be "dingy", but it "launched Green Day's career", and an "abundance of attitude and energy" "more than makes up for its lack of frills and alcohol."

Oliveto Cafe & Restaurant   22 | 23 | 23 | $10 |
5655 College Ave. (Shafter Ave.), Oakland, 510-547-5356;
www.oliveto.com
The "neighborhood secret is the downstairs cafe" say tipsters of "star" chef Paul Bertelli's "buzzy" double-decker Italian in Oakland's "trendy Rockridge district"; the "small" bar's the "place to schmooze" over a "great" glass of wine, and the "casual" room looks "European with bistro tables" just made for "reading the paper"; one caveat: "it's hard just to have a drink because the food's so good."

Pacific Coast Brewing Company   19 | 15 | 18 | $6

906 Washington St. (10th St.), Oakland, 510-836-2739;
www.pacificcoastbrewing.com

Expect "nothing too trendy" at this "solid" "downtown beer parlor" in the "spruced up" section of Old Oakland, just lots of "awesome house-brewed ales", "decent" pub grub from a recently expanded menu and a bit of televised sports; it's a "good after-work place" ("it's within stumbling distance and I often stumble") thanks to the "mellow" setting and "inviting" patio.

Paragon Bar & Cafe   19 | 19 | 17 | $9

Claremont Resort & Spa, 41 Tunnel Rd. (Claremont Ave.), Berkeley,
510-843-3000; www.paragonrestaurant.com

See review in City of San Francisco Directory.

PARAMOUNT THEATER   29 | 29 | 20 | $7

2025 Broadway (bet. 20th & 21st Sts.), Oakland, 510-465-6400;
www.paramounttheater.com

"Radio City Music Hall has nothing on this" 1931 Timothy Pfluger–designed "palace", a "stunning" "architectural masterpiece of the art deco era" in Downtown Oakland that's once again No. 1 for Decor and tops for Appeal in this *Survey*; "Friday night movie classics are the best $6 you can spend" and include newsreels and an organist, but whether you're seeing celluloid, a band or comedy show, "come early to mingle with the local hipsters" over a "drink in the downstairs bar", and be sure to "dress up and feel grand."

PARKWAY SPEAKEASY THEATER ≠   26 | 17 | 21 | $5

1834 Park Blvd. (E. 18th St.), Oakland, 510-814-2400;
www.picturepubpizza.com

"Have a brew, a view and a slice all at once" at this "Oakland institution" that's a "fun movie house with couches instead of theater seats"; it screens "an odd mix of second-run, cult and occasional art films", serves "good" grub and "great beers and wines" (Wednesday is two-for night) and provides "one of the best cheap dates around", though for fervent aflickcionados, it's "a reason to live"; N.B. Monday is 'Baby Brigade', an evening for parents and infants, while Saturday is *Rocky Horror* night.

PYRAMID BREWERY & ALEHOUSE   18 | 16 | 16 | $7

901 Gilman St. (8th St.), Berkeley, 510-528-9880
1410 Locust St. (Cypress St.), Walnut Creek, 925-946-1520
www.pyramidbrew.com

"One needn't dig too far to find a good" beer at this pair of "East Bay temples" to all things hopped and malted in Berkeley and Walnut Creek, both outposts of a "great" Seattle-based craft brewery; the "large" settings are "bright" and "sterile", but the pub fare's "reliable", the "tours are a plus" and "you can't go wrong" with the "excellent" ales.

Radio Bar   ∇ 22 | 18 | 22 | $6

435 13th St. (bet. Broadway & Franklin St.), Oakland,
510-451-2889

"Hipsters" broadcast their approval of this "rare pocket of chic in Downtown Oakland", now under new ownership, where the "bartenders are beautiful" and/or "hunky", the "stiff" "potables are flavorful" ("order the Key lime martini") and the decor is "dappled with red light" as befits the Ruby Room's sibling; even though it's "tiny" and can get "crowded", the "people having a great time on the dance floor" proclaim "pump up the volume!"

Raleigh's
18 | 15 | 13 | $5

2438 Telegraph Ave. (bet. Channing & Haste Sts.), Berkeley, 510-848-8652

The "outdoor beer garden is a big plus" at this Berkeley eatery and quaffery, a "perfect student hangout" since it's "only two blocks from campus"; followers find it a "fun frat-boy experience" with "cheap brews and decent food", while foes foam-ent it's all about "convenience" and warn against the "agonizingly slow service."

Ruby Room
▽ 18 | 16 | 19 | $6

132 14th St. (bet. Madison & Oak Sts.), Oakland, 510-444-7224

It's a "kitschy dive bar" that "knows what's up" say those sparkling over this "red-lit" Oakland "favorite" (Radio Bar's sister) and its "heavy-handed" pours, "bittersweet" staff and "always-changing" DJ and jukebox sounds; it's "perfect for the zeitgeist crowd" and other "young hipsters in black", but remains "grungy" and "cavelike" for others who find the aesthetic too perilously close to "your high-school friend's basement" for comfort.

Saddle Rack ⇪
— | — | — | M

42011 Boscell Rd. (Auto Mall Pkwy.), Fremont, 510-979-0477; www.thesaddlerack.com

Urban cowboys and -girls can get their kicks on the huge dance floor and take their licks from a buck-happy mechanical bull at this country music showplace in Fremont; headliners from Blake Shelton to the Bellamy Brothers share the schedule with house band Appaloosa and various DJs as honky-tonkers toy with the two-step, West Coast swing or line dances like the Rack Attack and Copperhead Road.

Schmidt's Tobacco & Trading Company ⇪
— | — | — | I

1492 Solano Ave. (Santa Fe Ave.), Albany, 510-525-1900

Like hanging in a "friend's living room", this Albany institution known affectionately as 'The Pub' boasts a "cozy fireplace and warm wood floors" that create a "chill atmosphere"; it's also a "rare haven" for folks who wish to "smoke in comfort" on its two large porches, and sells tobacco, cigars and "cheap pipes" to go with your beer, wine or coffee.

Shattuck Avenue Spats
19 | 18 | 17 | $7

1974 Shattuck Ave. (University Ave.), Berkeley, 510-841-7225

"Relax with your date" on "plush couches" while "nursing retro cocktails" such as 'Flossie's Chocolate Grog' at this "quiet", "cozy" Berkeley cafe that "looks as though a flea market exploded on the walls"; however, one person's "shabby chic" is another's "run-down frump", and when it comes to the "creative", "delicious libations" nobody prefers them "too pricey."

Shattuck Down Low
— | — | — | M

2284 Shattuck Ave. (Bancroft Way), Berkeley, 510-548-1159; www.shattuckdownlow.com

A "chill, underground vibe" combined with "beautiful", "classy" decor and a "velvety feel" make this Berkeley dance club "near the UC campus" a high point for partisans; it hosts some of the "best hip-hop, funk and soul in the East Bay" and offers "crazy karaoke on Tuesdays", and even critics who claim it's "cheesy" admit it's "good on the right night."

Skates on the Bay 23 | 22 | 20 | $10

100 Seawall Dr. (University Ave.), Berkeley, 510-549-1900;
www.r-u-i.com

"When the fog remains behind the Golden Gate" and "that evening sun goes down", the view across the Bay is "exquisite" from the "attractive" confines of this restaurant/bar in Berkeley's Marina; the "good wine list", "responsive staff" and "upscale" digs make for a "romantic" experience, but the "noisy" setting and large tabs have cheapskates equating it to an "overpriced prom date."

Spoontonic Lounge ∇ 24 | 23 | 20 | $10

2580 N. Main St., Suite A (3rd Ave.), Walnut Creek,
925-977-1888

"A real martini joint in a suburban basement" has tipplers touting this "strange, out-of-the-way place" that's Walnut Creek's answer to an "edgy San Francisco bar"; it's "hip without being snotty", with a "dimly lit, moody atmosphere", modern decor, eclectic crowd and "cheerful" bartenders who "pour really mean" cocktails that are "high-priced but excellent."

Starry Plough 19 | 11 | 17 | $6

3101 Shattuck Ave. (bet. Prince & Woolsey Sts.), Berkeley,
510-841-2082; www.starryploughpub.com

"Appealing bands" from national acts to Bay Area–based artists are on the lineup each week along with slam poets, Gaelic folkies, dancers and open-mike singer-songwriters at this "comfortable Irish-themed bar" in Berkeley; maybe it's the music or the "excellent selection" of 20 craft brews on draft that keep the atmosphere "über-casual", "relaxed" and "warm" around the edges; N.B. beer and wine only.

Stork Club ⊘ – | – | – | M

2330 Telegraph Ave. (bet. 23rd & 24th Sts.), Oakland, 510-444-6174;
www.storkcluboakland.com

It's "still punk rock" after all these years, and that's why this Oakland "dive" is so "wonderful" to those who are stork raving mad for the year-round Christmas decorations, "amazing" collection of Barbies behind the bar and eclectic lineup of "loud" local and touring indie bands; some clash over the "surly service and bad attitude" of the place, while others find nirvana in the "friendly staff that makes you feel at home."

Townhouse Bar & Grill ∇ 19 | 16 | 19 | $7

5862 Doyle St. (bet. 59th & Powell Sts.), Emeryville, 510-652-6151;
www.townhousebarandgrill.com

"Who'd figure a cool spot in Emeryville?" ask pleased patrons of this "hard-to-find" former bootlegger's haven and honky-tonk where "wonderful food" and "great wines by the glass" have replaced shots and a beer; the "decor and service are warm and fuzzy" and there's live jazz on Wednesday nights, but it still retains vestiges of its "old roadhouse atmosphere."

Trader Vic's – | – | – | E

9 Anchor Dr. (I-80), Emeryville, 510-653-3400;
www.tradervics.com

See review in City of San Francisco Directory.

Triple Rock Brewery
| 17 | 13 | 16 | $6 |

1920 Shattuck Ave. (Hearst Ave.), Berkeley, 510-843-2739;
www.triplerock.com
Berkeley's "original brewpub" (founded in 1986) "buzzes with
activity" on any given night with students and others attracted to
"excellent" "handcrafted ales", the "pleasant" rooftop deck for
"those warm East Bay evenings" and two huge plasma TVs;
complainers call it "completely unremarkable" with a "dull bar
scene", but the rock-ribbed contend "it's the place to be."

White Horse ⊅
| – | – | – | M |

6551 Telegraph Ave. (66th St.), Oakland, 510-652-3820;
www.whitehorsebar.com
A "diverse crowd" from "frat boys to bar trolls to cruisers" merges
at this "not-fancy" but "friendly" 1933 tavern in Oakland that's the
"only game in town" for a "laid-back" gay clientele; no one has
an "attitude" so it's "comfortable no matter what you want to do –
play pool, dance, talk, hang out by the fireplace", smoke in the back
room or just horse around, and it offers "great DJs on weekends."

Wildcard Bar & Grill
| – | – | – | E |

(fka Ibiza)
10 Hegenberger Rd. (98th Ave.), Oakland, 510-567-8945;
www.wildcardoakland.com
This massive, 35,000-sq.-ft. multiroomed sports bar and dance
palace near the Oakland airport claims to be the largest nightclub
in the Bay Area; sports fans scope games on projection TVs while
on weekends it's flush with club kids who come to groove indoors
or out by the pool; the ace up this former hotel's sleeve may be the
74 rooms still available and perfect for post-party retiring.

YOSHI'S AT JACK LONDON SQUARE
| 26 | 22 | 19 | $10 |

Jack London Sq., 510 Embarcadero W. (bet. Clay & Washington Sts.),
Oakland, 510-238-9200; www.yoshis.com
"That all-American combo of sushi and jazz" makes for a "winning"
concept at this "premier" club in Oakland's Jack London Square
that books a "constant stream" of "A-list talent" ("there's
something worthwhile every night") and provides an "excellent
sound system" in an "upscale" setting; the Japanese fare's a bit
"pricey" but "tasty" enough, and a dinner reservation guarantees
you the "best seats" and lets you "avoid the long line" outside.

A	D	S	C

Ana's Cantina

-	-	-	M

1205 Main St. (Spring St.), St. Helena, 707-963-4921
Loyalists of this lunch-only Mexican that's a "semi-dive" by night
applaud it as the "last neighborhood bar in St. Helena where
you can have a drink and not be worried about posing"; "great"
cocktails, "surprisingly decent music", karaoke on Thursdays and
a "funky" vibe make for good ol' "lowbrow", "honest fun."

AUBERGE DU SOLEIL

28	27	26	$11

*Auberge du Soleil, 180 Rutherford Hill Rd. (Silverado Trail), Rutherford,
707-963-1211; www.aubergedusoleil.com*
Enjoy a "spectacular sunset" and "astonishing views" of the
valley while sipping "a glass of champagne on the patio" of this
"casually chic" and "romantic as hell" Relais & Châteaux resort
in Rutherford; "the prices are huge" ("instead of a maitre d' they
have a loan officer"), but with "gorgeous decor, superior service"
and a "fabulous wine list", it's "great for a special treat", and on
"warm summer nights", it's "the perfect place to end your day" in
the Napa Valley.

Boca

-	-	-	E

340 Ignacio Blvd. (Rte. 101), Novato, 415-883-0901
The Argentine heritage of former Fifth Floor and Aqua chef George
Morrone takes center stage at his Novato steakhouse, which
serves up beef and cactus juice fit for after-work gauchos; done
up in stone, plank flooring and forged metal, it emulates an
authentic estancia; saddle up at the bar and dream of drifting the
high plains as you indulge in empanadas or a sip from the rotating
roster of wines by the glass.

Bouchon

25	23	22	$11

*6534 Washington St. (Yount St.), Yountville, 707-944-8037;
www.bouchonbistro.com*
You may be in Napa Valley but it sure "feels like Paris" at this
"wonderful" bistro, the "pretty" *petite soeur* of Thomas Keller's
French Laundry in Yountville; the "terrific wine list", "excellent"
Gallic food and extended hours make it "great for late-night
eats" and drinks, and a "world-class bartender" and "beautiful"
clientele of both "locals" and "out-of-towners" help ensure it's
"always a joy."

Buckeye Roadhouse

24	23	23	$9

*15 Shoreline Hwy./Hwy. 1 (west of Hwy. 101), Mill Valley, 415-331-2600;
www.buckeyeroadhouse.com*
The "cool lodge-type decor", fireplace and "clubby atmosphere"
of this circa-1937 Mill Valley restaurant "just off 101" appeal to
the "Marin locals" and tourists "on their way to the coast" who
pass by and can't help but turn their heads; it's "not for the low-
budget crowd", and the bar's always "packed", but after the
"hospitable staff" serves you a "stiff drink", you'll sure be "glad
that you came."

Café Amsterdam
– | – | – | M |

23 Broadway Blvd. (Bolinas Rd.), Fairfax, 415-256-8020;
www.cafeamsterdamfairfax.com

This "upscale" "hangout in Fairfax", now under new ownership, provides a "warm" atmosphere that its "cool" clientele considers conducive to a "cozy evening"; the draft "microbrews are always good" (ditto the "noshes") and the regular roster of live music every night includes rockabilly, alternative and "great folk acts with a world beat twist."

Café Society
▽ 22 | 22 | 19 | $10 |

1000 Main St. (1st St.), Napa, 707-256-3232;
www.cafesocietystore.com

Offering a "bit of Parisian clutter in Napa", this "friendly" "hangout" and boutique a stone's throw from the Opera House serves "gorgeous" lattes, beer, wine and light fare during the day and late into the evening on weekends in a "fabulous" setting; however, a few bourgeois carp that "it can't make up its mind if it's a cafe or a pricey interiors shop."

Caffe Cicero
– | – | – | M |

1245 First St. (Randolph St.), Napa, 707-257-1802;
www.caffecicero.com

"Groups with all kinds of tastes" will likely be happy at this Napa cafe, which is "one of the newer late-night places" in town to "grab a coffee", a "glass of good wine" or some "excellent" casual fare; it's often "crowded with locals on weekends" who come for classic movies or live acoustic music, and while the "service could be more focused", optimists opine that "hopefully it'll fulfill its potential."

Caffe Trieste ⊅
22 | 15 | 17 | $6 |

1000 Bridgeway St. (Caledonia St.), Sausalito, 415-332-7660;
www.caffetrieste.com

See review in City of San Francisco Directory.

Calistoga Inn Restaurant & Brewery
24 | 17 | 23 | $9 |

Calistoga Inn, 1250 Lincoln Ave. (Cedar St.), Calistoga, 707-942-4101;
www.calistogainn.com

Home to the Napa Valley Brewing Company, this "charming" pub in a circa-1822 Calistoga inn offers a "lovely little spot" to "quench your thirst" with "fine" craft brews (as well as the expected "fantastic wines"); "mucho ambiance", "elegant bar food" and live music Thursday–Saturday make for a "romantic" respite, and "weather permitting", you can quaff in the "excellent" garden.

Cole's Chop House
25 | 25 | 23 | $9 |

1122 Main St. (bet. 1st & Pearl Sts.), Napa, 707-224-6328

It "seems like a sin to have martinis in wine country", but this "sophisticated" Napa eatery "just screams out for ice-cold shaken gin"; the crowd's "weighted toward the higher end", meaning "you won't run into headbangers here" (it's just "too expensive"), but with "friendly bartenders" and a "warm" atmosphere, it's the "de facto locale for a swanky drink."

COPIA
22 | 20 | 19 | $11 |

500 First St. (Napa River), Napa, 707-259-1600; www.copia.org

Foodies feel they've "died and gone to heaven" at this Napa culinary museum offering "fun, varied" activities from exploring the "spectacular gardens" to dining on "excellent" food in the newly refurbished Julia's Kitchen to wine tastings to Thursday concert and Friday movie nights; a few critical cooks spoil the broth, proclaiming it's "pricey" and service is "slow", but boosters with a *bon appétit* maintain it's a "must-visit."

E&O Trading Company   20 | 21 | 18 | $8 |
2231 Larkspur Landing Circle (Old Quarry Rd.), Larkspur, 415-925-0303;
www.eotrading.com
See review in City of San Francisco Directory.

Frantoio   21 | 21 | 21 | $9 |
152 Shoreline Hwy./Hwy. 1 (west of Hwy. 101), Mill Valley,
415-289-5777; www.frantoio.com
"Watch olive oil being made" in the on-site press "while feasting like a king" or partaking of "the best lemon drops anywhere" ("a waiter told me so, and he was correct!") and some "great wines" in the lounge or "busy dining room" of this Mill Valley Italian located just off Highway 101; it has an "open and airy feeling" inside with a "garden view from the bar tables", and the "ample parking" out front is a definite bonus.

Guaymas   21 | 20 | 18 | $9 |
5 Main St. (Tiburon Blvd.), Tiburon, 415-435-6300;
www.guaymas.com
An "amazing bayfront location" in Tiburon "overlooking the ferry dock" makes this "casual Mexican" "worth the stop" day or night for "tasty" margaritas on the deck and "fab views of the city skyline" across the water; *si,* service is "slow" and prices are "huge", but amigos don't mind shelling out for the "fantastic setting"; P.S. "be careful about consumption as it's a long way back to the highway."

Henry's Cocktail Lounge ⌐   ∇ 18 | 10 | 17 | $7 |
823 Main St. (3rd St.), Napa, 707-252-9815
It "used to be a secret" but "not anymore" say the "serious drinkers" and other devotees of this "true dive" that's a "Napa institution"; it's "a happening" neighborhood hangout for locals and tourists alike"(plus it gets "packed to the rafters with young singles" some nights), and while "Henry may not still be with us, the current owners" keep his spirit alive and the "cheap, stiff" spirits flowing; N.B. a recent refurb may impact the Decor score.

Hurley's Restaurant & Bar   ∇ 21 | 23 | 23 | $9 |
6518 Washington St. (Yount St.), Yountville, 707-944-2345;
www.hurleysrestaurant.com
The "best place in Yountville to watch the world walk by" may be this "lively, fun bar" and eatery that's "quickly become a Napa Valley favorite" since opening in 2002; "high ceilings, dark wood and tile floors" highlight the indoor space while "huge windows" open onto a "beautiful patio" that's "rightfully popular"; the "good wine selection" is a given, but special events like "wild game week" supply something to "look forward to."

Hydro Bar & Grill   ∇ 18 | 15 | 20 | $8 |
1403 Lincoln Ave. (Washington St.), Calistoga, 707-942-9777
Hailed as a place to get hydrated in "Napa Valley where you don't have to order wine", this "friendly" "Calistoga nightspot" slakes your thirst with 20 microbrews on tap as well as local vintages and

"great" cocktails; "good live music" makes it "lots of fun" and draws "lots of crowds."

Insalata's
22 | 21 | 21 | $9

120 Sir Francis Drake Blvd. (Barber Ave.), San Anselmo, 415-457-7700; www.insalatas.com
"Delicious cocktails and food" along with "excellent service" are in abundance at this "comfortable", "lovely" restaurant in San Anselmo known for its California-influenced Med cuisine; don't expect a swinging singles scene, but do pull up dining-room chairs or one of the handful of barstools and give the limonatas, Tunisian Breezes and other creative libations a go.

LARK CREEK INN, THE
25 | 22 | 24 | $11

234 Magnolia Ave. (Madrone Ave.), Larkspur, 415-924-7766; www.larkcreek.com
Bradley Ogden's "destination" restaurant is an "epicurean institution" set in "a wonderful old Victorian" nestled "among California redwoods" in Larkspur; the fireplace-warmed bar is "cozy and romantic on rainy winter nights", and in summer the "gorgeous garden" beckons; of course, with so much "historical charm", it's also "the type of place one might propose marriage" – so go easy on the "wonderful wines."

Last Day Saloon
17 | 11 | 18 | $6

120 Fifth St. (Davis St.), Santa Rosa, 707-545-2343; www.lastdaysaloon.com
See review in City of San Francisco Directory.

Left Bank
21 | 21 | 19 | $9

507 Magnolia St. (Ward St.), Larkspur, 415-927-3331; www.leftbank.com
The "moneyed, mellow and middle-aged relax" over "well-poured drinks" and "tasty" food at this burgeoning "upscale" brasserie mini-chain with branches outside of San Francisco, where the "delightful decor" and "gracious" sidewalk seating provide a "slice of Parisian life"; *bien sûr,* service can be "slow" and the offerings are "pricey", but they must be doing something right, as they're always "bustling."

Marin Brewing Co.
17 | 14 | 16 | $6

Larkspur Landing Shopping Ctr., 1809 Larkspur Landing Circle (Sir Francis Drake Blvd.), Larkspur, 415-461-4677; www.marinbrewing.com
Despite its "suburban" location, this spacious brewpub is a "wonderful place to go in Larkspur for housemade beer" and some "great food"; locals "catch a game at the bar" or "mingle with twentysomethings after a movie", and there's "good people-watching" on the patio – it's just "too bad it's in a mall."

MARTINI HOUSE
26 | 27 | 24 | $10

1245 Spring St. (Hwy. 29), St. Helena, 707-963-2233; www.kuleto.com
With such "spectacular surroundings" and "unique" decor, Pat Kuleto's St. Helena restaurant "feels like you're at a rich friend's house"; the "patio is as charming as it gets", and the "beautiful downstairs bar with fireplace" offers an "interesting" atmosphere in which to "enjoy a pricey martini" or some "great wines"; sociable sorts insist the "tight quarters" make "meeting others a must."

Mustards Grill   24 | 19 | 22 | $10
7399 St. Helena Hwy. (bet. Oakville & Yountville), Yountville,
707-944-2424; www.mustardsgrill.com
"Quintessential Napa", this "little jewel" is a "popular" Yountville
"landmark for good reason", offering "lots of wonderful wine
choices" and serving "simple but perfectly prepared food to go
with it"; "you'll find industry people" and the "best conversation
available" at the "cozy" bar, and fans for whom it's a "favorite"
profess the "upscale but low-key" ambiance "just feels right."

Mystic Theatre   – | – | – | M
23 Petaluma Blvd. N. (B St.), Petaluma, 707-765-2121;
www.mystictheatre.com
This "gently shabby theater", a former vaudeville house built in
1911, is today a "truly funky place" with a "large dance floor" in
Downtown Petaluma where local and national rock, blues and
roots musicians perform; a "mixed crowd" maintains it "combines
with the attached McNear's Saloon" (which itself dates from
1886) to "form a great night out" featuring "high-caliber" acts and
"reasonably" priced cocktails.

Napa Valley Opera House   ▽ 21 | 23 | 20 | $12
1030 Main St. (1st St.), Napa, 707-226-7372; www.nvoh.org
Jack London and John Philip Sousa are among the celebrity
performers who graced the stage during the heyday of this
Downtown Napa monument to the arts erected in 1880; after a
"wonderful restoration", it's once again a "cultural hub" hosting
"great" theater, music and comedy acts on its second-floor main
stage and in the smaller Cafe Theatre downstairs.

19 Broadway   16 | 11 | 17 | $5
19 Broadway Blvd. (Bolinas Rd.), Fairfax, 415-459-1091;
www.19broadway.com
"Deep in the heart of hippiedom" lies this "homey club" in "sleepy
Fairfax" that since 1984 has filled its roster nightly with "good
local rock bands", "internationally known reggae acts", blues
artists and "great jazz"; though doubters deem it a "dive", the
adjacent tiki bar run by mixologist Mr. Vise Grip is a "most welcome"
addition, and the heated "patio for smokers" is a plus.

No Name Bar ⊟   ▽ 19 | 13 | 18 | $6
757 Bridgeway (Anchor St.), Sausalito, 415-332-1392
Admirers can't be anonymous at this "friendly", "old-time favorite"
in Sausalito that supplies a "local hangout in a town where there
are almost no locals"; it's a mere "sliver of a place", though you can
always "escape the live jazz and tourists" on the "tiny back patio,
a perfect oasis on a rare warm evening", but beware the "strong
drinks" ("'no name' is usually what I can remember when I leave").

PELICAN INN   25 | 25 | 19 | $7
10 Pacific Way (Hwy. 1), Muir Beach, 415-383-6000; www.pelicaninn.com
"All that's missing is a dog howling across the moors" at this
"fantastically atmospheric British pub" in a country inn "plopped
in the middle of the Marin hills" near Muir Beach; "granted, nothing
happens here at night" if you're not sleeping over, but its ye olde
Tudor decor makes it "a great place to fall into after a day at the
beach or a hike on Mt. Tam" and "let the time unfurl over a pint or
two" at this "special hideaway."

Piazza D'Angelo
– | – | – | E

22 Miller Ave. (Throckmorton Ave.), Mill Valley, 415-388-2000;
www.dangelocatering.com

The "charming atmosphere" pairs nicely with "good Italian food"
at this "popular" restaurant in Mill Valley; the "busy bar" doubles
as a "pickup" place for "the second-time-around crowd", meaning
"patrons tend to have baggage with them", and we're not talking
Louis Vuitton suitcases; despite being "too noisy" for some tastes,
it's still "a nice place to meet friends."

Pinot Blanc
▽ 22 | 21 | 21 | $11

641 Main St. (Mills Ln.), St. Helena, 707-963-6191; www.patinagroup.com

With its Provençal country inn–inspired decor and bright, airy
design, Joachim Splichal's St. Helena outpost is a "beautiful
spot" even if all you want is to sit at the bar with a "great" glass
of wine; the patio is "wonderful in warm months" and not so bad
on chilly nights, either, thanks to the outdoor fireplace.

Rancho Nicasio
– | – | – | M

1 Old Rancheria Rd. (Nicasio Valley Rd.), Nicasio, 415-662-2219;
www.ranchonicasio.com

"Sitting at the bar" or lounging out back in the spacious patio,
"you'll feel like you're in an old Western outpost" at this circa-
1940 bar, restaurant and music venue located "out in the country"
of West Marin; it's a bit of a drive from just about anywhere, but
the roster of local and touring roots, blues, swing and country artists
means it's always "worth the trip."

Saketini
18 | 15 | 16 | $9

3900 Bel Aire Plaza (Redwood Rd.), Napa, 707-255-7423

"The place to be seen in Napa", this "fun-filled" bar lures a "young"
crowd with DJs, occasional live bands and mixed drinks (including
its namesake) that'll "knock your socks off"; inevitably, it's a
"meat market" with "too much testosterone" and a "collegiate"
atmosphere, but its rep as one of "the 'in' places" in the wine
country (and drop-in visits from "Raiders players in the summer")
keeps it kicking.

Sam's Anchor Cafe
22 | 16 | 17 | $8

27 Main St. (Tiburon Blvd.), Tiburon, 415-435-4527;
www.samscafe.com

"On a sunny day, the beautiful people are out in full force" on the
deck of this Tiburon "institution" to soak up cocktails and the
"killer views" of the Bay, Alcatraz and the San Francisco skyline;
those who've pulled anchor say you pay for those panoramas
with "expensive drinks" and proximity to patrons who "party like
high-schoolers", but "great" cocktails, "excellent oysters" and
the "relaxing" atmosphere have made it a "must" for "well-heeled"
habitués since 1920.

Silverado Brewing Company
– | – | – | I

3020A N. St. Helena Hwy. (Stice Ln.), St. Helena, 707-967-9876;
www.silveradobrewingcompany.com

There's a "great selection" of "tasty", "affordable" house ales at
this "comfortable" roadside brewpub just north of St. Helena that's
a boon for those needing "to take a rest from wine while in Napa";
those at lagerheads say it's a "little boring", but hophounds hail it
as a "definite recommend."

Silverado Resort Lounge | 22 | 20 | 21 | $11 |
Silverado Resort, 1600 Atlas Peak Rd. (Hardman Ave.), Napa, 707-257-0200; www.silveradoresort.com
"Elegant surroundings", "good food" and "attentive service" are the hallmarks of this "chic" country club, spa and resort in Napa where the fireplace-lit lounge was once the living room of a historic mansion; outdoor seating overlooks the "gorgeous" golf course and green hills, though you may share the experience with a few "conventioneers"; N.B. recent renovations may impact the Decor score.

Silver Peso | ▽ 17 | 7 | 13 | $6 |
450 Magnolia Ave. (Cane St.), Larkspur, 415-924-3448
"Nothing beats" a night knocking back "stiff Manhattans or rum and cokes" and grooving to the 1,000-CD jukebox at this "perfect dive bar" (circa 1930) in the "swanky town" of Larkspur; it's not much on looks, though "you don't go here for the atmosphere" but to "hang out with locals" and the random "biker" or to hit the "fantastic" pool tables and shuffleboard.

SUSHI RAN | 26 | 20 | 22 | $11 |
107 Caledonia St. (bet. Pine & Turney Sts.), Sausalito, 415-332-3620; www.sushiran.com
"If you're hip, then you're here" at this "phenomenal" Sausalito restaurant with an attached wine bar serving what some raw-fishionados report is the "absolute best sushi in the Bay Area, period"; the "inevitable waits" are made endurable by sipping "excellent" vinos (30 by the glass) or a "great sake martini" in the "relaxed" setting and "chatting with the approachable Marinites."

Sweetwater Saloon | 24 | 18 | 16 | $6 |
153 Throckmorton Ave. (Madrona St.), Mill Valley, 415-388-2820; www.sweetwatersaloon.com
"You never know when your favorite band" will show up for an "unannounced gig" at this "tiny" Mill Valley "institution" where it's "not unusual to see" local legends in the audience as well; though there may be "no atmosphere", "every group spawned in the Bay Area has played here" so the stardust scattered by Jerry Garcia to John Lee Hooker since 1971 creates "good vibes" and the staff "couldn't be friendlier."

1351 Lounge | – | – | – | E |
1351 Main St. (Adams St.), St. Helena, 707-963-1969; www.1351lounge.com
"Cool lighting" and a "clientele of beautiful people" help make this St. Helena "fun spot" among the "swankiest in the valley" (Napa, that is); with live music and DJs, "hefty" infused vodka drinks (local Charbay is the brand of choice) and a weekly trivia night, it's a "good place for hipsters to hang out" in what some wine-ers wail is otherwise a pretty "pedestrian" town.

Tra Vigne | 24 | 24 | 23 | $11 |
1050 Charter Oak Ave. (Main St.), St. Helena, 707-963-4444; www.travignerestaurant.com
For a "relaxing" "Tuscan night in Napa Valley", this "romantic" St. Helena "must-stop" offers a "striking" setting with a "lush porch", terrace and courtyard and a "beautiful" interior as well as "outstanding, creative" Italian fare served by a "top-notch"

staff; its adjacent enoteca Cantinetta serves 60–120 "wonderful", "top-end" wines by the glass, and on summer Sundays visiting vintners showcase their wares.

Two AM Club ⌂　　　▽ 14 | 8 | 15 | $5
380 Miller Ave. (Montford Ave.), Mill Valley, 415-388-6036
"Crusty barflies", "Marin kids back in town" and hikers and bikers fresh from a day on nearby Mt. Tamalpais mix it up at this "neighborhood dive" "lovingly referred to as 'the Deuce'" on the outskirts of Mill Valley; it's been around since 1930 and gained some attention when featured on a Huey Lewis album cover (*Sports*), but today the "drinks and pool tables are the draw" more than any celebrity drop-ins.

Uva Trattoria & Bar　　　20 | 17 | 20 | $9
1040 Clinton St. (bet. Brown & Main Sts.), Napa, 707-255-6646;
www.uvatrattoria.com
A "lively", "wonderful atmosphere", "great wines" and "friendly service" are earning uvations for this "hip hot spot" in Downtown Napa that's becoming a "required stop" whether you're "spending the evening" or just passing through; there's a "nice-sized bar" serving "good" cocktails, "incredible" small plates and "excellent" live jazz (Wednesday–Sunday).

South of San Francisco

A	D	S	C

Agenda Restaurant & Lounge | 20 | 21 | 18 | $7 |

399 S. First St. (San Salvador St.), San Jose, 408-287-3991;
www.agendalounge.com

Whether you're seeking "a martini or a salsa dance" (Wednesday nights) or even a sit-down dinner, "there's something for everyone" at this multilevel and multifaceted San Jose restaurant, club and "mellow hangout" with a new banquet facility in the works; the dance floor gets "packed" with a "good mix of people" giving it up to jazz, reggae and "great old-school music", and though some consider its multiple agendas "strange", most counter "how could you go wrong with three different bars on three different floors?"

Almaden Feed & Fuel | – | – | – | M |

18950 Almaden Rd. (Almaden Expwy.), San Jose, 408-268-8950;
www.feedandfuel.com

"You'd think you were in a country roadhouse" holler the honky-tonkers tippling beer and bourbon (and tucking into steaks and 'cue) "with the locals" at this "San Jose tradition" (it was "originally a stagecoach stop"); the "great live" acoustic acts pick up the pace on weekends, making it especially "worth a visit when you're hiking" or biking in nearby Almaden Quicksilver County Park.

Antonio's Nut House | 18 | 10 | 13 | $4 |

321 S. California Ave. (Birch St.), Palo Alto, 650-321-2550

"Everyone throws caution to the wind" at this "popular" and "cheap, cheap, cheap" "Stanford hangout" that's "the best downmarket experience in upmarket Palo Alto"; "hard-drinking contractors sit elbow-to-elbow with computer geeks" in an "unpretentious atmosphere" that's abetted by the mounds of empty "shells on the floor" (the latter thanks to the "life-size rubber gorilla" dispensing free peanuts from his cage near the bar).

Avalon | – | – | – | M |

777 Lawrence Expwy. (Homestead Rd.), Santa Clara, 408-241-0777;
www.nightclubavalon.com

A colorful mural at the bar enlivens the drink-fetching experience and offers punchy counterpoint to the swanky, moody decor at this multiroomed Santa Clara hangout; occasional live rock bands and comedy shows spice up parties like 'College Thursdays' and Saturday's mix of house, hip-hop and Top 40 whose admission price includes a buffet.

Black Watch ⌀ | 17 | 10 | 17 | $6 |

141½ N. Santa Cruz Ave. (bet. Hwy. 9 & Main St.), Los Gatos,
408-354-2200

"Make sure you have a designated driver" when patronizing this "faux biker bar" in Los Gatos, as it's "a great place to get plowed" thanks to the "large", "incredible kamikazes" ("the best you'll ever have"); it "looks scary" and it can be "claustrophobic", yet it possesses an "odd charm" that keeps its loyalists lined up "out the door on busy weekends."

Blank Club, The   – ⎹ – ⎹ – ⎹ M
44 S. Almaden Ave. (Post St.), San Jose, 408-292-5265;
www.theblankclub.com
It's sort of "rave meets rock star" at this two-year-old nightclub in
Downtown San Jose; some surveyors report it attracts a "strange
gathering of people", though the "interesting music" – live punk
and alternative bands along with DJs spinning everything from
loungecore to '80s synth pop – wipes away any blank stares.

Blowfish Sushi to Die For   23 ⎹ 24 ⎹ 20 ⎹ $9
355 Santana Row (Stevens Creek Blvd.), San Jose, 408-345-3848;
www.blowfishsushi.com
See review in City of San Francisco Directory.

Blue Chalk Cafe   17 ⎹ 17 ⎹ 15 ⎹ $8
630 Ramona St. (bet. Forest & Hamilton Aves.), Palo Alto, 650-326-1020
"Yuppies", "townies" and "Stanford MBA students" "commingle
in the name of the almighty eight ball" at this "vast" double-storied
bar and restaurant in Palo Alto with a newly revised Eclectic menu;
it may get a bit too "crowded with would-be dot-commers savoring
the good old days" (or looking to hook up), but even though it's an
"after-work madhouse", it provides "plenty of seats" so "you can
always find a place" to sit and sip an "awesome margarita."

Branham Lounge ⊖   – ⎹ – ⎹ – ⎹ I
1116 Branham Ln. (Almaden Expwy.), San Jose, 408-265-5525
"Regulars" fill the stools at this "old-school San Jose lounge" that's
been serving 'em up since 1969 and is now under new ownership;
the "occasional young swingers and poseurs", though, drop in to
check out "the beautiful *Coming to America* show" performed at
the whim of the Neil Diamond–impersonating bartender who keeps
solitary men and women entertained.

Britannia Arms of Almaden   16 ⎹ 13 ⎹ 18 ⎹ $6
5027 Almaden Expwy. (Cherry Ave.), San Jose, 408-266-0550
173 W. Santa Clara St. (bet. N. Almaden Ave. & N. San Pedro St.),
San Jose, 408-278-1400
www.britanniaarms.com
Embrace "Boddington's, bangers and football" at this pair of
"friendly", British-style pubs in San Jose that offers an "authentic
taste of London" without having to cross the pond; a few gripe the
decor's "mediocre" and karaoke nights "so loud you can't even
think", but a "rockin' weekend crowd" would beg to differ, declaring
it's also "great for sports" and live music.

British Bankers Club   18 ⎹ 18 ⎹ 18 ⎹ $7
1090 El Camino Real (Santa Cruz Ave.), Menlo Park, 650-327-8769
The "gorgeous building" is a definite turn-on for mavens of this
"Menlo Park stalwart", a "great place for an after-work drink" with
"cool pub decor" and a "warm atmosphere"; later on, it "turns
into a club scene" with DJs, karaoke and live music, so "on the
right night" it's "energetic", but hits a sour note for some as it
escalates into a "meat market" with "gold diggers" "on the prowl";
N.B. a recent renovation may outdate the Decor score.

Café Niebaum-Coppola   19 ⎹ 22 ⎹ 19 ⎹ $10
473 University Ave. (bet. Cowper & Kipling Sts.), Palo Alto, 650-752-0350;
www.cafeniebaum-coppola.com
See review in City of San Francisco Directory.

California Billiard Club   ▽ 16 | 15 | 15 | $6
881 E. El Camino Real (Dale Ave.), Mountain View, 650-965-3100;
www.californiabilliardclub.com
"From serious pool tournaments to afternoon kids' parties", this
"large", "well-lit billiards club" in Mountain View "does a great
job" keeping sharks and scratchers satisfied; it also racks up the
"Saturday night date" crowd, and with "lots of tables" (34 in all),
there's room enough for everyone to get in the game (and "good
big-screen TVs to watch while you wait").

Cinebar   – | – | – | I
69 E. San Fernando St. (2nd St.), San Jose, 408-292-9562
This "drinkers' bar" in Downtown San Jose "belongs to the locals
and a few sly dive" devotees, as it has since 1928; if "you're
looking to network" or to dance, then "don't bother", but if you're
questing after a "stiff" belt and "good conversation", then you've
found your Shangri La.

Clooney's Pub   – | – | – | I
1189 Laurel St. (Brittan Ave.), San Carlos, 650-654-7937;
www.clooneyspub.com
See review in City of San Francisco Directory.

Compadres Old Adobe   15 | 14 | 17 | $6
(fka Compadres Mexican Bar & Grill)
3877 El Camino Real (Page Mill Rd.), Palo Alto, 650-858-1141
Though it feels like an "off-campus frat party", this "classic
Stanford hangout" also keeps local Palo Alto "amigos" and "after-
workers" coming in for its "great margaritas", huge selection of
"good top-shelf tequilas" and "decent" Southwestern fare; it's
"loud" and "crowded", but that's what happens in a "fun-filled
ambiance"; N.B. a recent redo outdates the Decor score.

Deep Restaurant & Lounge   – | – | – | M
87 N. San Pedro St. (W. St. John St.), San Jose, 408-287-3337;
www.deepsj.com
Don't be afraid of the dark or the Deep when you dive into the
party-friendly waters of this splashy new San Jose dance palace
with an adjacent seafood restaurant; the big, burly 10,000-sq.-ft.
space boasts four different rooms, featuring guest DJs spinning
Reggaeton, salsa, merengue and hip-hop, with an expansive
outdoor patio to boot; N.B. open Thursday–Saturday.

E&O Trading Company   20 | 21 | 18 | $8
96 S. First St. (San Fernando St.), San Jose, 408-938-4100;
www.eotrading.com
See review in City of San Francisco Directory.

Elephant Bar & Restaurant   18 | 19 | 16 | $8
1600 Old Bayshore Hwy. (bet. Broadway & Millbrae Ave.), Burlingame,
650-259-9585
499 E. Hamilton Ave. (Hwy. 17), Campbell, 408-871-8401
19780 Stevens Creek Blvd. (N. Portal Ave.), Cupertino, 408-865-0701
www.elephantbar.com
Herds of "singles" keep the scene "buzzing" at these "popular"
"jungle safari"–themed chain outposts that double as "decent
neighborhood bars"; thirsty explorers extol the "great drinks" and
"good people-watching", but dissidents stampede the "noisy"
ambiance and "prefab" interiors as "suburbia's attempt at hipness."

Empire Grill & Tap Room   20 | 21 | 19 | $9

651 Emerson St. (bet. Forest & Hamilton Aves.), Palo Alto, 650-321-3030

"Those looking for a quieter place" and maybe a fine pint or two gather at this "convivial upscale bar" that, as the name might imply, offers the "best tap selection in Downtown Palo Alto"; there's a "magical" "heated garden" as well, and while some whine it's "full of snotty Stanford brats", most applaud the "nice mix" of college kids, locals and "mellow thirtysomethings", adding "thank god the staff has finally moved beyond its dot-com attitude."

Evvia   24 | 23 | 23 | $10

420 Emerson St. (bet. Lytton & University Aves.), Palo Alto, 650-326-0983; www.evvia.net

Watch "Palo Alto's old and new money sipping wine" at this "lovely" "Silicon Valley power restaurant" (sister to San Francisco's Kokkari Estiatorio) serving "classy" cocktails and "wonderful Mediterranean food"; the "ambiance is excellent", but be warned there are only a handful of chairs at the "cute", "sophisticated bar", a "coveted" spot that "can be crowded" (and "deservedly so") "as people wait for tables."

Fanny & Alexander   17 | 15 | 15 | $8

1108 Burlingame Ave. (California Dr.), Burlingame, 650-343-5654
412 Emerson St. (University Ave.), Palo Alto, 650-326-7183
www.fannyalexander.com

"Get ready for the singles scene on steroids" assert survivors of this pair of "Silicon Valley yuppie" playgrounds offering DJs and "great outdoor areas"; since "rowdy" behavior and a "discouraging cover charge" happen all too often, detractors suggest "if you're this close to the city, then just keep going north"; N.B. the San Jose branch closed.

Faultline Brewing Company   16 | 17 | 16 | $7

1235 Oakmead Pkwy. (Lawrence Expwy.), Sunnyvale, 408-736-2739; www.faultlinebrewing.com

"Expect to see your coworkers" and perhaps "the founder of the next big thing" tipping back "great" housemade ales and "decent bar food" at this Sunnyvale brewpub; it "caters to the after-work crowd" ("heavy on the Silicon Valley vibes"), with patio seating and a "view of a lake" providing a brief respite for desk jockeys, though faultfinders fuss it "has no personality"; N.B. closed Saturday and Sunday.

Fibbar Magees   17 | 14 | 15 | $6

156 S. Murphy Ave. (bet. Evelyn & Washington Aves.), Sunnyvale, 408-749-8373; www.fibbars.com

Molly Magees

241 Castro St. (bet. Dana & Villa Sts.), Mountain View, 650-961-0108; www.fibbars.com

Neither Fibbar Magees in Sunnyvale nor Molly Magees in Mountain View may be "much to look at" but it sure is "fun to hang around" this pair of "appealing, authentic pubs"; filled with the "30-and-under" set, they're naturally "noisy and crowded" with folks getting fubar, especially on big-game days or weekend DJ parties, but overall they boast a "laid-back Irish feel" that makes them "great" for chilling with friends.

Forge in the Forest, The   – | – | – | E
Fifth & Junipero Aves., Carmel, 831-624-2233;
www.forgeintheforest.com
"A gracious drinking experience" awaits at this tree-canopied
Carmel bar and restaurant that's within "easy walking distance to
wherever you'll be" in town; the "beautiful" tavern's "awesome
atmosphere" derives from its roots as a blacksmith shop as well
as the literary stars who've bent elbows by the fireplace including
John Steinbeck and Henry Miller; N.B. there's now a new banquet
room for private parties.

GORDON BIERSCH   17 | 15 | 16 | $8
640 Emerson St. (bet. Forest & Hamilton Aves.), Palo Alto,
650-323-7723
33 E. San Fernando St. (bet. 1st & 2nd Sts.), San Jose,
408-294-6785
www.gordonbiersch.com
See review in City of San Francisco Directory.

Hedley Club   – | – | – | E
Hotel De Anza, 233 W. Santa Clara St. (Almaden Rd.), San Jose,
408-286-1000; www.hoteldeanza.com
"Downtown San Jose's exquisitely restored pink stucco De Anza
Hotel", which dates back to 1931 and once hosted guests from
Eleanor Roosevelt to Jack Dempsey, "deserves no less" than the
"cool atmosphere" of this art deco "treasure" gracing its ground
floor; you can listen to live music on Friday and Saturday nights,
enjoy a cigar on the outdoor patio or indulge in a cocktail "without
having to shout."

HIGHLANDS INN   28 | 28 | 24 | $11
Park Hyatt Carmel Highlands Inn, 120 Highlands Dr. (Hwy. 1),
Carmel, 831-620-1234; www.hyatt.com
From its perch over the Pacific with seats "overlooking rock cliffs,
swirling surf and sea otters", this circa-1917 Carmel resort is "an
enchanting way to experience the California coast"; vistaphiles
can partake of "gorgeous sunsets" from two "romantic" lounges
(one featuring live entertainment) or the "lovely" restaurant
and drink "luxe" wines served by a "great" staff; though it's no
longer independently owned, "not even Hyatt could dull the shine
on this classic."

Hog's Breath Inn   19 | 16 | 16 | $8
San Carlos St. (bet. 5th & 6th Aves.), Carmel, 831-625-1044;
www.hogsbreathinn.net
"Meet and mingle on the patio" of this Western-themed chuck
wagon, which is "still the place to see and be seen for outdoor
dining in Carmel" thanks to the high profile of former owner Clint
Eastwood; the good: "on an overcast day" it's hard to beat "sitting
outside" at a table "in front of a fireplace"; the bad: it's "as much
tourist attraction as bar"; and the ugly: it's "overpriced" and "over
the hill" say those whose day was definitely not made here.

Improv, The   ∇ 24 | 18 | 18 | $8
Jose Theatre, 62 S. Second St. (bet. E. San Fernando &
E. Santa Clara Sts.), San Jose, 408-280-7475; www.improv.com
Jolson and Houdini may have disappeared from its stage, but
"outstanding performances" still abound at this vaudeville-era

Jose Theatre that was renovated in 2002 ("South Bay finally did something right"); "lots of interesting" folks are here to have "fun" provided by the nationally known comedians, and it's definitely a "good first-date" destination.

Knuckles Sports Bar   17 | 14 | 17 | $8
Hyatt Rickeys, 4219 El Camino Real (Charleston Rd.), Palo Alto, 650-352-1234; www.hyatt.com
See review in City of San Francisco Directory.

Left Bank   21 | 21 | 19 | $9
635 Santa Cruz Ave. (Doyle St.), Menlo Park, 650-473-6543
1100-377 Santana Row (Olin Ave.), San Jose, 408-984-3500
1100 Park Pl. (David St.), San Mateo, 650-345-2250
www.leftbank.com
See review in North of San Francisco Directory.

Los Gatos Brewing Company   21 | 19 | 19 | $7
130G N. Santa Cruz Ave. (Grays Ln.), Los Gatos, 408-395-9929; www.lgbrewingco.com
This "upscale, barnlike brewpub" is located "in tony Los Gatos and feels like it", as it attracts "lots of young multimillionaires" for its "hopping weekend scene"; it's also a "nice place to celebrate a high-tech milestone with your team" or to simply "enjoy the beer and the youngish crowd", though keep in mind it can be "highly pretentious" despite having "not much style."

MacArthur Park   17 | 17 | 18 | $9
27 University Ave. (bet. Alma St. & El Camino Real), Palo Alto, 650-321-9990; www.macpark.com
See review in City of San Francisco Directory.

Max's Opera Cafe   16 | 14 | 16 | $8
1250 Old Bayshore Hwy. (Broadway), Burlingame, 650-342-6297
711 Stanford Shopping Ctr. (Sand Hill Rd.), Palo Alto, 650-323-6297
www.maxsworld.com
See review in City of San Francisco Directory.

NOLA   21 | 21 | 17 | $9
535 Ramona St. (bet. Hamilton & University Aves.), Palo Alto, 650-328-2722; www.nolas.com
"It's Mardi Gras every day at this popular Cajun restaurant" in Downtown Palo Alto, and the "young, exuberant" crowd of celebrants can be "as thick as a humid Louisiana night"; the "open, airy courtyard" is a "fun scene" in winter, and the outsider art in the interior evokes "Andy Warhol's childhood bedroom"; "classic New Orleans drinks" and other "volatile cocktails" keep it "rockin' at happy hour" and beyond.

Oasis   19 | 13 | 17 | $5
241 El Camino Real (Cambridge Ave.), Menlo Park, 650-326-8896; www.theoasisbeergarden.com
"History is literally carved into the decor" of this "venerable burger and beer joint" in Menlo Park "favored by Stanford students and alumni" who wade through "peanut shells on the floor" to sit at "graffiti"-engraved tables on "hard wooden benches" and reminisce over "cheap pitchers"; "yes, it's a dive", but that's "part of its charm", and "if you want ostentation, go elsewhere."

Old Pro

– | – | – | M

541 Ramona St. (bet. Hamilton & University Aves.), Palo Alto, 650-326-1446

"Satisfy that burger and beer craving" and "overdose on ESPN" at the same time with a visit to this rookie iteration of a "great sports bar" in Palo Alto; the original on El Camino Real was "a total dump", and though some feel the latest Pro is "trying too hard to make an impression", with a "good beer selection", expanded menu and 26 screens, this incarnation may be the "best place to watch a game on the Peninsula."

Palo Alto Bowl

15 | 11 | 15 | $6

4329 El Camino Real (San Antonio Rd.), Palo Alto, 650-948-1031; www.fun2spare.com

"Yay for drunken bowling" is the cheer on 'Thirsty Thursdays' at this Palo Alto pin parlor and singles magnet that attracts "geeks from Stanford and Silicon Valley"; while "the scenery isn't going to win" any awards, it also offers "great karaoke", and cynics sigh "it is what it is and in this town, that's refreshing."

Pedro's Restaurant & Cantina

15 | 16 | 16 | $7

316 N. Santa Cruz Ave. (Hwy. 9), Los Gatos, 408-354-7570
3935 Freedom Circle (Mission College Blvd.), Santa Clara, 408-496-6777
www.pedrosrestaurants.com

"Be prepared to rub elbows with Silicon Valley nerds" at this pair of Mexican cantinas whose convenient locations in Los Gatos and Santa Clara make them "after-work" "techie" magnets; the "house margaritas will knock you on your butt", but bashers boo it as a bit of "a poor man's happy-hour joint" with "spotty" service and "nothing-special" food.

Pisces

20 | 23 | 22 | $11

1190 California Dr. (Broadway), Burlingame, 650-401-7500; www.aqua-sf.com

Expect a "high level of satisfaction" from this "delightful" sister to SF's Aqua that's housed in an "old train station" next to the Caltrain tracks in Downtown Burlingame; it "feels sophisticated and homey at the same time", and the "small, comfortable" bar up front is a "great place for champagne and oysters" or a "first-date drink."

Restaurant at Mission Ranch, The

▽ 25 | 19 | 21 | $7

26270 Dolores St. (15th Ave.), Carmel, 831-625-9040; www.missionranchcarmel.com

Locals and in-the-know visitors alike believe there's "something special" about this 19th-century property in Carmel that's served time as a dairy farm, resort and officer's club before Clint Eastwood bought it in 1986, rescuing it from the bulldozers of developers; "head out to the patio and have a drink with a view" of the crashing waves and in the distance Point Lobos, or settle into the lounge for "great piano sing-alongs."

Rose & Crown Pub, The

18 | 11 | 17 | $5

547 Emerson St. (bet. Hamilton & University Aves.), Palo Alto, 650-327-7673

"Although dominated by Stanford grads and students, the scene" at this "hole-in-the-wall British pub" is "less yuppified than the rest of Palo Alto", and with "good beers on tap" (no liquor) and "tasty fish 'n' chips", it's "perfect for knocking back a few with friends"; there's jazz on Sundays, comedy on Mondays and Tuesday "trivia nights are a hoot", plus the "jukebox is awesome" all week long – just "beware errant darts."

Roy's   22 | 22 | 23 | $11 |
Inn at Spanish Bay, 2700 17 Mile Dr. (Congress Rd.), Pebble Beach, 831-647-7423; www.roysrestaurant.com
See review in City of San Francisco Directory.

Rudy's Pub   19 | 10 | 15 | $7 |
117 University Ave. (bet. Alma & High Sts.), Palo Alto, 650-329-0922; www.elbe-restaurant.com
"A perfect dive-bar escape in otherwise upscale Palo Alto", this "relaxed" pub serving German beers has a "neighborhood feel during the week"; Thursday through Saturday, though, "great dance music" including "really good hip-hop" transforms it into a "good-time" dance club that supporters call "one of the better singles scenes" around and critics chide as "cheesy."

Running Iron Restaurant & Saloon   – | – | – | M |
24 E. Carmel Valley Rd. (Via Contenta), Carmel Valley, 831-659-4633
The wild, wild West lives on at this long-running "informal" Carmel Valley eatery, a "great place for families" looking for a friendly meal and old thirsty cowboys; enjoy the outside patio or canter to the bar that seats a few dozen, not counting your horse, of course.

Spago Palo Alto   22 | 24 | 23 | $11 |
265 Lytton Ave. (bet. Bryant & Ramona Sts.), Palo Alto, 650-833-1000; www.wolfgangpuck.com
"Sidle up to the bar" of Wolfgang Puck's Palo Alto outpost and "feel like a venture capitalist" sipping "excellent" wines or "killer margaritas" in "posh", "lovely surroundings"; antagonists aver it's a "hoity-toity" "scene for power parents" who "brag about their kids' math tests", but it's still a "place to see and be seen."

Steelhead Brewing Company   20 | 18 | 18 | $6 |
333 California Dr. (Burlingame Ave.), Burlingame, 650-344-6050; www.steelheadbrewery.com
A "sporty crowd" gathers at this "cavernous" brewpub "in the heart of Downtown Burlingame" to sip "well-crafted" beers, watch the game and "shoot pool in the classy dark-wood hall" in the back; an outpost of the Oregon mother ship, it may be "typical" and "somewhat noisy", but it's certainly "good enough for the 'burbs", so "sink into one of the armchairs and lounge, baby!"

Stinger Lounge   – | – | – | M |
38 E. 25th Ave. (El Camino Real), San Mateo, 650-571-8486
"If you didn't know better, you'd think you were in a trendy SF spot" when you enter this slinky "little find" that sprouted up in 2003 "out in the middle of nowhere" in San Mateo; '60s-style decor, DJs spinning down-tempo and progressive house and a "good" cocktail menu attract a "dressy clientele" and produce a "great" vibe; N.B. try the wine tastings the first Monday of every month.

Stoa   – | – | – | E |
632 Emerson St. (Hamilton Ave.), Palo Alto, 650-328-2600; www.stoarestaurant.com
Recently relocated closer to Downtown Palo Alto, this revamped Peninsula staple still offers its trademark upscale vegetarian fare

(and now seafood as well) and also doubles as a *vin* venue; numerous selections by the glass or bottle are poured nightly in the elegant wine bar, which also boasts live jazz three nights a week.

St. Stephen's Green | 19 | 15 | 18 | $7 |
223 Castro St. (Villa St.), Mountain View, 650-964-9151; www.st-stephens-green.com
This "laid-back" Irish pub in the Peninsula attracts a "chilled-out" group of "after-workers" during the week with lots of beers on tap and a "great" staff, and becomes "quite the scene" from Thursday to Saturday nights with "DJs who know how to work a crowd"; though detractors declare it's "devoid of character", cynics say it's "not bad if you're unlucky enough to be going out" in Mountain View; N.B. the Los Altos branch closed.

Tamarine | – | – | – | E |
546 University Ave. (bet. Cowper & Webster Sts.), Palo Alto, 650-325-8500; www.tamarinerestaurant.com
Martini mavens seeking sophistication on suburban turf escape to this upscale Vietnamese lounge and restaurant in Palo Alto; the cocktail list brims with classics (try a Negroni, a stinger or a Pimm's Cup) and the small plates are built for sharing, so it's little wonder that the elegant bar buzzes from happy hour onward.

Tarpy's Roadhouse | 23 | 22 | 24 | $9 |
2999 Monterey-Salinas Hwy. (Canyon Del Ray Blvd.), Monterey, 831-647-1444; www.tarpys.com
Bask in the bucolic views from the "relaxing", "idyllic" garden patio or sit at the bar and soak up the feel of the 1917 homestead that forms the foundation of this Monterey restaurant; sure, it's a bit "out of the way", but the "service is great" and the "food always comes out right" at this "casual" but "classy place."

Tied House Cafe & Brewery | 18 | 15 | 18 | $7 |
954 Villa St. (bet. Bryant & Franklin Sts.), Mountain View, 650-965-2739
San Pedro Sq., 65 N. San Pedro St. (Santa Clara St.), San Jose, 408-295-2739
www.tiedhouse.com
These "casual microbreweries" in Mountain View and San Jose are "always a safe choice", attracting a "techie crowd" after work for "fresh suds" and "fried and salted grub"; the "pretty patios" are "great for groups", though on game night in Sharks territory the "large bar" gets entirely "packed" with folks who don't care that the decor's about as "charming as a train station waiting hall."

Trader Vic's | – | – | – | E |
4261 El Camino Real (Dinahs Ct.), Palo Alto; www.tradervics.com
See review in City of San Francisco Directory.

Trials Pub | – | – | – | M |
265 N. First St. (bet. Devine & Julian Sts.), San Jose, 408-947-0497; www.trialspub.com
Insiders insist this "awesome", "authentic British pub" is "one of San Jose's better-kept secrets" but the jury's jubilant over the "good selection" of beers on tap and "low-key" atmosphere with nary a TV in sight; its circa-1894 building previously served as a brothel, jail and railroad workers' residence, though these days the "little hole-in-the-wall" is simply a "gem."

23 Club ✍   – | – | – | M |
23 Visitacion Ave. (San Francisco Ave.), Brisbane, 415-467-7717
From the stuffed buffalo head over the stage to the Bud bottles
amassing at the tables, this Brisbane honky-tonk is the real deal, so
no wonder just about every country star of the '50s and '60s turned
beers into tears here; since falling from the hands of longtime
owners the DeMarco family, the joint has weathered changes,
and at press time had a new owner once again, but nevertheless
remains a one-of-a-kind spot for C&W, Cajun and rockabilly bands.

Zibibbo   23 | 23 | 21 | $10 |
430 Kipling St. (bet. Lytton & University Aves.), Palo Alto, 650-328-6722
The Palo Alto sister to SF's Azie and Lulu, this "bustling, upscale"
Mediterranean "surfed the dot-com wave but didn't crash" and
remains the "place to rub shoulders with the well-to-do" of the
Peninsula; there's a fireplace in the "romantic" garden for cool
evenings, a separate wine cafe offering over 60 by the glass and a
"dark", "refined bar" that's a "strong attraction in itself"; anywhere
you sit, it's "worth lingering" over a "great" drink or two.

Indexes

LOCATIONS
SPECIAL APPEALS

All nightspots are in San Francisco unless otherwise noted (E=East of San Francisco; N=North of San Francisco; S=South of San Francisco).

LOCATIONS

CITY OF SAN FRANCISCO

Bayview/Hunter's Point
Pound-SF
Space 550

Bernal Heights
Chaise Lounge
Liberty Cafe
Wild Side West

Castro
Badlands
Bar on Castro
Café
Cafe Flore
Daddy's
Harvey's
Lime
Men's Room
Metro City Bar
Midnight Sun
Mix
Moby Dick
Pendulum
2223 Restaurant
Twin Peaks
Whiskey Lounge

China Basin/Dogpatch
Cafe Cocomo
Dogpatch
Jelly's
Kelly's
Ramp
Sno-Drift
Sublounge

Chinatown
Bow Bow Lounge
Buddha Bar
Li Po
Mr. Bing's

Cow Hollow
Balboa Cafe
Bayside Sports
Betelnut Pejiu Wu
Black Horse Pub
Blue Light
Brazen Head
Bus Stop
City Tavern
Comet Club
Eastside West
Left/Albuquerque

Liverpool Lil's
Mas Sake
MatrixFillmore
Mauna Loa
Perry's
Rica

Downtown
Aqua
Bacchus Kirk
B44
Biscuits & Blues
BIX
Bubble Lounge
Cafe Bastille
Café Claude
Campton Place
Carnelian Room
C. Bobby's Owl Tree
Cityscape
Club EZ5
Cortez
E&O Trading Co.
850 Cigar Bar
Farallon
Fifth Floor
First Crush
Frisson
Gold Dust Lounge
Grand Cafe
Grandviews Lounge
Harrington's B&G
Harry Denton Starlight
House of Shields
Irish Bank
Johnny Foley's
John's Grill
Kokkari Estiatorio
La Scene
Le Central Bistro
Le Colonial
Lefty O'Doul's
London Wine
MacArthur Park
Mandarin Lounge
Michael Mina
Millennium
Myth
Occidental Cigar
Perry's
Pied Piper Bar
Plouf
Plush Room

Ponzu
Postrio
Punchline Comedy
Red Room
Redwood Room
Royal Exchange
Rubicon
Ruby Skye
Scala's Bistro
Seasons Bar
Tadich Grill
Tunnel Top
View Lounge
Voda
Warfield

Embarcadero

Americano
Beale St. B&G
Boulevard
butterfly
Chaya Brasserie
Equinox
Ferry Plaza Wine
Fog City Diner
Gordon Biersch
Grumpy's Pub
Houston's
La Suite
MarketBar
One Market
Ozumo
Palomino
Pier 23 Cafe
Shanghai 1930
Slanted Door
13 Views
Tonno Rosso

Fisherman's Wharf

Ana Mandara
Buena Vista
Fiddler's Green
Gary Danko
Hard Rock Cafe
Jack's Cannery Bar
Knuckles Sports
Lou's Pier 47
McCormick/Kuleto's
Red Jack
Suede

Glen Park

Glen Park Station

Haight-Ashbury/
Cole Valley

Club Deluxe
Eos

Finnegan's Wake
Gold Cane
Hobson's Choice
Kan Zaman
Kezar Bar
Kezar Pub
Magnolia Pub
Milk Bar
Murio's Trophy
Trax
Zam Zam

Hayes Valley/Civic Center

Absinthe
Hôtel Biron
Jade Bar
Jardinière
Marlena's
Martuni's
Michael's Octavia
Place Pigalle
Rickshaw Stop
Sauce
Soluna
Suppenküche
Trader Vic's
Zuni Cafe

Inner Richmond

Alpha Bar
Bitter End
Blue Danube Coffee
540 Club
Ireland's 32
Last Day Saloon
Pig & Whistle
Plough & Stars
RoHan Lounge
Would You Believe

Inner Sunset

Blackthorn Tavern
Canvas Cafe
Eldo's Grill
Fireside Bar
Little Shamrock
Mucky Duck
Yancy's

Japantown

Winterland

Laurel Heights

Cafe Lo Cubano

Lower Haight

An Bodhran
Cafe International
Mad Dog in Fog

Molotov
Movida Lounge
Nickie's BBQ
Noc Noc
Toronado
Underground SF

Marina

Ace Wasabi's
Bar None
Black Magic
Cozmo's Corner
Delaney's
Final Final
Gravity
Grove
HiFi
Horseshoe
Nectar Wine

Mission District

Alma
Amnesia
Andalu
Argus Lounge
Atlas Cafe
Attic Club
Beauty Bar
Benders
Bissap Baobab
Blondie's Bar
Blowfish Sushi
Bruno's
Cafe Macondo
Cama
Casanova
Cha Cha Cha
Circolo
Clooney's Pub
Dalva
Delirium Cocktails
Doc's Clock
Dovre Club
Dylan's
Elbo Room
Elixir
El Rio
Esta Noche
500 Club
Foreign Cinema
Hush Hush Lounge
Keane's 3300
Kilowatt
La Rondalla
Last Supper Club
Laszlo
Latin Amer. Club
Levende

Lexington Club
Liberties
Lone Palm
Luna Park
Make-Out Room
Monkey Club
Odeon
Oxygen Bar
Papa Toby's
Phoenix
Phone Booth
Pink
Puerto Alegre
Ramblas
Rite Spot Cafe
Roccapulco
Savanna Jazz
Skylark
Slow Club
Tokyo Go Go
Treat Street
12 Galaxies
Uptown
Whisper
Zeitgeist

Nob Hill

Big 4
C&L
Front Room
Lobby Lounge
Lobby/Ritz-Carlton
Tonga Room
Top of the Mark

Noe Valley

Bliss Bar
Dubliner
Noe's
Noe Valley Ministry

North Beach

Bamboo Hut
Beat Lounge
Bimbo's 365 Club
Bocce Cafe
Café Niebaum-Cop.
Café Prague
Caffè Greco
Caffe Puccini
Caffe Trieste
Capp's Corner
Centerfolds
Cobb's Comedy
Columbus Café
Crow Bar
Dolce
Enrico's Sidewalk

downtown
Freight & Salvage
Jupiter
La Peña Cultural
924 Gilman
Paragon
Pyramid Brewery
Raleigh's
Shattuck Ave. Spats
Shattuck Down Low
Skates on Bay
Starry Plough
Triple Rock Brewery

Concord
Elephant Bar

Emeryville
Kimball's East
Townhouse B&G
Trader Vic's

Fremont
Elephant Bar
Saddle Rack

Oakland
Alley
At Seventeenth

Ben & Nick's
Bench & Bar
Cafe Van Kleef
Cato's Ale House
Conga Lounge
Fat Lady
5th Amendment
Golden Bull
Heinold's Saloon
Kingman's
Luka's Taproom
Oliveto Cafe
Pacific Coast Brew.
Paramount Theater
Parkway Speakeasy
Radio Bar
Ruby Room
Stork Club
White Horse
Wildcard B&G
Yoshi's

Pleasant Hill
Left Bank

Walnut Creek
Pyramid Brewery
Spoontonic Lounge

NORTH OF SAN FRANCISCO

Calistoga
Calistoga Inn
Hydro B&G

Fairfax
Café Amsterdam
19 Broadway

Larkspur
E&O Trading Co.
Lark Creek Inn
Left Bank
Marin Brewing
Silver Peso

Mill Valley
Buckeye Roadhouse
Frantoio
Piazza D'Angelo
Sweetwater Saloon
Two AM Club

Napa
Café Society
Caffe Cicero
Cole's Chop House
COPIA
Henry's Cocktail

Napa Valley
Saketini
Silverado Resort
Uva Trattoria

Novato
Boca

Petaluma
Mystic Theatre

Rutherford
Auberge du Soleil

San Anselmo
Insalata's

Santa Rosa
Last Day Saloon

Sausalito
Caffe Trieste
No Name Bar
Sushi Ran

St. Helena
Ana's Cantina
Martini House
Pinot Blanc

Silverado Brewing
1351 Lounge
Tra Vigne

Tiburon
Guaymas
Sam's Anchor Cafe

West Marin/Olema
Pelican Inn
Rancho Nicasio

Yountville
Bouchon
Hurley's
Mustards Grill

SOUTH OF SAN FRANCISCO

Brisbane
23 Club

Burlingame
Elephant Bar
Fanny & Alexander
Max's Opera
Pisces
Steelhead Brew.

Campbell
Elephant Bar

Carmel/Monterey Peninsula
Forge in Forest
Highlands Inn
Hog's Breath Inn
Rest. at Mission Ranch
Roy's
Tarpy's Roadhouse

Carmel Valley
Running Iron

Cupertino
Elephant Bar

Los Gatos
Black Watch
Los Gatos Brewing
Pedro's

Menlo Park
British Bankers Club
Left Bank
Oasis

Mountain View
Cal. Billiard Club
Fibbar/Molly Magees
St. Stephen's
Tied House Cafe

Palo Alto
Antonio's Nut Hse.
Blue Chalk Cafe
Café Niebaum-Cop.
Compadres Adobe
Empire Grill

Evvia
Fanny & Alexander
Gordon Biersch
Knuckles Sports
MacArthur Park
Max's Opera
Nola
Old Pro
Palo Alto Bowl
Rose & Crown
Rudy's Pub
Spago Palo Alto
Stoa
Tamarine
Trader Vic's
Zibibbo

San Carlos
Clooney's Pub

San Jose
Agenda
Almaden Feed
Blank Club
Blowfish Sushi
Branham Lounge
Britannia Arms
Cinebar
Deep
E&O Trading Co.
Gordon Biersch
Hedley Club
Improv
Left Bank
Tied House Cafe
Trials Pub

San Mateo
Left Bank
Stinger Lounge

Santa Clara
Avalon
Pedro's

Sunnyvale
Faultline Brewing
Fibbar/Molly Magees

SPECIAL APPEALS

(Indexes list the best in each category. Multi-location
nightspots' features may vary by branch. For some
categories, schedules may vary; call ahead or check
Web sites for the most up-to-date information.)

Additions

Alpha Bar
Americano
At Seventeenth/E
Bacchus Kirk
Bar 821
Bench & Bar/E
Blur
Boca/N
Cafe Lo Cubano
Cama
C&L
Chaise Lounge
Cip
Circolo
Deep/S
Dolce
Eight
Element Lounge
Frisson
Gallery Lounge
Golden Bull/E
Jack Falstaff
La Suite
Levende
Lime
Luella
Luka's Taproom/E
Madrone Lounge
Michael Mina
Michael's Octavia
Mighty
Myth
Nectar Wine
Oola
Prive Lounge
Red Eye Lounge
Rica
Riptide
RX Gallery
Sauce
Soluna
Stoa/S
Swig
Tamarine/S
Tonno Rosso
Trader Vic's/E/S
222 Club
Underground SF
VinoVenue
Whiskey Thieves
Wildcard B&G/E
Winterland

After Work

Ace Wasabi's
Americano
Aqua
Attic Club
Badlands
Beale St. B&G
Bell Tower
BIX
Blue Chalk Cafe/S
British Bankers Club/S
Chaya Brasserie
Cosmopolitan
Crow Bar
Dave's
Dovre Club
E&O Trading Co./S
Empire Grill/S
Faultline Brewing/S
Ferry Plaza Wine
Finnegan's Wake
Fly
Gallery Lounge
Gold Dust Lounge
Gordon Biersch
Grumpy's Pub
Harrington's B&G
Harry's
Harvey's
Houston's
Il Pirata
Irish Bank
Jade Bar
Kate O'Brien's
Kezar Pub
London Wine
Luna Lounge
MacArthur Park
Marin Brewing/N
Moose's
Occidental Cigar

111 Minna
One Market
Oola
Ozumo
Pacific Coast Brew./E
Perry's
Pied Piper Bar
Pier 23 Cafe
Plouf
Rest. LuLu
Royal Exchange
San Fran. Brewing
Slanted Door
Specs Bar
St. Stephen's/S
Tadich Grill
Thirsty Bear Brewing
Tied House Cafe/S
Tonno Rosso
Tunnel Top
Varnish Fine Art
XYZ
Zeitgeist
Zuni Cafe

Art Bars

Atlas Cafe
Cafe Van Kleef/E
Cama
Canvas Cafe
Gallery Lounge
Hôtel Biron
Madrone Lounge
Make-Out Room
111 Minna
RX Gallery
Studio Z
Tamarine/S
Varnish Fine Art

Beautiful People

Absinthe
Amber
Ana Mandara
Aqua
bacar
Betelnut Pejiu Wu
BIX
Bliss Bar
Boulevard
Bubble Lounge
César/E
Cozmo's Corner
Dolce
Element Lounge
Farallon
Frisson

g bar
Jade Bar
Jardinière
Laszlo
Le Central Bistro
Le Colonial
Lime
MatrixFillmore
Mecca
Michael Mina
Myth
Ozumo
Postrio
Redwood Room
Rose Pistola
Ruby Skye
Shanghai 1930
Spago Palo Alto/S
Suede
Sushi Groove So.
1351 Lounge/N
Tonic

Biker Bars

Crow Bar
Eagle Tavern
Hole in the Wall
Lone Star
Thee Parkside
Toronado
Two AM Club/N
Zeitgeist

Blues

Beach Chalet
Biscuits & Blues
Boom Boom Rm.
Caffe Cicero/N
Club Deluxe
Hydro B&G/N
Ivy Room/E
Kimball's East/E
Last Day Saloon/N
Lou's Pier 47
19 Broadway/N
Rancho Nicasio/N
Riptide
Saloon
Slim's
Sweetwater Saloon/N

Bottle Service

At Seventeenth/E
Bambuddha Lounge
Circolo
Dolce
Element Lounge
Fluid

Frisson
Loft 11
Mezzanine
Paradise Lounge
Pink
Prive Lounge
Red Eye Lounge
Ruby Skye
Sno-Drift
Suede
suite one8one
Whisper
XYZ

Cabaret

AsiaSF
Aunt Charlie's
Café Society/N
Marlena's
Mecca
Plush Room
Purple Onion

Coffeehouses

Atlas Cafe
Bazaar Café
Blue Danube Coffee
Cafe Abir
Cafe Flore
Cafe International
Cafe Lo Cubano
Cafe Macondo
Café Prague
Café Royale
Caffè Greco
Caffe Puccini
Caffe Trieste/E/N
Grove
Mario's Bohemian
Orbit Room Cafe
Simple Pleasures
Steps of Rome

Comedy Clubs

Cobb's Comedy
Improv/S
Punchline Comedy
Purple Onion

Cross-Dressing

AsiaSF
Aunt Charlie's
Café
Divas
Esta Noche
Harvey's
N'Touch
Stud

Dancing

Agenda/S
Ashkenaz/E
AsiaSF
At Seventeenth/E
Badlands
Bamboo Hut
Bambuddha Lounge
Bench & Bar/E
Bimbo's 365 Club
Biscuits & Blues
Bissap Baobab
Blakes/Telegraph/E
Bohemia Bar
Boom Boom Rm.
Buzz 9
Cafe Cocomo
Cat Club
Cherry Bar
Circolo
Club EZ5
Club Hide
Club Six
Deep/S
Delirium Cocktails
Divas
DNA Lounge
Dolce
Elbo Room
Element Lounge
El Rio
Endup
Esta Noche
Factory 525
Fanny & Alexander/S
Fiddler's Green
Fillmore
Frisson
Glas Kat
Golden Bull/E
Gravity
Great Amer. Music
Harry Denton Starlight
Harvey's
HiFi
House of Shields
Hush Hush Lounge
Ireland's 32
Jelly's
Jillian's
Johnny Foley's
Kan Zaman
Kimo's
Levende
Lit Lounge
Luka's Taproom/E
Luna Lounge

Mad Dog in Fog
Madrone Lounge
Make-Out Room
MatrixFillmore
Metronome Dance
Mezzanine
Mighty
Milk Bar
Mitchell Bros.
Mystic Theatre/N
Nickie's BBQ
19 Broadway/N
N'Touch
Ozumo
Pink
Plough & Stars
Ramp
Rancho Nicasio/N
Red Eye Lounge
Rickshaw Stop
Roccapulco
Ruby Skye
Rudy's Pub/S
Saddle Rack/E
Saloon
1751 Social
Shanghai 1930
Shattuck Down Low/E
Skylark
Soluna
Space 550
St. Stephen's/S
Stud
Sublounge
Suede
suite one8one
Ten 15 Club
330 Ritch
Tonga Room
Tongue & Groove
Top of the Mark
12 Galaxies
Velvet Lounge
Whisper
White Horse/E
Wildcard B&G/E

Dives

Acme Bar/E
Alley/E
Aunt Charlie's
Branham Lounge/S
Cinebar/S
Clooney's Pub
Club Mallard/E
Doc's Clock
Eagle's Drift In

Expansion Bar
Final Final
Finnegan's Wake
500 Club
Glen Park Station
Gold Cane
Golden Bull/E
Grumpy's Pub
Ha Ra
Hotsy Totsy/E
Ireland's 32
Ivy Room/E
Keane's 3300
Lefty O'Doul's
Li Po
Mauna Loa
Men's Room
Mr. Bing's
Murio's Trophy
Odeon
Route 101
Sadie's Elephant
Saloon
Silver Peso/N
Stork Club/E
TK's
Trad'r Sam's
Treat Street
Two AM Club/N
Uptown
Would You Believe

DJs

Agenda/S
Amnesia
Ana's Cantina/N
Annie's Lounge
Ashkenaz/E
AsiaSF
At Seventeenth/E
Attic Club
Aunt Charlie's
Avalon/S
Bacchus Wine
Badlands
Bamboo Hut
Bambuddha Lounge
Bar on Castro
Beauty Bar
Bench & Bar/E
Bigfoot Lodge
Bissap Baobab
Blakes/Telegraph/E
Blank Club/S
Bliss Bar
Blowfish Sushi/S
Bohemia Bar

Boom Boom Rm.
Brainwash
Britannia Arms/S
British Bankers Club/S
Bruno's
Butter
butterfly
Buzz 9
Café
Cafe Cocomo
Cafe Van Kleef/E
Canvas Cafe
Casanova
Cat Club
Cherry Bar
Cinch Saloon
Club EZ5
Club Hide
Club Six
Comet Club
Daddy's
Dalva
Deep/S
Divas
DNA Lounge
Dolce
Eight
Element Lounge
El Rio
Endup
Esta Noche
Factory 525
Fiddler's Green
Frisson
Fuse
Gallery Lounge
g bar
Glas Kat
Gravity
Harry Denton Rouge
Harry Denton Starlight
Harry's
Hemlock Tavern
HiFi
House of Shields
Hush Hush Lounge
Jack Falstaff
Jelly's
Jillian's
Julie's Supper Club
Kate O'Brien's
Kelly's
Kingman's/E
Last Day Saloon/N
Laszlo
Levende
Lingba Lounge

Lion Pub
Lit Lounge
Loading Dock
Loft 11
Lost Weekend/E
Luka's Taproom/E
Make-Out Room
Mas Sake
MatrixFillmore
Mecca
Metro City Bar
Metronome Dance
Mezzanine
Midnight Sun
Mighty
Milk Bar
Monkey Club
Movida Lounge
Nickie's BBQ
19 Broadway/N
N'Touch
Olive Bar
111 Minna
Orbit Room Cafe
Oxygen Bar
Ozumo
Paradise Lounge
Pendulum
Pier 23 Cafe
Pink
Ponzu
Power Exchange
Prive Lounge
Public
Radio Bar/E
Red Devil
Red Eye Lounge
Redwood Room
Rickshaw Stop
Roccapulco
RoHan Lounge
Rosewood
Royale
Ruby Room/E
Ruby Skye
Rudy's Pub/S
RX Gallery
Sake Lab
Saketini/N
1751 Social
Shattuck Down Low/E
Skylark
Sno-Drift
Soluna
Space 550
Spoontonic Lounge/E
Stinger Lounge/S

St. Stephen's/S
Stud
Sublounge
Suede
suite one8one
Sushi Groove So.
Ten 15 Club
1351 Lounge/N
330 Ritch
Tongue & Groove
Tonic
Trader Vic's
Tunnel Top
222 Club
Underground SF
Varnish Fine Art
Velvet Lounge
Voda
Whisper
White Horse/E
Wildcard B&G/E
Wish

Drink Specialists
Beer
(* Microbrewery)
Albatross Pub/E
Amnesia
Beach Chalet*
Ben & Nick's/E
Bohemia Bar
Cato's Ale House/E
Dalva
E&O Trading Co.
Edinburgh Castle
Eldo's Grill*
Elixir
Empire Grill/S
Faultline Brewing/S
Gordon Biersch/S
Hydro B&G/N
Jack's Cannery Bar
Jupiter/E
Kennedy's Irish
Los Gatos Brewing/S
Lucky 13
Luka's Taproom/E
Mad Dog in Fog
Magnolia Pub*
Marin Brewing/N
O'Reilly's Irish Pub
Pacific Coast Brew./E
Pig & Whistle
Place Pigalle
Plough & Stars
Pyramid Brewery/E*
Rogue Ales*

Royal Exchange
Rudy's Pub/S
San Fran. Brewing*
Schmidt's Tobacco/E
Silverado Brewing/N*
Steelhead Brew./S*
Suppenküche
Thirsty Bear Brewing*
Tied House Cafe/S*
Tommy's Joynt
Toronado
Trials Pub/S
Triple Rock Brewery/E*
21st Amendment*

Champagne
Bubble Lounge
g bar
Nectar Wine

Cocktails
Absinthe
Alma
Amber
Anú
Aqua
Avalon Bar
bacar
Betelnut Pejiu Wu
Bissap Baobab
BIX
Blondie's Bar
Boulevard
British Bankers Club/S
Bruno's
Campton Place
César/E
Club Deluxe
Doc's Clock
Eight
Elite Cafe
Empire Grill/S
15 Romolo
Fifth Floor
Frisson
Fuse
Gary Danko
g bar
Habana
Harris'
Hobson's Choice
Jardinière
Julie's Supper Club
La Suite
Le Colonial
Lime
Lingba Lounge
Lion Pub

Luna Park
Lush Lounge
Mandarin Lounge
Martuni's
Michael Mina
Millennium
Monkey Club
Nola/S
Olive Bar
Oliveto Cafe/E
Orbit Room Cafe
Ozumo
Padovani's
Ponzu
Radio Bar/E
Red Room
Seasons Bar
Shattuck Ave. Spats/E
Slanted Door
Sublounge
Tommy's Mexican
Tony Nik's
Tosca Cafe
Voda
Washington Sq. B&G
Whiskey Lounge
Zam Zam
Zuni Cafe

Sake
Ace Wasabi's
Bacchus Wine
Blowfish Sushi/S
Mas Sake
Ozumo
Paragon/E
Sake Lab
Shanghai 1930
Sushi Groove So.
Sushi Ran/N
Tokyo Go Go

Wine Bars
Azie
Bacchus Wine
Bubble Lounge
Café Niebaum-Cop.
Eos
Ferry Plaza Wine
First Crush
Hôtel Biron
Liberty Cafe
London Wine
Nectar Wine
Padovani's
Stoa/S
Sushi Ran/N
Tamarine/S

Tra Vigne/N
Varnish Fine Art
VinoVenue

Wine by the Glass
bacar
Bacchus Wine
Boulevard
Bubble Lounge
Café Niebaum-Cop./S
COPIA/N
Cortez
Cosmopolitan
Eos
Farallon
Ferry Plaza Wine
Fifth Floor
First Crush
Gary Danko
g bar
Hawthorne Lane
Hôtel Biron
Jardinière
Lark Creek Inn/N
La Suite
Liberty Cafe
London Wine
Luella
Mandarin Lounge
Martini House/N
Michael Mina
Millennium
Moose's
Nectar Wine
Padovani's
Pisces/S
Ponzu
Rest. LuLu
Rubicon
Stoa/S
Sushi Ran/N
Tamarine/S
Top of the Mark
Tra Vigne/N
2223 Restaurant
Varnish Fine Art
VinoVenue
Zibibbo/S
Zuni Cafe

Enter at Your Own Risk
Aunt Charlie's
Bus Stop
Clooney's Pub
Dogpatch
Ha Ra
Hole in the Wall
Hotsy Totsy/E

Li Po
Molotov
Mr. Bing's
Mucky Duck
Power Exchange
Powerhouse

Expense-Accounters
Absinthe
Americano
Ana Mandara
Aqua
bacar
Bacchus Kirk
Betelnut Pejiu Wu
Big 4
BIX
Boca/N
Boulevard
Bubble Lounge
Buckeye Roadhouse/N
Campton Place
C&L
Carnelian Room
Elite Cafe
Equinox
Farallon
Fifth Floor
Frisson
Gary Danko
g bar
Grand Cafe
Grandviews Lounge
Harris'
Harry Denton Starlight
Hawthorne Lane
Hedley Club/S
Jardinière
Kokkari Estiatorio
Lark Creek Inn/N
La Scene
La Suite
Le Central Bistro
Le Colonial
Lobby Lounge
Lobby/Ritz-Carlton
Mandarin Lounge
MatrixFillmore
Maya
Michael Mina
Moose's
One Market
Ozumo
Padovani's
Pied Piper Bar
Pisces/S
Postrio

Redwood Room
Rose Pistola
Roy's
Rubicon
Seasons Bar
Shanghai 1930
Spago Palo Alto/S
Tonno Rosso
Top of the Mark
Town Hall
Trader Vic's
Winterland
XYZ

Eye-Openers
(Serves alcohol before
8 AM on most days)
500 Club
Gino & Carlo
Old Rogue

Fine Food Too
Absinthe
Acme Chophouse
Ana Mandara
Aqua
Auberge du Soleil/N
Avalon Bar
Azie
bacar
Bacchus Kirk
Betelnut Pejiu Wu
B44
Big 4
Bissap Baobab
BIX
Blowfish Sushi
Boca/N
Boulevard
Bruno's
Buckeye Roadhouse/N
Cafe Bastille
Café Claude
Cafe Lo Cubano
Campton Place
C&L
Carnelian Room
César/E
Cha Cha Cha
Circolo
COPIA/N
Cortez
Cosmopolitan
downtown/E
Eastside West
Elite Cafe
Eos

Farallon
Fifth Floor
Florio
Fog City Diner
Foreign Cinema
Frisson
Gary Danko
Grand Cafe
Harris'
Hawthorne Lane
Highlands Inn/S
Jardinière
Julie's Supper Club
Kokkari Estiatorio
Lark Creek Inn/N
La Scene
Last Supper Club
La Suite
Le Central Bistro
Le Colonial
Lefty O'Doul's
Liberties
Liberty Cafe
Lime
Luella
Luna Park
Martini House/N
Maya
Michael Mina
Millennium
Moose's
Myth
Oliveto Cafe/E
One Market
Oola
Original Joe's
Padovani's
Pisces/S
Plouf
Ponzu
Postrio
Public
Ramblas
Ramp
Rancho Nicasio/N
Rasselas Jazz Club
Rest. LuLu
Rose Pistola
Roy's
Rubicon
Sauce
Scala's Bistro
Shanghai 1930
Slanted Door
Slow Club
Spago Palo Alto/S
Stoa/S

Suppenküche
Tamarine/S
Tommy's Mexican
Tonno Rosso
Town Hall
Townhouse B&G/E
21st Amendment
2223 Restaurant
Whiskey Lounge
Winterland
XYZ
Yoshi's/E
Zibibbo/S
Zuni Cafe

Fireplaces
Albatross Pub/E
Auberge du Soleil/N
Bacchus Kirk
Beckett's Irish Pub/E
Big 4
Bitter End
Blue Chalk Cafe/S
Boca/N
Buckeye Roadhouse/N
Cliff House
Club Mallard/E
Compadres Adobe/S
Divas
Dylan's
Eagle Tavern
Endup
Evvia/S
Fibbar/Molly Magees/S
Fiddler's Green
500 Club
Foreign Cinema
g bar
Glen Park Station
Guaymas/N
Harrington's B&G
Harris'
Hedley Club/S
Highlands Inn/S
Hog's Breath Inn/S
Houston's
Ireland's 32
Jack's Cannery Bar
Johnny Foley's
Kezar Pub
Knuckles Sports/S
Kokkari Estiatorio
Lark Creek Inn/N
Left Bank/N
Lion Pub
Little Shamrock
Lobby/Ritz-Carlton

MacArthur Park
Martini House/N
MatrixFillmore
Mauna Loa
Men's Room
Nola/S
Plouf
Rancho Nicasio/N
Rasselas Jazz Club
Rest. at Mission Ranch/S
Riptide
Running Iron/S
Schmidt's Tobacco/E
Seasons Bar
Silverado Resort/N
Skates on Bay/E
Sno-Drift
Swig
Tarpy's Roadhouse/S
Townhouse B&G/E
Trials Pub/S
222 Club
Whiskey Lounge
Whisper
White Horse/E
Wild Side West
Zibibbo/S

Frat House

Abbey Tavern
Bar None
Bayside Sports
Blue Chalk Cafe/S
Blue Light
Bus Stop
City Tavern
Comet Club
850 Cigar Bar
Fiddler's Green
Final Final
Fuse
Gordon Biersch/S
Greens Sports Bar
Hard Rock Cafe
Horseshoe
Ireland's 32
Irish Bank
Jack's Cannery Bar
Jupiter/E
Kate O'Brien's
Last Day Saloon
Marin Brewing/N
Mars Bar
Noe's
North Star Cafe
Perry's
Raleigh's/E

Redwood Room
Royal Oak
Ruby Skye
Sam's Anchor Cafe/N
Savoy Tivoli
Shanghai Kelly's
Shattuck Down Low/E
Velvet Lounge
Zeke's Sports B&G

Games

Bowling

Albany Bowl/E
Palo Alto Bowl/S

Darts

Abbey Tavern
Albany Bowl/E
Albatross Pub/E
Almaden Feed/S
An Bodhran
Antonio's Nut Hse./S
Bar None
Bayside Sports
Bitter End
Black Horse Pub
Blackthorn Tavern
Black Watch/S
Blue Chalk Cafe/S
Bohemia Bar
Branham Lounge/S
Britannia Arms/S
Clooney's Pub
Conn. Yankee
Crow Bar
Dogpatch
Dylan's
Eagle's Drift In
Eagle Tavern
E&O Trading Co.
Edinburgh Castle
Elixir
Fibbar/Molly Magees/S
Final Final
Finnegan's Wake
540 Club
Glen Park Station
Harrington's B&G
Ireland's 32
Kennedy's Irish
Kezar Pub
Kilowatt
Last Day Saloon
Little Shamrock
Mad Dog in Fog
Marin Brewing/N
Mucky Duck
Old Rogue

Special Appeals

Pacific Coast Brew./E
Palo Alto Bowl/S
Pelican Inn/N
Phoenix
Pig & Whistle
Pilsner Inn
Plough & Stars
Red Jack
Rose & Crown/S
Rudy's Pub/S
Saddle Rack/E
San Fran. Brewing
Starry Plough/E
Stork Club/E
Thirsty Bear Brewing
TK's
Trials Pub/S
21st Amendment
White Horse/E
Yancy's
Zeke's Sports B&G

Pinball
Acme Bar/E
Albany Bowl/E
Antonio's Nut Hse./S
Benders
Bitter End
Black Watch/S
Blakes/Telegraph/E
Bohemia Bar
Bottom of Hill
Brainwash
Café
Cal. Billiard Club/S
Cinch Saloon
Club Mallard/E
Crow Bar
Daddy's
Eagle Tavern
Elbo Room
Endup
Finnegan's Wake
500 Club
Greens Sports Bar
HiFi
Hole in the Wall
Kennedy's Irish
Kezar Pub
Kilowatt
Last Day Saloon
Lexington Club
Lucky 13
Luka's Taproom/E
Moby Dick
Molotov
Mucky Duck
Murio's Trophy

Noe's
Oasis/S
Old Pro/S
Palo Alto Bowl/S
Pilsner Inn
Powerhouse
Red Jack
Riptide
Route 101
Sadie's Elephant
Stork Club/E
Stud
Treat Street
Two AM Club/N
Uptown
Whiskey Thieves
White Horse/E
Wild Side West
Zeitgeist

Pool Halls
Albany Bowl/E
Cal. Billiard Club/S

Pool Tables
Abbey Tavern
Acme Bar/E
Albatross Pub/E
Ana's Cantina/N
Annie's Lounge
Antonio's Nut Hse./S
Argus Lounge
At Seventeenth/E
Avalon/S
Bacchus Kirk
Bar None
Bayside Sports
Bench & Bar/E
Benders
Blakes/Telegraph/E
Blondie's Bar
Blue Chalk Cafe/S
Blue Light
Bohemia Bar
Bottom of Hill
Bubble Lounge
Bus Stop
Buzz 9
Café
Café du Nord
Café Royale
Cal. Billiard Club/S
Casanova
Cherry Bar
Cinch Saloon
Cinebar/S
Clooney's Pub/S
Club Mallard/E

Columbus Café
Crow Bar
Delirium Cocktails
Divas
Dogpatch
Dovre Club
Eagle's Drift In
Eagle Tavern
Edinburgh Castle
Elbo Room
Esta Noche
Fibbar/Molly Magees/S
Finnegan's Wake
540 Club
Fly
Gino & Carlo
Gold Cane
Golden Bull/E
Greens Sports Bar
Ha Ra
Hemlock Tavern
Hole in the Wall
Horseshoe
Hotsy Totsy/E
Ireland's 32
Ivy Room/E
Jack's Cannery Bar
Kelly's
Kennedy's Irish
Kezar Pub
Kilowatt
Knuckles Sports
Last Day Saloon
Latin Amer. Club
Lucky 13
Luka's Taproom/E
Marlena's
Mars Bar
Mauna Loa
Mix
Moby Dick
Molotov
Mucky Duck
Mystic Theatre/N
North Star Cafe
N'Touch
Old Pro/S
Phone Booth
Pig & Whistle
Pilsner Inn
Place Pigalle
Plough & Stars
Power Exchange
Powerhouse
Raleigh's/E
Route 101
Ruby Room/E

Ruby Skye
Saddle Rack/E
Sadie's Elephant
Savoy Tivoli
Shattuck Down Low/E
Silver Peso/N
Steelhead Brew./S
Stud
Thirsty Bear Brewing
330 Ritch
Treat Street
12 Galaxies
Two AM Club/N
Uptown
White Horse/E
Wildcard B&G/E
Wild Side West
Zeitgeist
Zeke's Sports B&G

Trivia Nights

Albatross Pub/E
Beale St. B&G
Beckett's Irish Pub/E
Benders
Bitter End
Britannia Arms/S
Chieftain Irish Pub
Dylan's
Edinburgh Castle
540 Club
Harvey's
Mad Dog in Fog
Pig & Whistle
Rose & Crown/S
Sadie's Elephant
1351 Lounge/N
Wilde Oscar's

Gay

(See also Lesbian)
Aunt Charlie's
Badlands
Bar on Castro
Bench & Bar/E
Café
Cafe Flore
Cinch Saloon
Daddy's
Divas
Eagle Tavern
Endup
Esta Noche
Harvey's
Hole in the Wall
Loading Dock
Lone Star
Lush Lounge

Special Appeals

Marlena's
Martuni's
Mecca
Men's Room
Midnight Sun
Mix
Moby Dick
N'Touch
Pendulum
Pilsner Inn
Powerhouse
Stud
Trax
Twin Peaks
Whiskey Lounge
White Horse/E

Group-Friendly
Albany Bowl/E
Ashkenaz/E
AsiaSF
Ben & Nick's/E
Bruno's
Butter
Café du Nord
Canvas Cafe
Cat Club
Cliff House
Compadres Adobe/S
COPIA/N
DNA Lounge
Eagle Tavern
Edinburgh Castle
Elephant Bar/E/S
Endup
Enrico's Sidewalk
Factory 525
Fillmore
Fly
Freight & Salvage/E
Glas Kat
Gordon Biersch/S
Great Amer. Music
Guaymas/N
Harry Denton Starlight
Il Pirata
Ireland's 32
Jack's Cannery Bar
Kelly's
Kennedy's Irish
Kilowatt
Last Day Saloon
Lefty O'Doul's
Make-Out Room
Marin Brewing/N
Mint Karaoke
MoMo's

Pacific Coast Brew./E
Padovani's
Palo Alto Bowl/S
Pier 23 Cafe
Pound-SF
Pyramid Brewery/E
Roccapulco
Ruby Skye
Saddle Rack/E
Slim's
Space 550
Steelhead Brew./S
Studio Z
Ten 15 Club
Thirsty Bear Brewing
Tied House Cafe/S
Tommy's Joynt
Tonga Room
12 Galaxies
23 Club/S
Whisper
Zeitgeist
Zeke's Sports B&G

Grown-Ups
Absinthe
Ana Mandara
Aqua
Ashkenaz/E
Atlas Cafe
Auberge du Soleil/N
Avalon Bar
bacar
Bacchus Kirk
Bazaar Café
Big 4
Boca/N
Boulevard
Brazen Head
Buckeye Roadhouse/N
Café Niebaum-Cop./S
Caffe Puccini
Caffe Trieste/N
Campton Place
C&L
Cityscape
downtown/E
Elite Cafe
Empire Grill/S
Eos
Equinox
Farallon
Fifth Floor
First Crush
Freight & Salvage/E
Gary Danko
Grand Cafe

Grandviews Lounge
Harris'
Hawthorne Lane
Hedley Club/S
Highlands Inn/S
Jardinière
Jazz at Pearl's
Kimball's East/E
Kokkari Estiatorio
La Scene
Lobby Lounge
Lobby/Ritz-Carlton
London Wine
Mandarin Lounge
Metronome Dance
Michael Mina
Millennium
Moose's
One Market
Pacific Coast Brew./E
Padovani's
Paramount Theater/E
Pied Piper Bar
Postrio
Rest. at Mission Ranch/S
Rubicon
Seasons Bar
Shanghai 1930
Simple Pleasures
Slanted Door
Spago Palo Alto/S
Top of the Mark
Tosca Cafe
Town Hall
Trader Vic's
Twin Peaks
VinoVenue
Whiskey Lounge
Winterland
Yoshi's/E
Zuni Cafe

Happy Hour

Acme Chophouse
Amnesia
An Bodhran
Annie's Lounge
Attic Club
Badlands
Bamboo Hut
Bar None
Bar on Castro
Bayside Sports
Beale St. B&G
Ben & Nick's/E
Benders
Bigfoot Lodge

Bissap Baobab
Black Horse Pub
Blue Chalk Cafe/S
Bohemia Bar
Brainwash
Britannia Arms/S
Butter
Café
Café du Nord
Café Prague
Café Society/N
Canvas Cafe
Casanova
Chaya Brasserie
Chieftain Irish Pub
Cinch Saloon
Club Deluxe
Club EZ5
Columbus Café
Comet Club
Cosmopolitan
Crow Bar
Daddy's
Dalva
Delaney's
Delirium Cocktails
Doc's Clock
Dovre Club
Dylan's
E&O Trading Co.
Eastside West
Edinburgh Castle
850 Cigar Bar
Eldo's Grill
Esta Noche
Fanny & Alexander/S
Final Final
Fish Bowl
540 Club
500 Club
Fly
Front Room
g bar
Gold Dust Lounge
Greens Sports Bar
Harry's
Hedley Club/S
Hemlock Tavern
Henry's Cocktail/N
Hotel Utah
House of Shields
Hush Hush Lounge
Hydro B&G/N
Il Pirata
Ireland's 32
Jade Bar
Kennedy's Irish

Kezar Bar
Kilowatt
Kingman's/E
Last Day Saloon/N
Latin Amer. Club
Lexington Club
Lit Lounge
Liverpool Lil's
Lone Star
Los Gatos Brewing/S
Lost Weekend/E
Lou's Pier 47
Lucky 13
Lush Lounge
MacArthur Park/S
Mad Dog in Fog
Magnolia Pub
Marin Brewing/N
Mauna Loa
Mecca
Metro City Bar
Midnight Sun
Milk Bar
Mix
Monkey Club
Movida Lounge
Murio's Trophy
No Name Bar/N
Old Pro/S
111 Minna
One Market
O'Reilly's Irish Pub
Papa Toby's
Pedro's/S
Pendulum
Perry's
Pied Piper Bar
Pier 23 Cafe
Plough & Stars
Ponzu
Pyramid Brewery/E
Radio Bar/E
Raleigh's/E
Red Jack
Rite Spot Cafe
Rogue Ales
RoHan Lounge
Route 101
Sadie's Elephant
Sake Lab
Saketini/N
San Fran. Brewing
Savanna Jazz
Spoontonic Lounge/E
Stinger Lounge/S
Thee Parkside
Thirsty Bear Brewing

1351 Lounge/N
Tied House Cafe/S
Tonga Room
Tonic
Tony Nik's
Toronado
Trax
Treat Street
Tunnel Top
12 Galaxies
21st Amendment
2223 Restaurant
Varnish Fine Art
Whiskey Lounge
Wilde Oscar's
Yancy's
Zeitgeist
Zeke's Sports B&G

Hotel Bars
Auberge du Soleil
  Auberge du Soleil/N
Basque Hotel
  15 Romolo
Calistoga Inn
  Calistoga Inn/N
Campton Place Hotel
  Campton Place
Claremont Resort & Spa
  Paragon/E
Clift Hotel
  Redwood Room
Commodore Hotel
  Red Room
Fairmont Hotel
  Tonga Room
Four Seasons Hotel
  Seasons Bar
Galleria Park Hotel
  Perry's
Grand Hyatt Hotel
  Grandviews Lounge
Hilton San Francisco
  Cityscape
Hotel Adagio
  Cortez
Hotel De Anza
  Hedley Club/S
Hotel Griffon
  Tonno Rosso
Hotel Majestic
  Avalon Bar
Hotel Milano
  Padovani's

Hotel Monaco
  Grand Cafe
Hotel Palomar
  Fifth Floor
Hotel Vitale
  Americano
Huntington Hotel
  Big 4
Hyatt at Fisherman's Wharf
  Knuckles Sports
Hyatt Regency Hotel
  Equinox
  13 Views
Hyatt Rickeys
  Knuckles Sports/S
Inn at Spanish Bay
  Roy's/S
Laurel Inn
  g bar
Mandarin Oriental Hotel
  Mandarin Lounge
Mark Hopkins InterContinental
  Hotel
  Top of the Mark
Marriott Hotel
  View Lounge
Palace Hotel
  Pied Piper Bar
Park Hyatt Carmel Highlands
  Inn
  Highlands Inn/S
Phoenix Hotel
  Bambuddha Lounge
Prescott Hotel
  Postrio
Renaissance Stanford Court
  Hotel
  Lobby Lounge
Ritz-Carlton
  Lobby/Ritz-Carlton
Savoy Hotel
  Millennium
Serrano Hotel
  Ponzu
Silverado Resort
  Silverado Resort/N
Sir Francis Drake Hotel
  Harry Denton Starlight
  Scala's Bistro
Warwick Regis Hotel
  La Scene
Westin St. Francis
  Michael Mina

W Hotel
  XYZ
York Hotel
  Plush Room

Irish

Abbey Tavern
An Bodhran
Beckett's Irish Pub/E
Chieftain Irish Pub
Delaney's
Dovre Club
Dubliner
Fibbar/Molly Magees/S
Fiddler's Green
Ireland's 32
Irish Bank
Johnny Foley's
Kate O'Brien's
Kennedy's Irish
Liberties
Little Shamrock
Old Rogue
O'Reilly's Irish Pub
Phoenix
Plough & Stars
St. Stephen's/S
Wilde Oscar's

Jazz Clubs

Beat Lounge
BIX
Bruno's
Café Claude
Enrico's Sidewalk
5th Amendment/E
Jazz at Pearl's
Kimball's East/E
Rasselas Jazz Club
Savanna Jazz
Shanghai 1930
Washington Sq. B&G
Yoshi's/E

Jukeboxes

Abbey Tavern
Acme Bar/E
Albany Bowl/E
Almaden Feed/S
Alpha Bar
Ana's Cantina/N
An Bodhran
Annie's Lounge
Antonio's Nut Hse./S
Anú
Argus Lounge
Bacchus Kirk
Bar None

Special Appeals

Bayside Sports
Beale St. B&G
Bitter End
Black Magic
Blackthorn Tavern
Blakes/Telegraph/E
Blondie's Bar
Blue Chalk Cafe/S
Blue Light
Blur
Bohemia Bar
Boom Boom Rm.
Bow Bow Lounge
Branham Lounge/S
Bus Stop
Café Royale
Caffe Puccini
Cal. Billiard Club/S
Casanova
Chieftain Irish Pub
Cinch Saloon
Cinebar/S
Clooney's Pub/S
Club Mallard/E
Crow Bar
Dalva
Dave's
Delaney's
Delirium Cocktails
Dogpatch
Dovre Club
Dubliner
Dylan's
Elixir
El Rio
Expansion Bar
Fibbar/Molly Magees/S
Fiddler's Green
15 Romolo
5th Amendment/E
Final Final
Finnegan's Wake
Fish Bowl
540 Club
500 Club
Frankie's Bohemian
Gino & Carlo
Glen Park Station
Gold Cane
Greens Sports Bar
Ha Ra
Hemlock Tavern
Hobson's Choice
Horseshoe
Hotel Utah
Hotsy Totsy/E
Il Pirata

Irish Bank
Ivy Room/E
Jack's Cannery Bar
Julie's Supper Club
Keane's 3300
Kennedy's Irish
Kezar Pub
Kilowatt
Kimo's
La Rondalla
Last Day Saloon
Left/Albuquerque
Lexington Club
Liberties
Li Po
Lucky 13
Madrone Lounge
Marlena's
Mauna Loa
Men's Room
Mighty
Mix
Molotov
Movida Lounge
Mr. Bing's
Mucky Duck
Murio's Trophy
Mystic Theatre/N
Noe's
No Name Bar/N
North Star Cafe
Old Pro/S
Old Rogue
Orbit Room Cafe
O'Reilly's Irish Pub
Pacific Coast Brew./E
Phoenix
Phone Booth
Pier 23 Cafe
Pig & Whistle
Pilsner Inn
Plough & Stars
Puerto Alegre
Radio Bar/E
R Bar
Red Jack
Riptide
Rite Spot Cafe
Rose & Crown/S
Route 101
Royale
Ruby Room/E
Rudy's Pub/S
Running Iron/S
Sadie's Elephant
Saloon
Savoy Tivoli

Shanghai Kelly's
Silver Peso/N
Stork Club/E
St. Stephen's/S
Thee Parkside
TK's
Toronado
Tosca Cafe
Trad'r Sam's
Treat Street
Triple Rock Brewery/E
Tunnel Top
Twin Peaks
Two AM Club/N
Uptown
Vesuvio
Whiskey Thieves
White Horse/E
Wilde Oscar's
Wild Side West
Would You Believe
Yancy's
Zam Zam
Zeitgeist
Zeke's Sports B&G

Karaoke Bars

Ana's Cantina/N
Annie's Lounge
Bow Bow Lounge
Divas
Mint Karaoke
N'Touch
Shattuck Down Low/E

Latin

Alma
Ana's Cantina/N
Boca/N
Cafe Lo Cubano
Compadres Adobe/S
Esta Noche
La Peña Cultural/E
La Rondalla
Maya
Pedro's/S
Puerto Alegre
Roccapulco
Tommy's Mexican

Lesbian

(See also Gay)
Café
Cafe Flore
Chaise Lounge
Cherry Bar
Lexington Club

White Horse/E
Wild Side West

Live Entertainment

(See also Blues, Cabaret,
Comedy Clubs, DJs, Jazz
Clubs, Karaoke Bars, Piano
Bars, Spoken Word, Strip
Clubs)
Abbey Tavern (Irish)
Ana Mandara (jazz)
An Bodhran (Irish)
Ashkenaz/E (varies)
Atlas Cafe (bluegrass)
Avalon Bar (big band/swing)
bacar (jazz)
Bazaar Café (guitar/vocals)
Beale St. B&G (lingerie nights)
Beckett's Irish Pub/E (varies)
Benders (acoustic)
Bimbo's 365 Club (varies)
Bissap Baobab (African bands)
Black Magic (open mike)
Blackthorn Tavern (varies)
Blue Danube Coffee (varies)
Bocce Cafe (jazz/piano)
Bottom of Hill (varies)
Bubble Lounge (jazz)
Café Amsterdam/N (varies)
Cafe Bastille (jazz)
Café du Nord (bands)
Café Royale (varies)
Caffe Trieste/E (opera)
Calistoga Inn/N (open mike)
Chaya Brasserie (jazz)
Chieftain Irish Pub (Irish)
Dogpatch (jazz)
downtown/E (jazz)
Dylan's (jazz/open mike)
Eagle's Drift In (varies)
Eagle Tavern (varies)
E&O Trading Co. (jazz)
Elbo Room (varies)
Eldo's Grill (jazz/salsa)
Fibbar/Molly Magees/S (Irish)
Fillmore (rock)
Fish Bowl (acoustic)
Foreign Cinema (films)
Freight & Salvage/E (varies)
Gold Dust Lounge (bands)
Great Amer. Music (rock)
Hard Rock Cafe (rock)
Harris' (jazz)
Harvey's (drag)
Hedley Club/S (jazz)
Hôtel Biron (jazz)
Hotel Utah (varies)

Houston's (jazz)
Ireland's 32 (Irish)
Irish Bank (Irish)
Jack's Cannery Bar (guitar)
Jardinière (jazz)
Johnny Foley's (comedy/jazz)
Jupiter/E (jazz)
Kan Zaman (belly dancing)
Keane's 3300 (poetry)
Kimo's (varies)
La Rondalla (mariachi)
Last Day Saloon (varies)
Le Colonial (jazz)
Left Bank/E/N (jazz)
Lefty O'Doul's (piano)
Lobby Lounge (piano)
Lobby/Ritz-Carlton (piano)
Mad Dog in Fog (varies)
Mandarin Lounge (piano)
Marin Brewing/N (varies)
Metronome Dance (varies)
Moose's (jazz)
Mucky Duck (varies)
Mystic Theatre/N (varies)
Napa Valley/N (blues/jazz)
No Name Bar/N (jazz)
Odeon (varies)
Old Rogue (varies)
Original Joe's (piano)
Palo Alto Bowl/S (DJs)
Papa Toby's (varies)
Paragon/E (jazz)
Paramount Theater/E (varies)
Pedro's/S (mariachi)
Pelican Inn/N (varies)
Pig & Whistle (varies)
Plough & Stars (bluegrass/Irish)
Pound-SF (rock)
Puerto Alegre (mariachi)
Ramblas (jazz)
Ramp (salsa/world)
Rick's (Hawaiian)
Rite Spot Cafe (varies)
Rose & Crown/S (comedy/jazz)
Rose Pistola (jazz)
Saddle Rack/E (country)
San Fran. Brewing (varies)
Simple Pleasures (varies)
Stork Club/E (indie)
Thee Parkside (varies)
Tonga Room (varies)
Tongue & Groove (varies)
Top of the Mark (varies)
Town Hall (guitar)
Townhouse B&G/E (jazz trio)
12 Galaxies (varies)
23 Club/S (cajun/rockabilly)

Uva Trattoria/N (guitar/jazz)
Velvet Lounge (bands)
View Lounge (jazz)
Wilde Oscar's (varies)
Zuni Cafe (piano)

Meat Markets

Badlands
Balboa Cafe
Bar None
Bar on Castro
Bench & Bar/E
Betelnut Pejiu Wu
Blue Light
Bus Stop
Café
Cat Club
City Tavern
Comet Club
Cosmopolitan
Cozmo's Corner
Daddy's
Deep/S
Eastside West
Factory 525
Fanny & Alexander/S
Farallon
Fiddler's Green
Final Final
Gordon Biersch/S
Harry Denton Rouge
Harry Denton Starlight
Harry's
Harvey's
Horseshoe
Ireland's 32
Jillian's
Left/Albuquerque
Lexington Club
Mars Bar
MatrixFillmore
Metro City Bar
MoMo's
Pendulum
Perry's
Powerhouse
Red Devil
Redwood Room
Shanghai Kelly's
Steps of Rome
Stud
Suede
Thirsty Bear Brewing
Velvet Lounge

Neighborhood Scenes

Acme Bar/E
Amnesia

Special Appeals

Annie's Lounge
Argus Lounge
Atlas Cafe
Attic Club
Aunt Charlie's
Bar 821
Bazaar Café
Bell Tower
Benders
Bitter End
Black Horse Pub
Black Watch/S
Blue Danube Coffee
Bow Bow Lounge
Brainwash
Buddha Bar
Casanova
C. Bobby's Owl Tree
Chaise Lounge
Cinch Saloon
Club Mallard/E
Conn. Yankee
Dalva
Dave's
Delaney's
Doc's Clock
Dogpatch
Dubliner
Dylan's
Eagle's Drift In
Elixir
Expansion Bar
Finnegan's Wake
500 Club
Frankie's Bohemian
Gino & Carlo
Glen Park Station
Gold Cane
Golden Bull/E
Grove
Hotsy Totsy/E
Ivy Room/E
Keane's 3300
Kezar Bar
Kezar Pub
Last Day Saloon
Latin Amer. Club
Lingba Lounge
Li Po
Little Shamrock
Liverpool Lil's
Lone Palm
Mad Dog in Fog
Make-Out Room
Men's Room
Moby Dick
Molotov

Movida Lounge
Mr. Bing's
Mucky Duck
Murio's Trophy
Noe's
No Name Bar/N
Old Rogue
Phone Booth
Pig & Whistle
Pilsner Inn
Place Pigalle
Red Jack
Rite Spot Cafe
Route 101
Sadie's Elephant
Schmidt's Tobacco/E
Simple Pleasures
Specs Bar
Thee Parkside
TK's
Tony Nik's
Trax
Treat Street
Twin Peaks
Uptown
Wild Side West
Would You Believe

Outdoor Spaces

Garden
Atlas Cafe
Bocce Cafe
Eagle Tavern
Empire Grill/S
Frantoio/N
Frisson
Jupiter/E
Lobby/Ritz-Carlton
Mad Dog in Fog
Pacific Coast Brew./E
Pilsner Inn
Rancho Nicasio/N
Rosewood
Spago Palo Alto/S
Tied House Cafe/S
Wild Side West
Zeitgeist

Patio/Terrace
Acme Chophouse
Agenda/S
Almaden Feed/S
Ana Mandara
Atlas Cafe
Auberge du Soleil/N
Bambuddha Lounge
Bazaar Café
Beale St. B&G

Special Appeals

Blondie's Bar
Blue Chalk Cafe/S
Blue Danube Coffee
Boca/N
Bottom of Hill
Britannia Arms/S
British Bankers Club/S
Bubble Lounge
Buckeye Roadhouse/N
Café
Café Amsterdam/N
Café Claude
Cafe Cocomo
Cafe Flore
Cafe International
Café Niebaum-Cop./S
Café Rouge/E
Cafe Van Kleef/E
Cal. Billiard Club/S
Cinch Saloon
Clooney's Pub/S
Club Hide
Club Mallard/E
Compadres Adobe/S
Conn. Yankee
Cosmopolitan
Deep/S
Eagle Tavern
E&O Trading Co./N
Eight
850 Cigar Bar
Elephant Bar/E/S
El Rio
Endup
Enrico's Sidewalk
Factory 525
Faultline Brewing/S
Fibbar/Molly Magees/S
Finnegan's Wake
540 Club
Foreign Cinema
Forge in Forest/S
Frantoio/N
g bar
Glen Park Station
Gold Cane
Gordon Biersch/S
Greens Sports Bar
Guaymas/N
Harrington's B&G
Heinold's Saloon/E
Hemlock Tavern
Highlands Inn/S
Hog's Breath Inn/S
Houston's
Hurley's/N
Il Pirata

Jack's Cannery Bar
Jelly's
Jillian's
Jupiter/E
Kate O'Brien's
Kelly's
Kennedy's Irish
Kezar Pub
Lark Creek Inn/N
La Suite
Le Colonial
Left Bank/S
Liberty Cafe
Liverpool Lil's
Lone Star
Lost Weekend/E
Lucky 13
MacArthur Park/S
Mad Dog in Fog
Marin Brewing/N
Marlena's
Mars Bar
Martini House/N
Maya
Metro City Bar
Mix
MoMo's
Mystic Theatre/N
19 Broadway/N
Nola/S
No Name Bar/N
Oasis/S
Old Pro/S
O'Reilly's Irish Pub
Palomino
Papa Toby's
Paragon
Pedro's/S
Pendulum
Piazza D'Angelo/N
Pier 23 Cafe
Pilsner Inn
Pinot Blanc/N
Pound-SF
Powerhouse
Pyramid Brewery/E
Raleigh's/E
Ramp
Rancho Nicasio/N
Red Jack
Rest. at Mission Ranch/S
Rica
Rose & Crown/S
Rudy's Pub/S
Running Iron/S
Sam's Anchor Cafe/N
Savoy Tivoli

Schmidt's Tobacco/E
Silverado Resort/N
Space 550
Spago Palo Alto/S
Spoontonic Lounge/E
Steelhead Brew./S
suite one8one
Sushi Ran/N
Tarpy's Roadhouse/S
Thee Parkside
330 Ritch
Tied House Cafe/S
Town Hall
Townhouse B&G/E
Tra Vigne/N
Triple Rock Brewery/E
Voda
Whisper
Wildcard B&G/E
Wild Side West
Zibibbo/S

Sidewalk
Absinthe
Antonio's Nut Hse./S
Bacchus Wine
Bell Tower
Betelnut Pejiu Wu
B44
Blue Danube Coffee
Bouchon/N
Cafe Abir
Cafe Bastille
Cafe Flore
Cafe Lo Cubano
Café Niebaum-Cop.
Café Royale
Café Society/N
Cafe Van Kleef/E
Caffe Cicero/N
Caffe Puccini
Caffe Trieste
César/E
Chaya Brasserie
City Tavern
Eastside West
Fat Lady/E
Fog City Diner
Grove
Grumpy's Pub
Harry's
Irish Bank
Knuckles Sports/S
Left/Albuquerque
Left Bank/S
Liberties
Lou's Pier 47
Mario's Bohemian

MarketBar
Martuni's
MatrixFillmore
Michael's Octavia
Nectar Wine
Noe's
Oliveto Cafe/E
Orbit Room Cafe
Perry's
Pisces/S
Purple Onion
Red Eye Lounge
Riptide
Rogue Ales
Rose Pistola
San Fran. Brewing
Simple Pleasures
Slow Club
Steps of Rome
Trials Pub/S
Zuni Cafe

Waterside
Gordon Biersch
Guaymas/N
Heinold's Saloon/E
Jelly's
Kelly's
La Suite
Lou's Pier 47
MarketBar
McCormick/Kuleto's
Pier 23 Cafe
Ramp
Sam's Anchor Cafe/N
Skates on Bay/E
Slanted Door

People-Watching
Ace Wasabi's
Bar on Castro
Betelnut Pejiu Wu
Blondie's Bar
Bubble Lounge
Café
Cafe Bastille
Café Claude
Cafe Flore
Caffè Greco
Caffe Puccini
Caffe Trieste
Canvas Cafe
Dubliner
El Rio
Endup
Enrico's Sidewalk
Florio
Frisson

Grove
Guaymas/N
Harvey's
Hemlock Tavern
Hobson's Choice
Jardinière
Jupiter/E
Kelly's
Le Colonial
Lefty O'Doul's
MatrixFillmore
Metro City Bar
Michael Mina
Moose's
Oliveto Cafe/E
111 Minna
O'Reilly's Irish Pub
Papa Toby's
Pilsner Inn
Ramp
Red Devil
Redwood Room
Rose Pistola
Ruby Skye
San Fran. Brewing
Savoy Tivoli
Spago Palo Alto/S
Steps of Rome
Tommy's Joynt
Tonga Room
Trader Vic's
Tunnel Top
Twin Peaks
Zuni Cafe

Piano Bars
Alley/E
Big 4
Cosmopolitan
Martuni's
Max's Opera/S
Rest. at Mission Ranch/S
Seasons Bar

Pub Grub
Albatross Pub/E
Atlas Cafe
Beckett's Irish Pub/E
Clooney's Pub/S
Dylan's
Fibbar/Molly Magees/S
Ireland's 32
Kennedy's Irish
Kezar Pub
Little Shamrock
Liverpool Lil's
Mad Dog in Fog
Magnolia Pub

Marin Brewing/N
O'Reilly's Irish Pub
Pacific Coast Brew./E
Pelican Inn/N
Pyramid Brewery/E
Rose & Crown/S
Schmidt's Tobacco/E
Starry Plough/E
St. Stephen's/S
Trials Pub/S
Wilde Oscar's

Punk Bars
Benders
Bottom of Hill
Casanova
Crow Bar
Doc's Clock
Golden Bull/E
Hemlock Tavern
Kilowatt
Kimo's
Lucky 13
Molotov
924 Gilman/E
Sadie's Elephant
Stork Club/E
Thee Parkside
Toronado
Treat Street
Zeitgeist

Quiet Conversation
Albatross Pub/E
Atlas Cafe
Avalon Bar
Big 4
Cafe Flore
Café Prague
Caffe Puccini
Caffe Trieste/E/N
C. Bobby's Owl Tree
Chaise Lounge
Cityscape
Cliff House
Equinox
15 Romolo
Fifth Floor
Frantoio/N
Grandviews Lounge
Highlands Inn/S
Hôtel Biron
Jillian's
Liberty Cafe
Lobby/Ritz-Carlton
Mandarin Lounge
McCormick/Kuleto's
Michael Mina

Original Joe's
Pedro's/S
Postrio
Rubicon
Seasons Bar
Shattuck Ave. Spats/E
Simple Pleasures
Tamarine/S
Tonno Rosso
Tosca Cafe
Twin Peaks
Wild Side West

Roadhouses

Almaden Feed/S
Annie's Lounge
Casanova
Cinch Saloon
Ivy Room/E
Lone Star
Rancho Nicasio/N
Sweetwater Saloon/N
Thee Parkside
Toronado
23 Club/S
Two AM Club/N

Romantic

Ana Mandara
Auberge du Soleil/N
Avalon Bar
Beach Chalet
Big 4
Bliss Bar
Bruno's
Bubble Lounge
Café du Nord
Caffe Trieste
Campton Place
Enrico's Sidewalk
Equinox
Farallon
15 Romolo
Fifth Floor
Hedley Club/S
Highlands Inn/S
Hog's Breath Inn/S
Hôtel Biron
Kokkari Estiatorio
Lark Creek Inn/N
La Suite
Le Colonial
Lobby/Ritz-Carlton
Michael Mina
Pelican Inn/N
Pied Piper Bar
Plush Room
Red Room

Seasons Bar
13 Views
Tony Nik's
Top of the Mark
Tosca Cafe
Vesuvio

Sleepers
(Good to excellent ratings,
but little known)

Cafe Macondo
Café Society/N
Dylan's
540 Club
Heinold's Saloon/E
Hole in the Wall
Improv/S
Lobby Lounge
Metronome Dance
Millennium
924 Gilman/E
Odeon
Pinot Blanc/N
Powerhouse
Radio Bar/E
Rest. at Mission Ranch/S
Spoontonic Lounge/E
Tarpy's Roadhouse/S
Uptown

Spoken Word

Brainwash
Cafe International
Canvas Cafe
Edinburgh Castle
La Peña Cultural/E

Sports Bars

Bar None
Bayside Sports
Britannia Arms/S
Bus Stop
Cal. Billiard Club/S
Chieftain Irish Pub
City Tavern
Conn. Yankee
Dubliner
Final Final
Gino & Carlo
Gold Cane
Gordon Biersch/S
Greens Sports Bar
Horseshoe
Houston's
Kezar Pub
Knuckles Sports/S
Mix
Molotov

Mucky Duck
Murio's Trophy
Noe's
Old Pro/S
Silver Peso/N
Wildcard B&G/E
Zeke's Sports B&G

Strip Clubs

Centerfolds
Gold Club
Larry Flynt's
Lusty Lady
Mitchell Bros.

Suits

Americano
Aqua
Bacchus Kirk
Big 4
BIX
Boulevard
Bubble Lounge
Campton Place
C&L
Carnelian Room
Chaya Brasserie
850 Cigar Bar
Empire Grill/S
Equinox
Farallon
Fifth Floor
Gary Danko
g bar
Gordon Biersch/S
Grandviews Lounge
Harrington's B&G
Harris'
Hawthorne Lane
Houston's
Jardinière
Kokkari Estiatorio
Le Central Bistro
Lobby Lounge
Lobby/Ritz-Carlton
London Wine
Mandarin Lounge
Michael Mina
Moose's
Occidental Cigar
One Market
Ozumo
Pied Piper Bar
Pisces/S
Postrio
Royal Exchange
Seasons Bar

Tadich Grill
Top of the Mark
View Lounge
Washington Sq. B&G
XYZ

Swanky

Absinthe
Americano
Ana Mandara
Aqua
Avalon Bar
bacar
Bacchus Kirk
Betelnut Pejiu Wu
B44
Big 4
Bimbo's 365 Club
BIX
Bliss Bar
Boulevard
Bruno's
Bubble Lounge
butterfly
Campton Place
C&L
Carnelian Room
Chaya Brasserie
Cip
Club Deluxe
Club EZ5
Cortez
Cosmopolitan
Eastside West
Eight
Elite Cafe
Evvia/S
Farallon
Fifth Floor
Fluid
Foreign Cinema
Frisson
Gary Danko
g bar
Grand Cafe
Grandviews Lounge
Harris'
Harry Denton Starlight
Hawthorne Lane
Hedley Club/S
Hôtel Biron
Jade Bar
Jardinière
Kokkari Estiatorio
Lark Creek Inn/N
La Scene
La Suite

Laszlo
Le Colonial
Lime
Lobby Lounge
Lobby/Ritz-Carlton
Mandarin Lounge
Mecca
Michael Mina
Millennium
Monkey Club
Moose's
Olive Bar
Oliveto Cafe/E
One Market
Ozumo
Padovani's
Paramount Theater/E
Pied Piper Bar
Pink
Pisces/S
Plush Room
Ponzu
Postrio
Public
Red Room
Redwood Room
Rose Pistola
Roy's
Rubicon
Scala's Bistro
Seasons Bar
Shanghai 1930
Slanted Door
Suede
Sushi Ran/N
13 Views
Tonic
Tonno Rosso
Tony Nik's
Top of the Mark
Town Hall
View Lounge
Washington Sq. B&G
Winterland
Wish
XYZ

Theme Bars
Bamboo Hut
Beauty Bar
Bench & Bar/E
Bigfoot Lodge
Bissap Baobab
Butter
C. Bobby's Owl Tree
Cherry Bar
Conga Lounge/E

E&O Trading Co./S
Farallon
Fat Lady/E
Habana
Hôtel Biron
Lingba Lounge
Max's Opera
Nola/S
Oxygen Bar
Pied Piper Bar
Pink
Red Room
Rick's
Ruby Room/E
Shanghai 1930
Sno-Drift
Tonga Room
Trader Vic's/E/S
Trad'r Sam's
Voda

Transporting Experiences
Americano
Bamboo Hut
Beach Chalet
Bigfoot Lodge
Bimbo's 365 Club
Bissap Baobab
Boom Boom Rm.
Boulevard
Cafe Van Kleef/E
Capp's Corner
Carnelian Room
C. Bobby's Owl Tree
Club Deluxe
Edinburgh Castle
Farallon
Forge in Forest/S
Frisson
Grand Cafe
Hedley Club/S
Heinold's Saloon/E
Jade Bar
John's Grill
Le Colonial
Lefty O'Doul's
Noc Noc
111 Minna
Oxygen Bar
Paramount Theater/E
Parkway Speakeasy/E
Pelican Inn/N
Plush Room
Ponzu
Rancho Nicasio/N
Red Room
Saddle Rack/E

Shanghai 1930
Sno-Drift
Tonga Room
Tosca Cafe
Trader Vic's
23 Club/S
Vesuvio
Zam Zam

Trendy
Ace Wasabi's
Alpha Bar
Amber
bacar
Beauty Bar
Betelnut Pejiu Wu
BIX
Bliss Bar
Bubble Lounge
Butter
Buzz 9
Cip
Club Deluxe
Club Six
Dalva
DNA Lounge
Dolce
Eight
15 Romolo
Foreign Cinema
Frisson
Fuse
Harry Denton Rouge
Jade Bar
Luna Park
Madrone Lounge
MatrixFillmore
Mezzanine
Mighty
Monkey Club
Noc Noc
111 Minna
Oxygen Bar
Paradise Lounge
Radio Bar/E
Red Devil
Red Room
Redwood Room
Rosewood
Ruby Skye
RX Gallery
Sake Lab
Skylark
Sno-Drift
Spoontonic Lounge/E
Sublounge
Suede

Sushi Groove So.
Swig
Tony Nik's
Tunnel Top
Velvet Lounge
Wildcard B&G/E

Under 21
Albany Bowl/E
Alpha Bar
Ashkenaz/E
Atlas Cafe
Bazaar Café
Blue Danube Coffee
Cafe Abir
Cafe International
Cafe Lo Cubano
Cafe Macondo
Caffe Trieste/E/N
Cal. Billiard Club/S
E&O Trading Co./N
Elephant Bar/E/S
Frisson
Grove
Hard Rock Cafe
La Suite
Levende
Lime
Luella
Luka's Taproom/E
Michael's Octavia
924 Gilman/E
Palo Alto Bowl/S
Rica
Simple Pleasures
Soluna
Stoa/S
Tamarine/S
Tonno Rosso
Trader Vic's/E/S

Velvet Rope
AsiaSF
Fuse
g bar
HiFi
Kelly's
Power Exchange
Redwood Room
Roccapulco
Ruby Skye
Ten 15 Club
Tonic
Whisper

Views
Americano
Auberge du Soleil/N

Special Appeals

Beach Chalet
butterfly
Carnelian Room
Chaya Brasserie
Cityscape
Cliff House
Equinox
Grandviews Lounge
Guaymas/N
Harry Denton Starlight
Highlands Inn/S
Insalata's/N
Kelly's
La Suite
Lou's Pier 47

MarketBar
McCormick/Kuleto's
Metro City Bar
Palomino
Pier 23 Cafe
Rest. at Mission Ranch/S
Sam's Anchor Cafe/N
Silverado Resort/N
Skates on Bay/E
Slanted Door
13 Views
Tonno Rosso
Top of the Mark
View Lounge

Alphabetical
Page Index

Restaurant locations are indicated by the following abbreviations: East of San Francisco=E; North of San Francisco=N; South of San Francisco=S.

Alphabetical Page Index

Alphabetical Page Index

Alphabetical Page Index

Alphabetical Page Index

Alphabetical Page Index

Alphabetical Page Index

Wine Vintage Chart

This chart is designed to help you select wine to go with your meal. It is based on the same 0 to 30 scale used throughout this *Survey*. The ratings (prepared by our friend **Howard Stravitz**, a law professor at the University of South Carolina) reflect both the quality of the vintage and the wine's readiness for present consumption. Thus, if a wine is not fully mature or is over the hill, its rating has been reduced. We do not include 1987, 1991–1993 vintages because they are not especially recommended for most areas. A dash indicates that a wine is either past its peak or too young to rate.

	'85	'86	'88	'89	'90	'94	'95	'96	'97	'98	'99	'00	'01	'02	'03
WHITES															
French:															
Alsace	24	–	22	28	28	27	26	25	25	26	25	26	27	25	–
Burgundy	26	25	–	24	22	–	28	29	24	23	26	25	23	27	24
Loire Valley	–	–	–	–	24	–	20	23	22	–	24	25	23	27	26
Champagne	28	25	24	26	29	–	26	27	24	24	25	25	26	–	–
Sauternes	21	28	29	25	27	–	21	23	26	24	24	24	28	25	26
Germany	25	–	25	26	27	25	24	27	24	23	25	24	29	27	–
California (Napa, Sonoma, Mendocino):															
Chardonnay	–	–	–	–	–	–	–	24	26	25	25	24	27	29	–
Sauvignon Blanc/Semillon	–	–	–	–	–	–	–	–	–	25	25	23	27	28	26
REDS															
French:															
Bordeaux	24	25	24	26	29	22	26	25	23	25	24	28	26	23	24
Burgundy	23	–	21	24	26	–	26	28	25	22	28	22	24	27	–
Rhône	25	19	27	29	29	24	25	23	24	28	27	27	26	–	25
Beaujolais	–	–	–	–	–	–	–	–	–	–	23	24	–	25	28
California (Napa, Sonoma, Mendocino):															
Cab./Merlot	27	26	–	21	28	29	27	25	28	23	26	23	27	25	–
Pinot Noir	–	–	–	–	–	–	–	–	24	24	25	24	26	29	–
Zinfandel	–	–	–	–	–	–	–	–	–	–	–	–	26	26	–
Italian:															
Tuscany	–	–	–	–	25	22	25	20	29	24	28	26	25	–	–
Piedmont	–	–	–	27	28	–	23	27	27	25	25	28	23	–	–